PHOTOSHOP CS2
RAW

Using Adobe Camera Raw, Bridge, and Photoshop
to Get the Most ouf of Your Digital Camera

PHOTOSHOP CS2
RAW

Using Adobe Camera Raw, Bridge, and Photoshop to Get the Most out of Your Digital Camera

Mikkel Aaland

O'REILLY®

BEIJING • CAMBRIDGE • FARNHAM • KÖLN • PARIS • SEBASTOPOL • TAIPEI • TOKYO

Photoshop CS2 RAW BY MIKKEL AALAND

Editor: **Colleen Wheeler**

Production Editor: **Philip Dangler**

Technical Editors: **Cris Rys and Doug Nelson**

Author's Assistants: **Peter Burian and Ed Schwartz**

Cover Design: **Mike Kohnke**

Interior Design: **Michael Kavish**

Graphic Production: **Jan Martí**

Published by O'Reilly Media, Inc., 1005 Gravenstein Highway North, Sebastopol, CA 95472.

O'Reilly books may be purchased for educational, business, or sales promotional use. Online editions are also available for most titles (*safari.oreilly.com*). For more information, contact our corporate/institutional sales department: 800.998.9938 or *corporate@oreilly.com*.

Print History: March 2006, First Edition.

0-596-00851-1

[F]

Printed in Canada.

To my Dad

Acknowledgments

I've been involved with digital photography for over 20 years, and the greatest pleasure has come from working with a community of generous, big-hearted people. For this book, I want to especially thank the following people, who shared their wisdom, knowledge, and work so freely.

From Adobe: Thomas Knoll, Kevin Connor, Cris Rys, Jeff Chien, John Peterson, Bryan O'Neil Hughes, Jon Petersen, and John Worthington.

Contributing photographers: Peter Burian, John Carnett, John McDermott, Luis Delgado Qualtrough, Maggie Hallahan, Jack Holm, Peter Krogh, Richard Morgenstein, Michael Reichmann, Mark Richards, Derrick Story, and Martin Sundberg. (On the next page, I've included a photographer's contributor list with contact information. I encourage you to check out the photograpers' work and see for yourself why I am so honored to have them associated with this book.)

From O'Reilly, which very patiently supported my efforts: Tim O'Reilly, Mark Brokering, Laurie Petrycki, Robert Eckstein, Steve Weiss, Colleen Wheeler, and Mike Kohnke.

The design and layout of this book is groundbreaking and for that, I profusely thank Michael Kavish and Jan Martí, who went way beyond what was expected of them. Lori Barra, of TonBo designs, was also supportive.

I want to also thank Bill Atkinson for his advice and help. We had several lively conversations that informed a lot of the material in this book. Thanks also to Dave Coffin, Eric Hyman, Fred Shippey, Dave Drum, Bruce Yelaska, Cheryl Parker, Jonathan Chester, Rudy Burger, Michael Borek, Andrew Tarnowka, Saurabh Wahi, Mike Haney, Paul Saffo, Leo Laporte, Suzanne Kantra Kirschner, Tom Kunhardt, Martin Evening, Lynne Browne, and Paul Kellogg.

Peter Burian and Ed Schwartz both assisted me in various research capacities, and I really enjoyed the collaboration with these fine men. Doug Nelson did an over-the-top job of technical editing, which I really appreciated.

Neil Salkind and David Rogelberg of Studio B watched out for my best interests, as usual. And finally, thanks to my wife, Rebecca, and two daughters, who make all this worthwhile.

Mikkel Aaland
San Francisco, 2006

Contributors

Peter Burian is a freelance photographer, editor, and author based in Toronto, Canada. His outdoor, travel, nature, and active lifestyle photographs are available as stock for editorial and advertising use via *www.peterkburian.com*.

John Carnett is Popular Science magazine's award-winning staff photographer of 14 years. See more of John's work at *www.carnettphoto.com*.

John McDermott is a San Francisco–based freelance photographer who shoots globally for corporate, advertising, and editorial clients. His work can be seen at *www.mcdfoto.com*.

Luis Delgado Qualtrough is a photographer whose prints, books, and installations have been shown extensively in the USA, Mexico, and Europe. His work is held at the San Francisco Museum of Modern Art, the Houston Museum of Fine Art, Lehigh University, Stanford University, and the Bibliothéque Nationale in Paris as well as in many private collections. His work can also be seen at *www.ladq.com*.

Maggie Hallahan is a San Francisco–based freelance photographer, who shoots both for editorial and corporate clients. Her work can be seen at *www.maggiehallahan.com*.

Jack Holm is a former professor at Rochester Institute of Technology (RIT) and is currently a senior scientist at Hewlett-Packard. He can be contacted at *jack.holm@hp.com*.

Peter Krogh owns and operates a full-service commercial photography studio in the Washington, DC area. Peter is both an award-winning photographer and author. His work can be seen at *www.peterkrogh.com*.

Richard Morgenstein is a location photographer based in San Francisco, specializing in environmental portraiture. You can see more of his work at *www.morgenstein.com*.

Michael Reichmann is a world-renowned nature photographer and photographic educator based in Toronto, Canada. His landscape and wildlife photography is widely collected and exhibited. Michael is the publisher and primary author of The Luminous Landscape web site, *www.luminouslandscape.com*, where you can see more of his work.

Mark Richards is an award-winning corporate and editorial photographer who specializes in people and lifestyle photography. To see more of his work, visit *www.markrichards.com*.

Derrick Story has over 20 years of professional photography experience and has authored several books on digital photography. His work can be seen at *www.thedigitalstory.com*.

Martin Sundberg is an award-winning photographer specializing in portraiture and extreme sports. His work can be seen at *www.martinsundberg.com*.

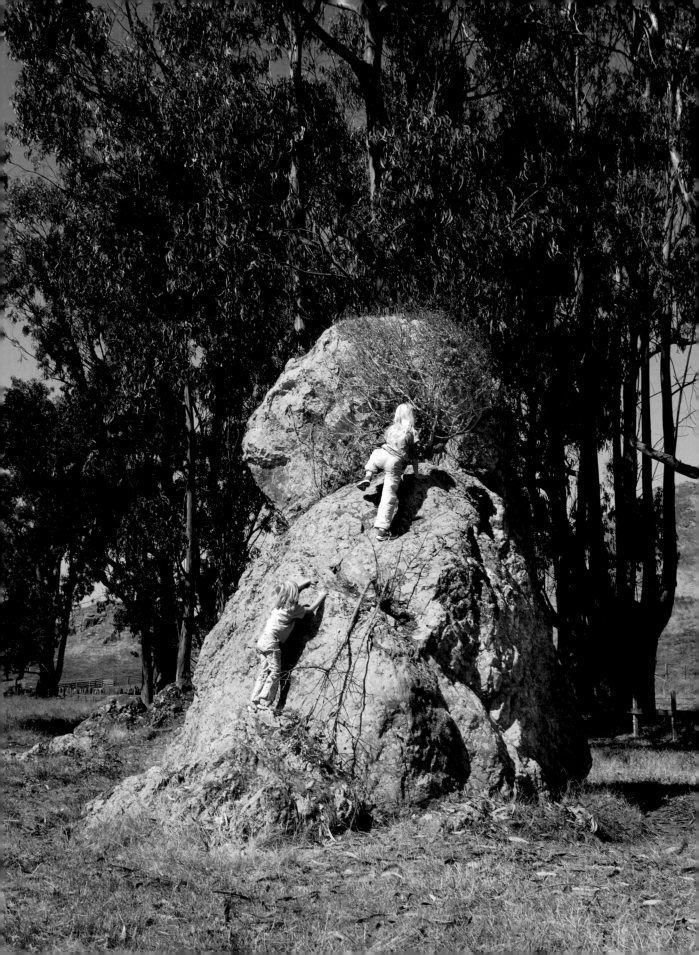

Contents

FOREWORD   xiii

INTRODUCTION   xv

CHAPTER 1   **Shooting & Importing RAW**   1

When to Shoot RAW   2

Critical Digital Camera Settings   5

Correct Exposure   8

Including a Color Target   9

Importing Images to Bridge with Import Camera   11

CHAPTER 2   **Using Adobe Bridge to Trash, Edit & Sort RAW Files**   15

Launching Bridge   16

Editing a Photo Session   23

Renaming Files   32

CHAPTER 3   **Using Adobe Camera Raw**   35

Updating Camera Raw   36

Workflow Options   38

Editing with Camera Raw   40

An Overview of Camera Raw Tools   44

Camera Raw Preview and Analysis Tools   51

Camera Raw Tabs   53

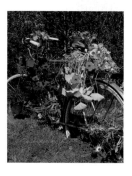

CHAPTER 4 Using Camera Raw Adjust & Curve Controls 57

Using Camera Raw Auto Adjustments 58

Customizing Camera Raw Default 60

Evaluating an Image in Camera Raw 63

Manually Adjusting White Balance 72

Manually Mapping Tone 76

Using Camera Raw Curve for More Control 82

Finishing Up Adjustments with Photoshop 89

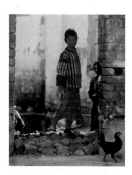

CHAPTER 5 Advanced Tonal Control 93

Advanced Tonal Control with Camera Raw and Photoshop 94

Part One: Creating Multiple Versions of the Same RAW File 95

Part Two: Blending in Photoshop 99

Extending Dynamic Range 102

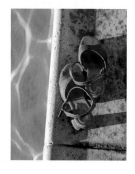

CHAPTER 6 Sharpening RAW Smartly 113

RAW Sharpening 101 114

Sharpening with Adobe Camera Raw 117

Using Photoshop's Smart Sharpen 123

Sharpening High ISO Images with Reduce Noise 129

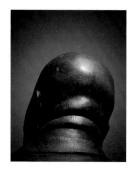

CHAPTER 7 Reducing Noise, Correcting Chromatic Aberrations & Controlling Vignetting 131

About Noise 132

Using Camera Raw to Reduce Noise 133

Using Photoshop's Reduce Noise Filter 137

About Chromatic Aberrations 142

Diminishing or Adding Vignetting 147

CHAPTER 8   **Better Black & White Images with RAW**   149

RAW Is Inherently Grayscale   150

Using Camera Raw to Generate Black & White Images   151

Advanced Localized Black & White Control   158

CHAPTER 9   **Archiving & Working with DNG**   165

Archive Strategy: Hedging Your Bets   166

Saving DNG Files   167

Converting to DNG with Camera Raw   171

Using Adobe DNG Converter   176

CHAPTER 10   **Converting & Delivering RAW**   179

Using Bridge + Image Processor to Convert RAW Files   180

Applying Custom Camera Raw Settings to Multiple Images   185

Using Camera Raw's Save Command   188

Automating Contact Sheets, Picture Package & Web Photo Gallery   191

Using Batch & Actions   194

Writing Custom Scripts   199

Index   200

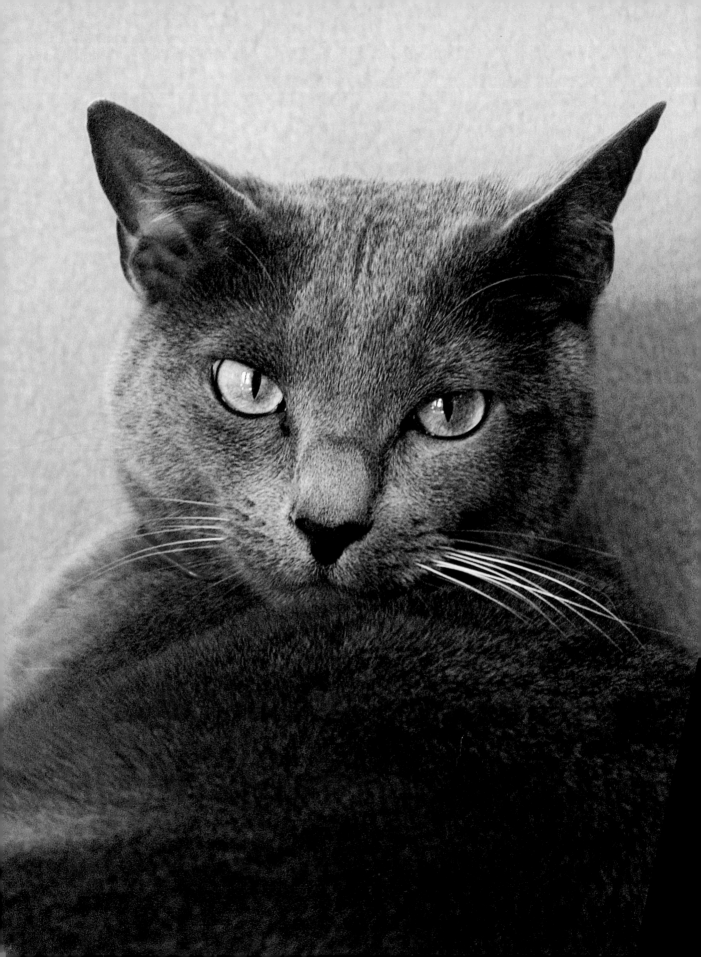

Foreword

The first five years of the twenty-first century have brought with them a revolution in photography. Although film isn't quite dead yet, and likely will remain in use for some years to come, both amateur and professional photographers have embraced digital photography with a vengeance.

In this book, Mikkel Aaland has combined a creative photographer's sensitivity with a widely published author's clarity of expression and has produced an eminently readable, in-depth look at the most powerful image processing tools that are currently available to photographers. Mikkel helps us understand not only how these tools work, but also why they do what they do.

The creative control that the chemical darkroom offered had its appeal, but the cost, space requirements, and necessity of working in the dark, in isolation from others, diluted this appeal considerably for many. Dealing with sometimes potentially toxic chemicals also raised concerns. Today, a prosumer-level DSLR, when combined with a contemporary photo-quality inkjet printer, can produce images not just equal to, but superior to, those that were possible in the darkroom as little as a decade ago.

But although the tools have changed, from enlargers and chemical trays to computers and desktop printers, the photographer still needs familiarity and skills with the appropriate tools. For most pros, and many serious amateurs, the software tools of choice are Photoshop CS2 and Camera Raw, Photoshop's built-in raw file processing program. When combined with the integrated Adobe Bridge program, photographers have a complete photographic imaging processing studio on their computer.

The arrival of digital image capture brought with it a new concept—that of the RAW file. While JPEG files have their place, and are convenient for snapshots, reportage, and use on the Web, anyone doing digital photography with an eye toward image quality will likely prefer to shoot in RAW mode.

In a RAW file, all of the settings that get "baked" into the image when one sets a camera to shoot a JPEG file are "tagged" to the file, but don't affect it. This gives the photographer great freedom to extract the best possible quality from that file, without having to commit to contrast, saturation, color balance, and sharpening settings at the time of exposure.

The RAW file gives photographers the equivalent of a latent image on film; one that is recorded but as yet unprocessed. The beauty of that file is that one can "develop" it over again any number of times, as one's skills, tools, and needs grow and change. Learning how to get the most from one's raw images is a learning process, and this book will help both newcomers and more experienced users along that path.

Michael Reichmann, photographer and publisher of www.luminous-landscape.com
Toronto, 2006

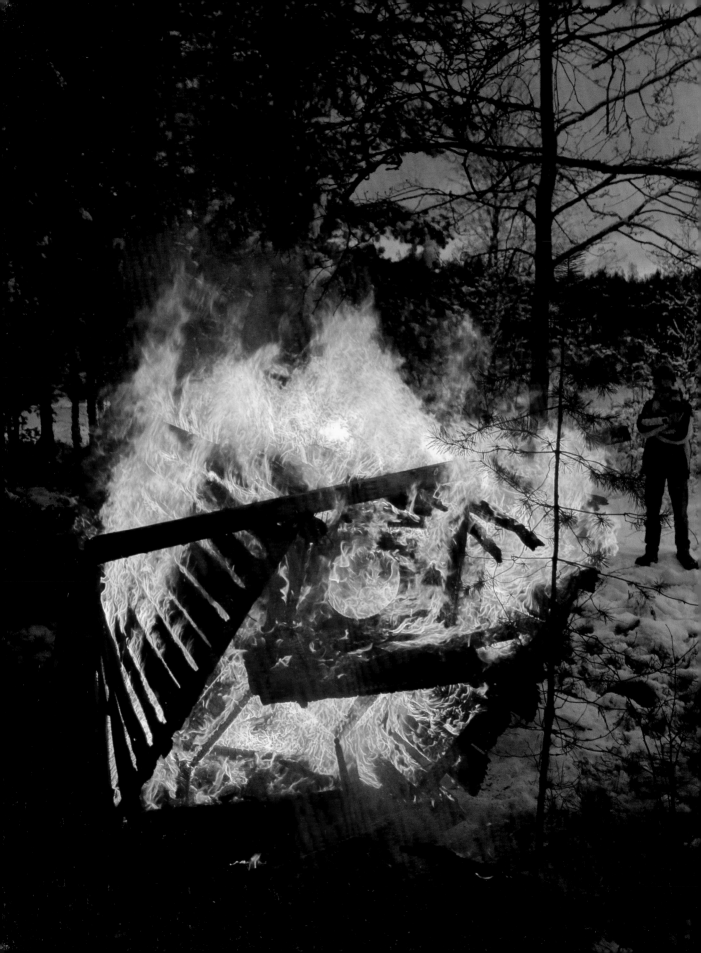

Introduction

RAW Power

I get really excited when I talk about the unprocessed RAW data generated by digital cameras. RAW data is the holy grail of digital photography, and you don't need to be a professional photographer to appreciate its potential—you just need a digital camera that saves the RAW data, a computer, Photoshop CS2, and, of course, this book! The fact is, anyone who is serious about digital photography and wants to produce the best possible picture will benefit from shooting and processing RAW.

If you shoot RAW, use Photoshop CS2, and want great images, this book is for you!

RAW is often described as a digital negative. The negative in traditional photography is considered the underlying source from which any number of prints (or interpretations) can be produced. You can take a negative to the corner drugstore and get a decent (but uninspired) print, or you can take the same negative into a darkroom and apply skill and tender loving care to produce something remarkable.

The same holds true for RAW files. You can let your digital camera interpret the RAW data and produce a JPEG or TIFF, or you can do the work yourself.

If you do it yourself, the payoffs are great:

- Non-destructive and complete control over white balance and color tint

- Dramatic control over tonal distribution

- Reversible sharpening and detail application

- Full advantage of future improvements in colormetric conversion technology

Having said all this, RAW—and consequently this book—is not for everyone. Not only do you need a digital camera that saves and captures RAW, but you need a powerful computer with lots of storage. Even though you can automate RAW conversion to a certain degree, time is a consideration. The RAW data must be touched, molded, and shaped before it takes form. It takes skill to do this right, and that is where this book comes in.

RAW- & Photoshop CS2-Centric

This book is both RAW- and Photoshop CS2-centric. When I say RAW, I'm talking about the unadulterated data that comes from a digital camera. When I say Photoshop CS2, I'm actually talking about three separate working environments: Bridge, Camera Raw, and Photoshop. All three of these components ship under the product name Photoshop CS2 and together, they'll take you just about anywhere you want to go with your RAW data.

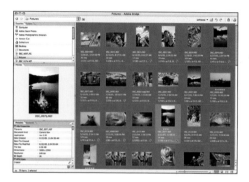

Bridge is a central organizer for your images, the command center for Adobe's Creative Suite, and a gateway to either Camera Raw or Photoshop.

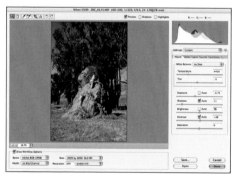

Camera Raw is the primary RAW processing application that launches from either Bridge or Photoshop.

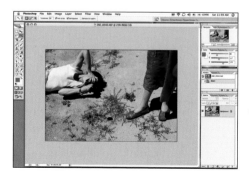

Photoshop...well, Photoshop is Photoshop, the world-class image editing and processing application. In this familiar environment, you can apply localized editing and processing to your converted RAW images and do whatever else is necessary to take them to their final, perfect form.

Platform Differences

Photoshop CS2 runs equally well on both the Mac and PC platforms. There is very little difference between the two. I work on a Mac, but I've made every possible effort to make this a PC-friendly book as well. When keyboard commands differ between platforms, I've noted the differences. I've also adopted the right-click shortcut to replace the keyboard Ctrl-/click command. This action—which often brings up a contextual menu—is long familiar to PC users, and most new Mac mice now operate similarly.

Comments and Questions

Please address comments and questions concerning this book to the publisher:

O'Reilly Media, Inc.
1005 Gravenstein Highway North
Sebastopol, CA 95472
(800) 998-9938 (in the United States or Canada)
(707) 829-0515 (international or local)
(707) 829-0104 (fax)

We'll list errata, examples, and any additional information at:

http://www.oreilly.com/catalog/photoshopraw/

To comment or ask technical questions about this book, send email to:

bookquestions@oreilly.com

Digital media artists—from the hobbyist photographer to the graphics designer and digital video producer—can find a wealth of informative and instructional articles, books, guides, and media content at O'Reilly's Digital Media site. For more creative inspiration, visit us at:

http://digitalmedia.oreilly.com/

For more information about our books, conferences, Resource Centers, and the O'Reilly Network, see our main web site at:

http://www.oreilly.com

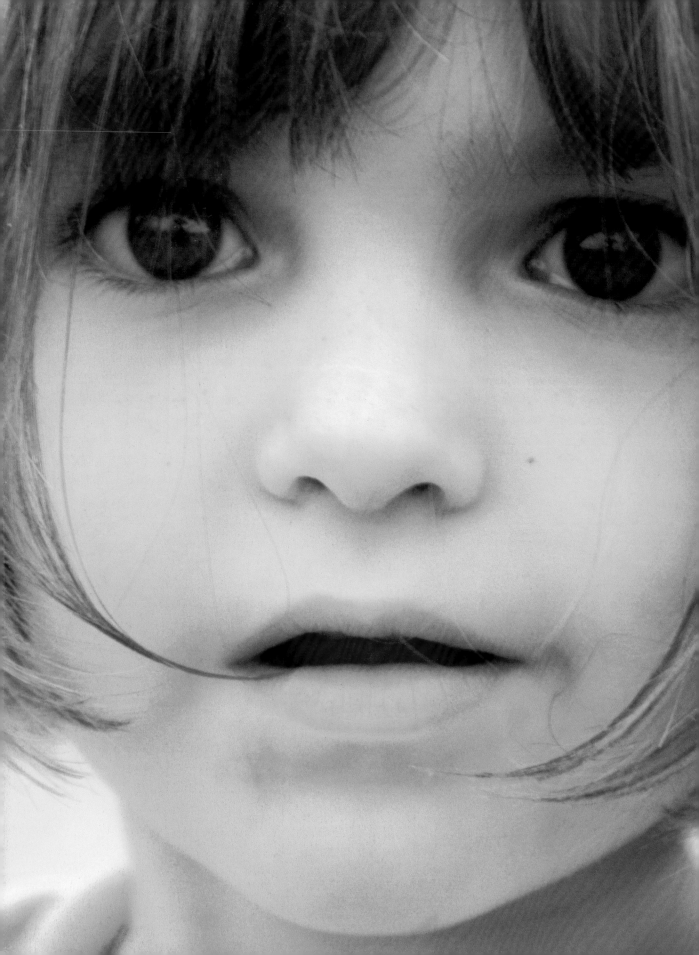

CHAPTER ONE

Shooting & Importing RAW

Long before you fire up your computer and transfer your image files from your digital camera, you must make important decisions that will affect your entire workflow. It's not always necessary to shoot and save RAW files. There are times when a JPEG works just fine. The question then is: when do you shoot RAW? There is also the question of the importance of various digital camera settings. When you shoot RAW, some settings, like ISO and exposure, are critical. Other settings, such as white balance and sharpening, aren't. This chapter highlights some of the more important choices you'll need to make, and provides guidelines that should make everything that follows go smoother. It'll also give you a cool way to make downloading your digital images to Bridge easier and more efficient.

Chapter Contents

When to Shoot RAW

Critical Digital Camera Settings

Correct Exposure

Including a Color Target

Importing Images to Bridge with Import Camera

1

When to Shoot RAW

It's helpful to understand that not every shot warrants the flexibility and quality of RAW, especially when you consider storage limitations and the extra work it takes downstream to convert and process the RAW files into formats that can be printed or otherwise shared.

Let me share a personal example with regard to making the RAW vs. JPEG choice. I was recently in Iceland, working on a travel story. I brought my wife and daughters, and mixed work with pleasure. Here are a couple photos of the family enjoying the famous Blue Lagoon, a unique geothermal spa just outside Reykjavik. *Figure 1-1*

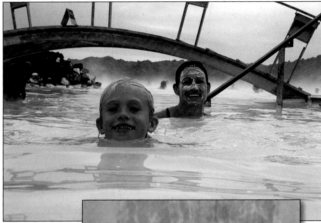

Figure 1-1

These are family mementos, snapshots if you will, meant for the family album. *Figure 1-2* I didn't want to fill my memory card, since I was going to have limited opportunities to download it to my laptop, and I had plenty of shooting ahead of me. In this case, I set my camera file preferences to JPEG with the highest quality setting. The saved file size was only 2.5MB and I could shoot to my heart's content with little worry of quickly filling my 1GB memory card.

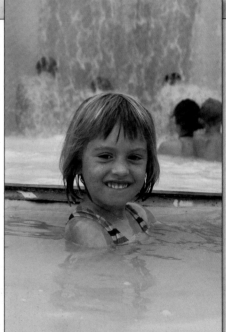

Figure 1-2

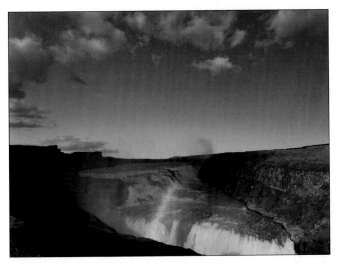

Figure 1-3

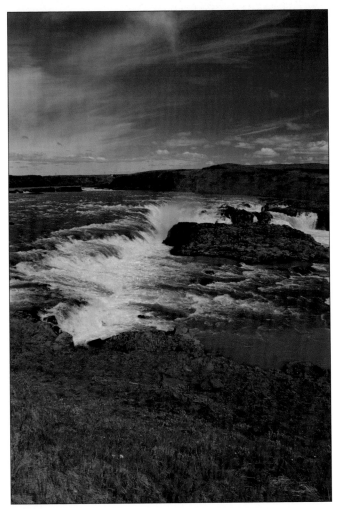

Figure 1-4

Later in the day, while touring the rugged terrain outside Reykjavik, we stopped at Gullfoss, Europe's most powerful waterfall. With this breathtaking scene in front of me, my concern for quality and flexibility increased, and I switched my file setting from JPEG to RAW. *Figure 1-3* In the past, I might have used a medium-format camera for this kind of shot. The act of changing my file format setting helped put me in a more deliberate mood, and I took time to carefully frame the shot and pay attention to detail. The resulting file size was 9.5MB, considerably larger than a JPEG would have been.

For now, changing file formats is a part of my work process, just like changing f-stops and shutter speeds. Every photographer comes up with their own criteria and rationale for shooting RAW. I've heard many event photographers say they avoid the RAW format altogether when shooting conventions and other such "grip and grin" situations. They are perfectly satisfied with the quality of JPEGs, which don't require post-processing like RAW files do. Wedding photographers, on the other hand, tend to shoot and archive RAW files, giving them maximum flexibility for extracting various sizes and quality options later in order to meet their clients' wishes. Almost every nature photographer I know shoots and archives RAW, which makes sense, since quality is such an important aspect of that kind of shooting. *Figure 1-4* Sports photographers I talk to shoot a combination of RAW and JPEG, depending on the capabilities of their equipment and the situation.

RAW vs. JPEG

In an ideal world—a world of the not-so-distant future—there will be little or no additional cost associated with the decision to shoot RAW. Digital camera memory will be so cheap that file size won't matter. Digital cameras will easily save both a RAW and a JPEG file—or other file formats of choice. (If Adobe is successful in integrating their DNG file format into common usage, digital cameras will also provide DNG as a file choice.) Camera processing time will be reduced significantly so there will be no "backlog," as RAW files are saved to memory. Computer processing power will be so great that it won't take any more time to manage and process your RAW files than a click of the mouse. More applications and operating systems will recognize and display RAW images—much as they universally read and recognize JPEG or TIFF files today. This ideal world isn't with us quite yet—even though more and more digital cameras offer a RAW+JPEG choice. And since it isn't, I suggest the following guidelines for determining if you should use the RAW format.

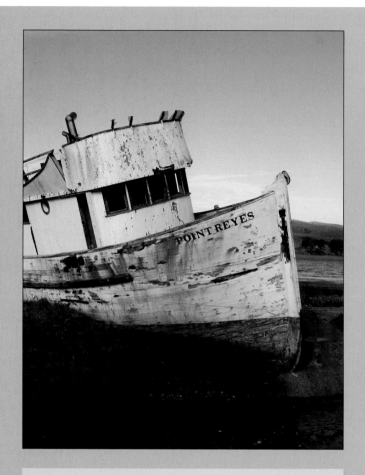

Shoot RAW if:

- *Technical quality is critical*
- *and memory is plentiful*
- *and processing time available.*

Shoot JPEG if:

- *Capture speed is an issue*
- *or memory is limited*
- *or time is of the essence for processing.*

(Many digital cameras will only save a few RAW files before temporarily "freezing" as RAW data is written to memory.)

Shooting and saving RAW adds built-in flexibility from a processing point of view. But the degree of flexibility is dependent on making the right choices as often as possible up front, even before you shoot. In short, some camera settings are critical, and others aren't.

Critical Digital Camera Settings

Here are what I consider to be the critical camera settings when you're shooting and saving RAW:

- File format
- Exposure
- ISO

File Format

This one is obvious; if you don't set you camera to save RAW, well, you won't get a RAW file with all its benefits. *Figure 1-5*

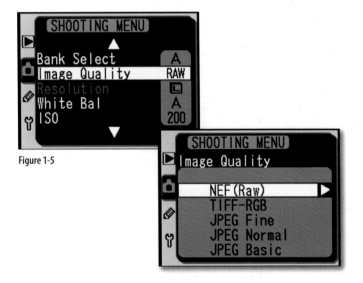

Figure 1-5

Exposure

As I'll explain in the following section, there is a common misconception that you don't have to worry about exposure when you shoot RAW. True, you have more margin of error with RAW. But only to a degree. (More on the subject of exposure correction later in Chapter 4.) *Figure 1-6*

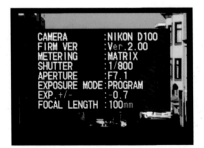

Figure 1-6

ISO

Just because you shoot RAW doesn't change the fundamental fact that quality is compromised at higher ISOs. The higher the ISO, the more electronic noise. This isn't necessarily bad. You just need to know ISO settings can make a noticeable difference. (In Chapter 7, I'll explain how to work with high ISOs from a processing point of view.) *Figure 1-7*

Here are the issues I don't consider to be quite as important when shooting RAW:

- White balance
- Sharpening
- Color Space

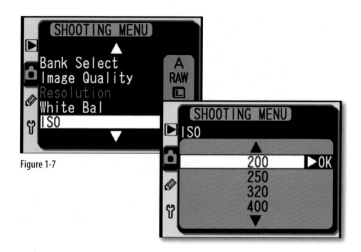

Figure 1-7

White Balance

I put this in the less-critical category with qualification. Yes, it's true, white balance can be determined later in Adobe Camera Raw with no quantifiable consequence. However, getting a correct white balance setting up front can streamline the process later. *Figure 1-8*

Sharpening

It doesn't matter what you set your camera sharpening setting to: Camera Raw ignores your settings and applies an optional setting of its own. However, if you shoot RAW+JPEG, your sharpening settings will apply to the JPEG file. Common wisdom is to turn sharpening to its minimum, and leave it as a last step in processing, just before printing. I go into great detail about process sharpening in Chapter 6. *Figure 1-9*

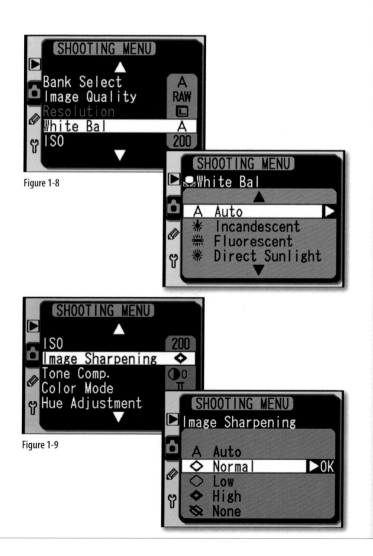

Figure 1-8

Figure 1-9

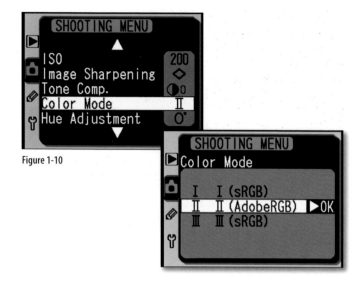

Figure 1-10

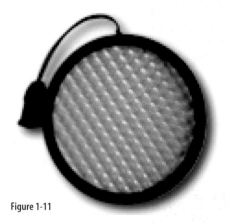

Figure 1-11

Color Space

Again, it doesn't matter which color space you set your digital camera to—be it commonly offered Adobe RGB or sRGB. Whatever color space you set can be changed later without consequence in Camera Raw. Color space determines which of the visible colors are available for your image. Some color spaces, like Adobe RGB, are wider and encompass more colors than, say, sRGB, which offers a more limited gamut of color. Keep in mind, if you shoot RAW+JPEG, the camera-selected color space is applied to the JPEG—and can't be changed later without degrading the image. *Figure 1-10*

In most single–light source shooting situations, I rely on my camera's Auto White Balance setting. When lighting sources are mixed—i.e., tungsten and florescent lights—I use the ExpoDisc Digital White Balance filter shown here, and create a custom white balance setting. You can achieve a custom white balance setting with a simple gray card, but I find the results achieved with the ExpoDisc far superior. It's available for around $75 at camera stores and online at www.expoimaging.net. Figure 1-11

Correct Exposure

It's a common misconception that you don't have to worry about exposure when you shoot RAW. Sure, you have more exposure latitude with RAW—some photographers swear they get two to three more exposure stops when they shoot RAW. But as you'll see later in Chapter 4, the further your image is from the correct exposure, the more work you'll have to do in Camera Raw or Photoshop to get it right.

Getting the correct exposure—as most photographers know—can either be very difficult or a piece of cake. It depends on the subject, the light, and the camera's capabilities. Fortunately, almost all digital cameras come with built-in features that help determine whether or not you are in the ballpark: LCD previews, histograms, and over/under exposure warnings. I encourage you, if you haven't already, to familiarize yourself with these handy tools and use them faithfully. (My book, *Shooting Digital*, goes into the subject of exposure in great detail.)

LCD Preview

The LCD preview will tell you if you got the shot, but shouldn't be relied on as an indictor of correct exposure. *Figure 1-12*

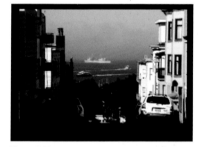

Figure 1-12

Histogram

Camera histograms are a very good indicator of exposure. *Figure 1-13* Properly exposed images will produce a well-distributed histogram, shifted slightly more to the right, without clipped highlights.

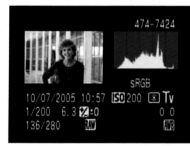

Figure 1-13

Over/Under Exposure Warnings

Flashing Over/Under exposure warnings are distractive, but at a glance you'll know if your highlights are too light or your shadows too dark. *Figure 1-14*

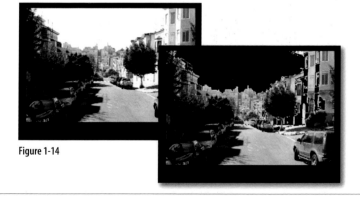

Figure 1-14

When it is possible or practical, I find it very useful to include a gray card or a color target—such as the GretagMacbeth color test chart—in at least one representative shot. You can find these targets at professional camera stores or on the web. (Keyword: "Buy. Photo. Gray Cards" or "GretagMacbeth.") The GretagMacbeth target should cost around $50 each, but gray cards are much less expensive, ranging from $10–$20.

Including a Color Target

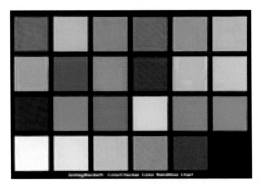

Figure 1-15

Figure 1-16

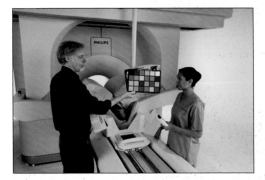

Figure 1-17

Not only does the GretagMacbeth color test chart provide a quantifiable color baseline, but as you can see, the chart also includes a white target and various shades of gray, which are useful for fine-tuning your tone mapping and white balance settings in Camera Raw. *Figure 1-15*

Gray cards such as the ones shown here, make a larger target and are therefore more useful for outdoor, "in-the-field" shots. Gray cards are useful on the shooting side for determining correct exposure and white balance in tricky lighting conditions, and later, as a target, for fine-tuning white balance settings in Camera Raw. *Figure 1-16*

Placement of the GretagMacbeth color target is easy and most effective in a studio environment with controlled lighting. Simply place the target so the studio lights strike it evenly. *Figure 1-17* Unless you change the type of lighting—i.e. from stroke to tungsten—all you need is one sample shot with the target. Using a target—be the GretagMacbeth color target or a gray card—outdoors under varying lighting conditions is trickier. As the light changes you'll need to reshoot the target to reflect the changes.

Later, when I open my files in Camera Raw. I use targets in either of two ways: if I've included a GretagMacbeth color card in the shot, I simply hold up the actual color target next to my monitor and compare the colors with those on my screen and manually make adjustments. *Figure 1-18* This is a very crude and inaccurate method, but sometimes it's all I need. Other times I simply use a gray card (or one of the neutral colored boxes at the bottom of the GretagMacbeth color card) as a target for determining correct white balance. I'll discuss this further in Chapter 5.

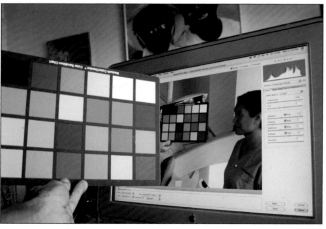

Figure 1-18

Every digital camera produces images with a specific color bias. Camera Raw compensates for this by referring to color profiles specific to a particular camera. Depending on your taste and your camera, the default Camera Raw setting may produce satisfactory results. If it doesn't, you can create custom settings for Camera Raw that will help assure consistent and satisfactory results. Figure 1-19 I'll show you more on this in Chapter 4.

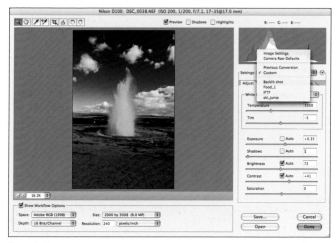

Figure 1-19

Many photographers simply attach their digital camera or memory card to a computer and manually transfer the image files to disc. You can also use a ready-made Adobe script to automatically import images from your digital camera to Bridge. It's called Import Camera, and it's available for free. (Of course, if you are comfortable with scripting language, you can write your own. Refer to the Adobe web site for more on writing custom scripts.)

Importing Images to Bridge with Import Camera

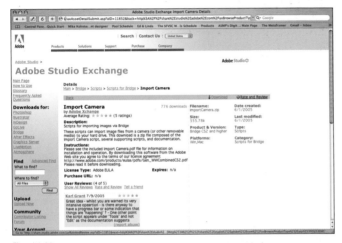

Figure 1-20

Downloading and using the Import Camera script takes a little bit of effort, but once you get the general concept and basic procedure you'll see how the tedious task of importing, renaming, and backing-up can be done in a snap without ever leaving the Bridge environment. Start by downloading the script from *http://share.studio.adobe.com. Figure 1-20*

(In Chapter 10, I'll show you ways to automate other tasks such as file conversion and resizing as well.)

Once you've downloaded the latest version of the Import Camera script, here's what to do:

1. The script file is *ImportCamera_BR.jsx*. Place the script in the Adobe StartupScripts folder. (Since the location of this folder varies from platform to platform, I suggest you search on your computer for .jsx files or "StartupScripts" to find the appropriate location.)

2. You'll also need to place three other files that come with the download into the start up scripts folder: *AdobeLibrary1.jsx, AdobeLibrary2.jsx,* and *AdobeLibrary3.jsx*. (The file AdobeScriptManger should already be loaded on your computer. If it isn't, use the AdobeScriptManager file that came with the Import Camera download.) *Figure 1-21*

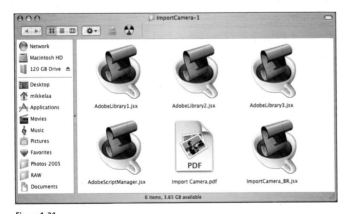

Figure 1-21

3. If you are using the full Creative Suite place the *ImportCamera_BR.jsx* file in the Workflow Automation Scripts folder, which is a sub folder of the startup scripts folder.

4. Once you have copied all of the files to their assigned locations, restart Bridge. A new menu item, "Import from Camera…" should appear in the Tools menu. *Figure 1-22*

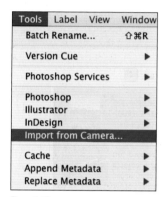

Figure 1-22

What you do next depends on how you want to download your images from your camera. Here is the general procedure:

1. Select Import from Camera (Tools > Import from Camera). You should get a dialog box that looks like the one shown here. *Figure 1-23*

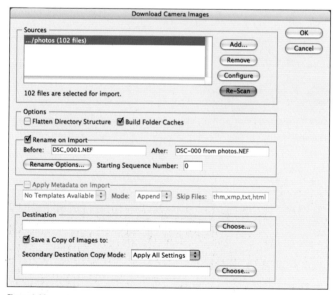

Figure 1-23

2. Navigate to the source and select it. If no source is available, this won't be an option.

3. Choose to Rename on Import and/or Apply Metadata on Import.

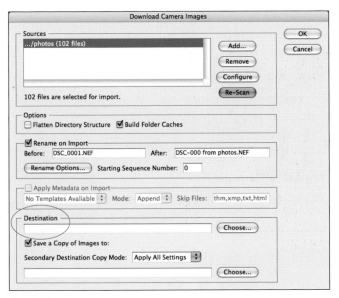

Figure 1-24

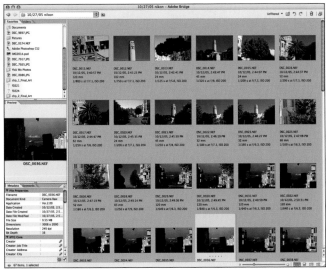

Figure 1-25

4. Select a Destination. If you want to create a backup at the same time, select "Save a Copy of Images" to: You will need to choose a secondary location for the backup. *Figure 1-24* You can also select Apply All Settings or Source File Backup. If you select the former, all the custom renaming and metadata settings will be applied to the backup as well. If you select Source File Backup, the original files will be copied as a backup, not the custom settings which will be only applied to the primary download. This is handy if you want to rename a batch of images for convenience and yet, at the same time, retain the original file names and metadata for archiving purposes. It can, however, be confusing having to sets of the same files with different names, so beware.

5. You won't have a choice—common to other import applications—of erasing original files after downloading. Some photographers who use the script complain about this omission, however, I would never want my original files erased until I was absolutely sure they had transferred correctly. So I don't miss this option.

Once you select OK, downloading begins. The Bridge temporarily freezes up. There is no progress indicator telling you how long you'll have to wait. Download time depends on the size of the files, the size of the media, and the processing speed of your computer, not to mention the options you choose. When the downloading is complete you get the following message: Import Complete. You are done downloading. Examine the files in Bridge and make sure they imported properly. *Figure 1-25* Then go ahead and use your camera to erase the files on the card.

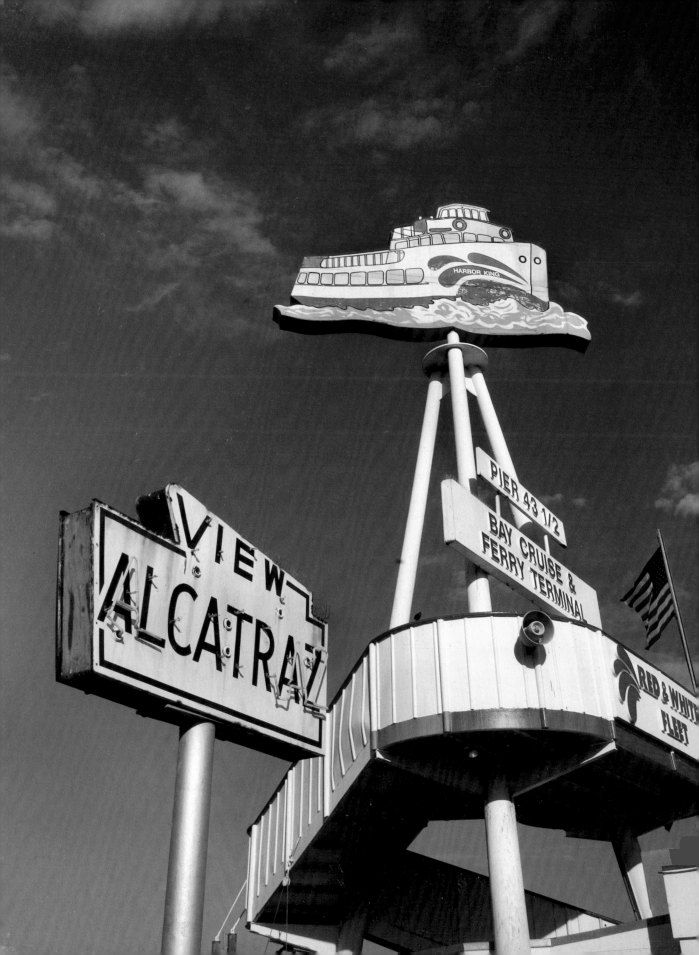

CHAPTER TWO

Using Adobe Bridge to Trash, Edit & Sort RAW Files

Adobe Bridge is roughly analogous to a traditional light table, and is therefore the perfect environment for trashing, editing, and sorting your RAW files. Let's take a look at how to use this standalone application to do this, and then, in subsequent chapters, we'll delve more deeply into the actual processing of RAW data using the other two distinct editing/processing environments: Photoshop and Camera Raw.

Chapter Contents

Launching & Viewing Images in Bridge

Editing a Photo Session

Checking for Image Sharpness & Exposure

Editing Based on Metadata

Labeling, Rating & Adding Keywords

Renaming Files

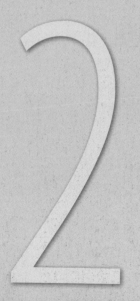

Launching Bridge

Bridge is a standalone application that launches separately from Photoshop CS2. It shares many of the attributes of the File Browser found in earlier versions of Photoshop, but it has more features and is designed to act as a central hub not only for Photoshop, but also for all of Adobe's Creative Suite products.

To open Bridge from within Photoshop:

1. Open Photoshop.

2. Select File > Browse.

You can also open Bridge from within Photoshop by clicking on the Bridge icon found in the Options bar. *Figure 2-1*

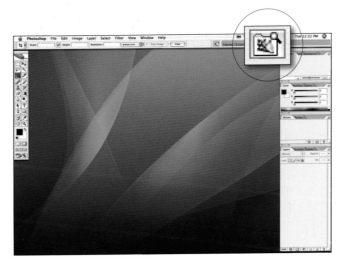

Figure 2-1

If you want Bridge to launch automatically whenever you launch Photoshop, you must change Photoshop default preferences. To do this:

1. Open Photoshop Preferences. (On a Mac, choose Photoshop > Preferences > General; on a PC, Edit > Preferences. Or use the shortcut Cmd/Ctrl-K.)

2. Check the box next to "Automatically Launch Bridge". *Figure 2-2*

The next time you launch Photoshop, Bridge will launch as well.

> *Since Bridge is an independent application, it can also be launched at any time directly from your desktop or Start menu.*

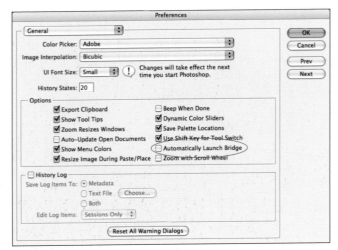

Figure 2-2

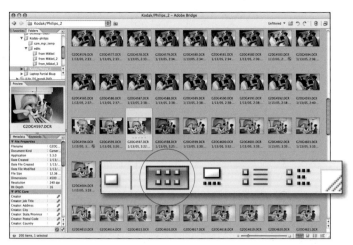

Figure 2-3

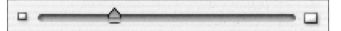

Figure 2-4

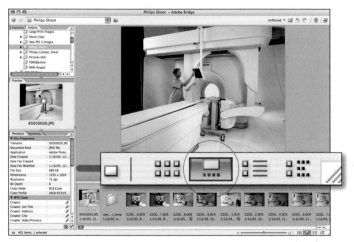

Figure 2-5

Viewing Images in Bridge

There are several options for viewing images in Bridge:

- You can view images as small thumbnails. For this view, select the indicated icon found at the bottom right of the Bridge window or choose View > Thumbnails. *Figure 2-3*

(You can increase the size of the thumbs incrementally by using the slider found at the bottom of the window, although this will increase the time required to open them. *Figure 2-4*)

- You can also use Bridge's Filmstrip view. *Figure 2-5* Selected images will appear magnified in the top window. For this view, select the indicated icon found at the bottom right of the Bridge window or choose As Filmstrip from the View menu.

You can view images in a Detailed view. *Figure 2-6* Images will appear alongside camera EXIF data. For this view, select the indicated icon found at the bottom right of the Bridge window or choose View > As Details.

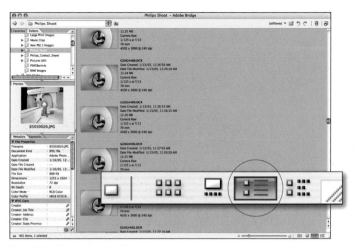

Figure 2-6

• You can also view "Versions and Alternates." *Figure 2-7* For this view, select the indicated icon found at the bottom right of the Bridge window or choose View > As Versions and Alternates. Versions and alternates will appear only if you have created a version. (Versions are shareable snapshots of various stages of a project. You can only create versions if you own and use the full Adobe Creative Suite 2.)

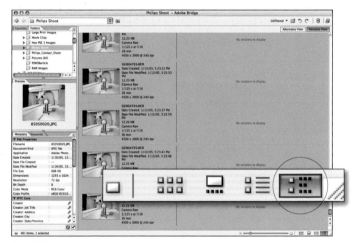

Figure 2-7

• Finally, you can view images as a slide show. Select View > Slide Show. *Figure 2-8*

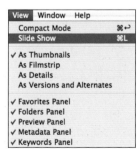

Figure 2-8

To properly orient images, use the right and left arrows at the top-right of the Bridge window or use the contextual menu, right-click, and choose the appropriate rotate command. Figure 2-9

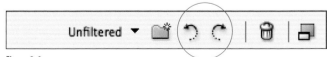

Figure 2-9

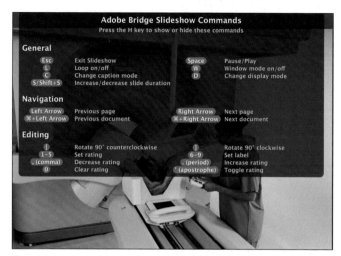

Figure 2-10

The slideshow will begin once you hit the spacebar. Clicking the mouse puts the slideshow into pause mode and subsequent clicks advance the show. The slideshow will display selected images. If no images are selected, the slideshow will display all the images in a folder.

You can control display characteristics and edit directly from within the slide show with keyboard commands. Pressing the H key shows these commands. *Figure 2-10* To hide the displayed commands, press the H key again. To quit the slide show, wait until the last slide is displayed, or hit the Esc key at any time. If you want to avoid looking at non-graphic files in your slide show, select View > Show Graphic Files only.

CHANGING THE BACKGROUND COLOR

Although the default neutral gray background is advisable for viewing most images whether they are color or black and white, you can darken or lighten the thumbnails background in the Bridge preferences. (Bridge > Preferences > General) *Figure 2-11*

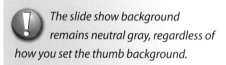

The slide show background remains neutral gray, regardless of how you set the thumb background.

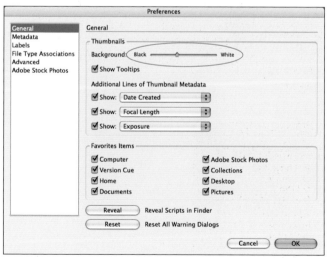

Figure 2-11

DISPLAY PERFORMANCE ISSUES

What happens if thumbnails, or "thumbs" for short, don't appear, or appear slowly? *Figure 2-12* The thumbs are actually generated by the Camera Raw plug-in so the problem may be that your version of Camera Raw does not support one of your RAW files. You'll need to periodically check the Adobe web site to make sure you are using the latest version of Camera Raw. (At the Adobe site you can sign up to be notified by email when new versions of Camera Raw become available.)

You may notice when Camera Raw is open and hosted by Bridge, Bridge stops generating new file thumbs. You can get around this by having Photoshop host Camera Raw instead. That way, even though you can continue working in Camera Raw, Bridge thumbs will be generated in the background. To understand what I'm talking about when I say "hosted" see sidebar titled: "Who Is the Host?"

Don't be surprised if it takes a while for RAW file thumbs to appear, especially when viewing them for the first time. A lot of processing is happening the background, and even the fastest computer may seem slow. Once the thumbs are created and cached, the next time you open the folder, they will appear quickly. (When Camera Raw creates a thumb it caches the small image separately from the original image file.)

(If you click on a RAW file whose thumb hasn't yet been generated, Bridge stops generating the other thumbs and prioritizes that file. When the thumb has been generated it resumes where it left off.) *Figure 2-13*

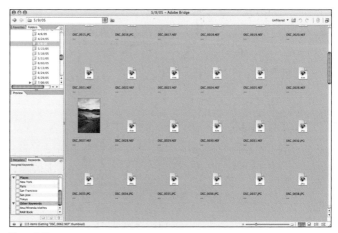

Figure 2-12

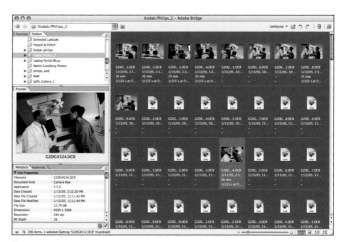

Figure 2-13

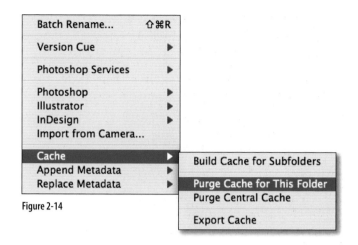

Figure 2-14

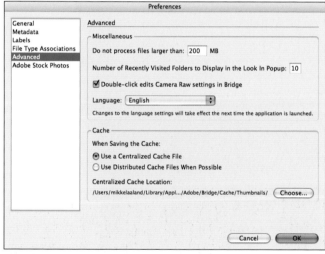

Figure 2-15

In rare cases, thumb files can become corrupted and won't display. In this case, you have no simple choice but to purge the thumb cache and have Camera Raw start over by building new thumbs. To do this select Tools > Cache and select either Purge Cache for This Folder or Purge Central Cache. *Figure 2-14* This purges the Bridge cache, but not the Camera Raw XMP or database data, nor does it purge the Camera Raw cache, which can be done via Camera Raw preferences. A warning: purging the Bridge cache can also purge labels and ratings, which are cached along with the thumbs.

> *The Bridge cache stores thumbnails, previews, and metadata for all file types. In the Advanced Bridge Preferences you can choose whether to use a Centralized Cache File, or use Distributed Cache Files. Figure 2-15 For the sake of simplicity, keep the default setting, which is Use a Centralized Cache File.*

Who Is the Host?

When you open a RAW file from Bridge you can choose the host. Your choice can make a difference in performance. If you select a RAW file, then select Cmd/Ctrl-R, or File > Open in Camera Raw, the Camera Raw host is Bridge. If you select a RAW file, then select Command+O, or File > Open With > Adobe Photoshop CS2, the Camera Raw host becomes Photoshop. You can actually have two Camera Raw windows open at the same time, one hosted by Bridge, the other by Photoshop.

How can you tell who's the host just by looking? If the Done button is the active selection it tells you Bridge is the host. *Figure 2-16* If Open is the active selection it tells you Photoshop is the host. *Figure 2-17*

It's true; when Bridge hosts Camera Raw, thumb production in Bridge stops until you close Camera Raw. However, as you will see in Chapter 9, when Bridge hosts Camera Raw and, say, you convert a batch of RAW files to the Adobe DNG format from using Camera Raw Save Options, you can close Camera RAW while the conversion occurs completely in the background and Bridge remains operable. If Photoshop hosts Camera Raw, and you convert a batch of RAW files to Adobe DNG and close Camera Raw before the conversion is finished, Photoshop becomes inoperative during the conversion. In short, most of the time, it's best to host Camera Raw from Bridge. This will keep the work area of Photoshop operational and, for the most part, it won't affect Bridge functionality when background processing is carried out by Camera Raw.

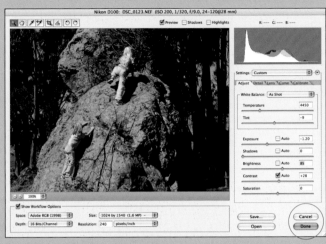

Figure 2-16

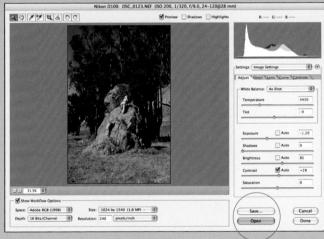

Figure 2-17

Getting from point A (a folder filled with RAW images stored on a photographer's hard drive) to point B (a finished image) requires several incremental steps, the first of which is culling the good shots from the bad. Sometimes this simply means identifying and trashing obvious shooting mistakes; other times it requires confirmation of focus and useable exposure.

Editing a Photo Session

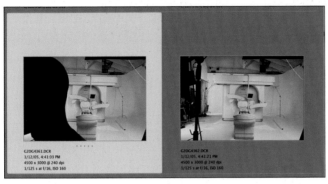

Figure 2-18

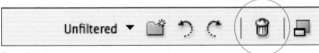

Figure 2-19

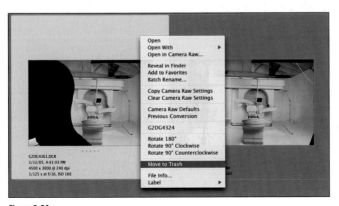

Figure 2-20

Deleting Images

To illustrate how to use Bridge to do this, I'll use images I recently took on assignment for Philips Medical systems.

The first thing I'll do before showing the client the images is delete the obviously bad ones; for example, the shot at the top left of the screen containing my wayward assistant. *Figure 2-18*

To delete images from Bridge and your hard drive:

1. Select the unwanted image. (Select multiple images by shift-clicking. Select non-adjacent images by Command-clicking.)

2. Click the trashcan icon found in the upper-right corner of the Bridge window. Alternatively you can hit the Delete key. *Figure 2-19*

You can also delete images via a contextual menu. Select an image or images, right-click, and select Move to Trash. (In Windows, select Send to Recycle Bin). *Figure 2-20* You can retrieve a trashed image from the Trash or Recycle Bin (as long as it hasn't been emptied).

Checking for Image Sharpness

Next I'll check for image sharpness. Sometimes out-of-focus shots are blatantly obvious; other times the unsharpness is a result of subtle camera or subject movement and doesn't show up in standard Bridge viewing options. *Figure 2-21* (Sharpness—or edge contrast—as it relates to RAW image processing is another subject, which I cover in Chapter 6.) If possible, it's always best to cull out unacceptable images early on in the editing process, before anyone gets too attached to the image and chooses it above other sharper ones.

Even though Bridge offers more viewing options than its predecessor, the File Browser, I'll be frank: it's not always easy to tell if an image is adequately sharp from within Bridge. You'll need to enlarge the image in question to its greatest magnification.

To do this:

1. Using the Thumbnail view, select an image.

2. Slide the slider on the bottom right of the Bridge window to the right as far as possible.

You can get a slightly greater magnified view by selecting the Filmstrip view and sliding the slider to the left. This will greatly decrease the size of the thumbnails, but also give you the largest possible magnification. *Figure 2-22*

The most magnification possible is available via the Slide Show option (View > Slide Show). When you choose this option, a single image fills your entire screen.

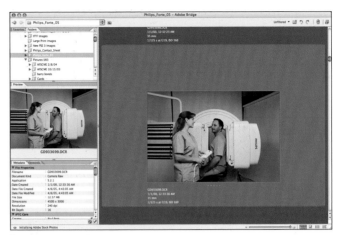

Figure 2-21

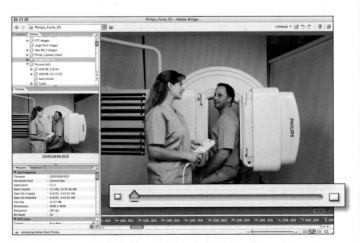

Figure 2-22

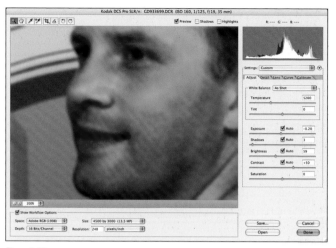

Figure 2-23

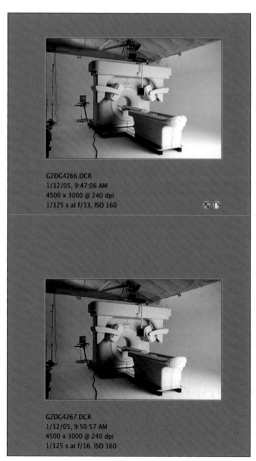

Figure 2-24

If you have any doubts about the sharpness of an image, open the image in Camera Raw (by double-clicking on the image in Bridge). Then use the much more powerful magnification and viewing tools available in Camera Raw (as I have done with the image shown here) to illustrate a very subtle, but clearly blurry image that is apparent only clearly at 100% or higher magnification. *Figure 2-23* When you are finished examining the image in Camera Raw, select the Cancel button to quickly bring you back to Bridge. (In Chapter 3, I'll show you how to cull and edit a photo session using Camera Raw.)

Checking Exposure

Images that are radically under- or overexposed can also be deleted. Bridge doesn't offer a histogram or other exposure checking tools, so you will need to rely on purely visual clues for this initial sorting. In order to check exposure from within Bridge, be sure your Camera Raw settings are set properly. For instance, look at the two shots shown here. *Figure 2-24*

These images look as if they were shot using the same exposure. But they weren't. As you can see by the EXIF data, the top image was shot at f/13 and the bottom image was shot at f/16. The images appear the same because the Camera Raw Defaults was set to automatically adjust and correct exposure. The Bridge thumbnail—which is generated in the background by the Camera Raw plug-in—is based on that auto adjustment rather than the actual exposure.

To change the Camera Raw Defaults setting and produce thumbnails which reflect different exposures:

1. Open any RAW image in Camera Raw. (File > Open in Camera Raw or double-click the image.)

2. In the flyout menu to the right of Settings, deselect Use Auto Adjustments. (Cmd/Ctrl-U toggles the Auto Adjustments settings.) *Figure 2-25*

3. Select Save New Camera Raw Defaults from the flyout menu.

4. Select Done.

Here are the same two images after toggling the Auto Adjustments; you can now see the images look different, allowing you to make an informed decision based on their different exposures. *Figure 2-26*

If Camera Raw was originally set to Use Auto Adjustments when all your thumbnails were first generated, and you changed your Camera Raw Defaults setting as outlined above, you will want to purge your Bridge thumb cache. Select Tools > Cache > Purge Cache for This Folder... Now all the new thumbnails will reflect the original camera settings. Use this method judicially, as it may also purge some ratings and labels.

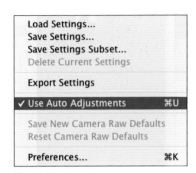

Figure 2-25

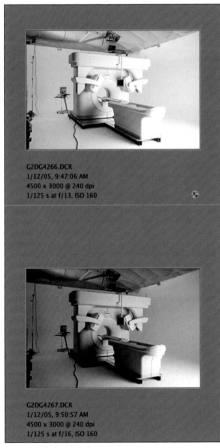

Figure 2-26

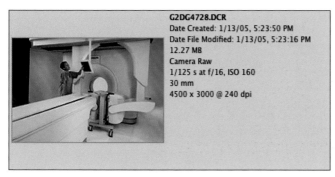

Figure 2-27

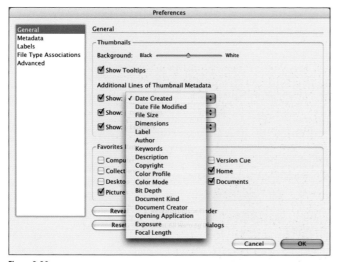

Figure 2-28

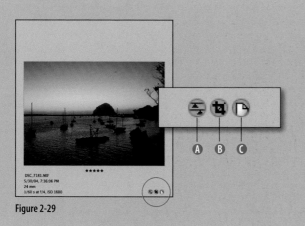

Figure 2-29

Editing Based on Metadata

Most of the time, editing decisions are based on visual considerations, but sometimes EXIF and other metadata can also inform your decision. Is there enough resolution, for example? What kind of file is it? What kind of camera was used? What ISO was used? And so on. When you view images in Bridge using the Detail mode, some (but not all) of this data is viewable. *Figure 2-27* These details also appear in other view modes when you hold your cursor over a thumbnail.

You can customize what metadata is displayed this way, up to a point. To change what is displayed, open the Bridge preferences (Bridge > Preferences > General) and under Additional Lines of Thumbnail Metadata, select the items you wish to display from the three pop-up menus. Each list has the same choices—basically, you get to pick three. *Figure 2-28* You may note that ISO is not an option, however, if you select Exposure, ISO will be included along with f-stop and shutter speeds. You can always view other Metadata by scrolling through the Metadata Tab or selecting File > File Info.

Thumb Icons Revealed

You can tell the status of your RAW file by looking at its thumb in Bridge. Here is a RAW file thumb revealed. Figure 2-29

A *Indicates Camera Raw settings have been applied.*

B *Indicates Camera Raw cropping*

C *Indicates file is open in Photoshop*

Understanding Metadata

Metadata is any data embedded in an image file that has been generated by you, your camera, or an application. EXIF metadata, for example, is data generated by a digital camera that contains such information as camera manufacturer, camera exposure time, f-stop, shutter speed, ISO, etc. Photoshop and Bridge display EXIF data via File > File Info and refer to the data as Camera Data 1 and Camera Data 2. Figure 2-30

EXIF data can also be viewed in the Bridge Metadata panel (View > Metadata panel). Figure 2-31 IPTC Core and XMP data, on the other hand, contain a wide range of contextual information, such as copyright and/or image description. You can also access this information using File > File Info and selecting the IPTC Contact (Figure 2-32), or in Bridge's Metadata panel. Figure 2-33

While you can easily use Photoshop and Bridge to add IPTC and XMP data to an image file and even create custom templates, EXIF data is generated by your camera and is generally not editable using Bridge or Photoshop CS2.

A typical RAW file contains EXIF data and you can add other metadata via File Info. However, it's important to remember that once you convert your RAW file to another file format or try to read IPTC or XMP metadata created in Photoshop CS2 in another application, the metadata may or may not survive the conversion or transition. I will address this potential problem later in Chapter 10.

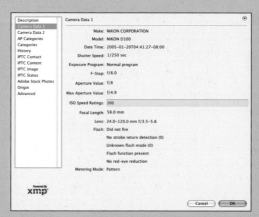

Figure 2-30

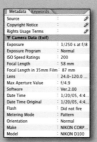

Figure 2-31

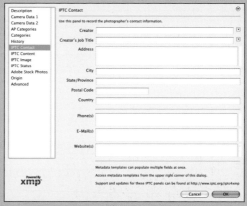

Figure 2-32

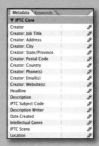

Figure 2-33

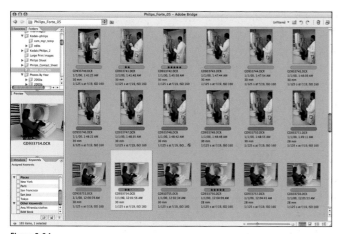

Figure 2-34

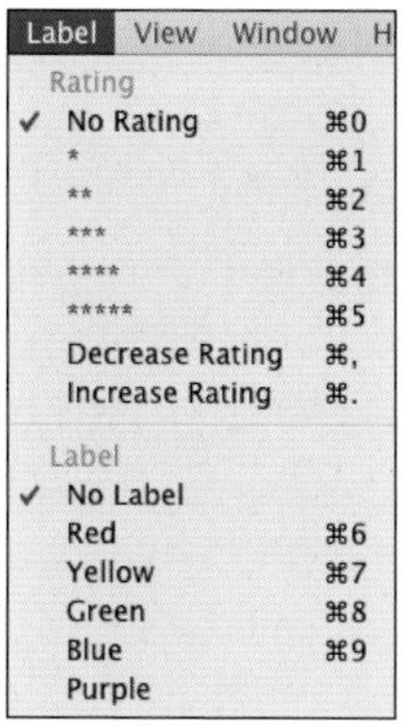

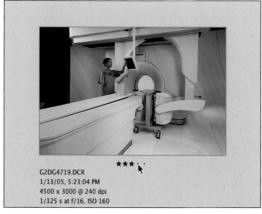

Figure 2-35

Labeling, Rating & Adding Keywords

As a final step in my editing process, I'll label and/or rate the images according to importance or category. Since I don't know exactly what the client is looking for, I will only cull out images that I feel are clearly weak. Since these images aren't necessarily awful, I won't trash them. Because they may contain something that may prove useful later, I'll keep them waiting in the wings, but away from the client's eyes.

In the old File Browser you could "flag" images to separate them from the rest. Adobe has now turned to traditional workflow for inspiration, using stars and colors instead of a flag. You can assign, for example, five stars to an image that is a definite "keeper," four to a lesser one, and so on. You can also "group" images by color. *Figure 2-34*

To assign stars to an image or images:

1. Select the image. Select multiple images by holding the command key while clicking. Cmd/Ctrl-A selects all the images in a folder.

2. Assign a star value via the Label menu. *Figure 2-35* Or use a keyboard command (shown in the Label menu). Use Label > Decrease (Cmd/Ctrl-,) or Label Increase (Cmd/Ctrl+.) to incrementally change the rating.

You can also assign stars directly under the thumb by clicking on the dots. *Figure 2-36* All the selected thumbs will be similarly rated. Remove individual stars by clicking on them. Remove all stars by clicking to the left of the first star. This is all too easy to do accidentally, so beware.

Figure 2-36

Color Labels are also added via the Label menu (with corresponding keyboard commands). Color Labels can be used to flag files to be trashed or otherwise categorized. Once you have created a star rating or color label, you can sort your images accordingly. Select the pop-up menu at the top of the Bridge browser window and choose the sorting criteria. *Figure 2-37*

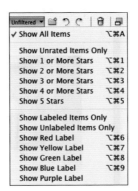
Figure 2-37

It's also very easy to add a keyword from Bridge. Keywords are embedded in the image file as metadata and add another layer of flexibility to image searches and accessibility.

To add a keyword in the Bridge:

1. Select the Keywords tab in the browser window. Several presets will appear. *Figure 2-38*

•   To delete a keyword, select the word and either click the trashcan icon at the bottom of the window, or select Delete from the pop-up list that appears when you click the arrow in the upper-right of the Keyword window.

•   To add new keywords to the list, click the New Keywords icon at the bottom of the Keywords window or select New Keyword from the pop-up menu. You can also add new Keyword sets. *Figure 2-39*

•   To add a keyword to an image file, simply select an image, and, in the Keywords window, click the box next to the word(s) you wish to include. Add keywords to more than one image by selecting multiple images in the Bridge browser window and then selecting the desired keywords.

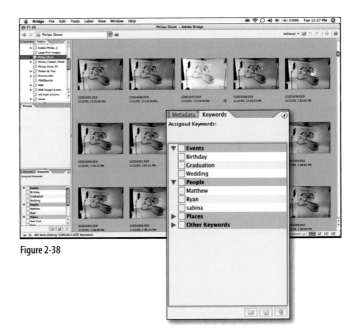
Figure 2-38

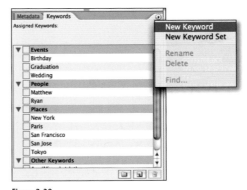
Figure 2-39

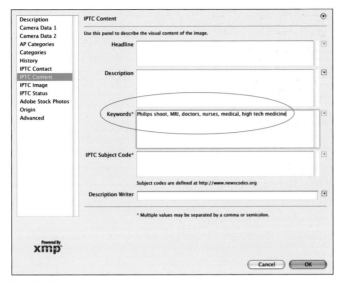

Figure 2-40

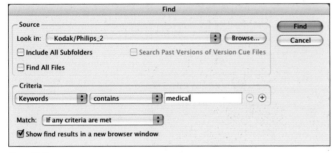

Figure 2-41

- To remove keywords from an image, select the image(s) and deselect the keyword(s). You can also edit or remove keywords from within the File Info dialog box (File > File Info). Or, go to IPTC Content, which contains the Keywords text field. *Figure 2-40*

- To search by keyword, select Edit > Find from Bridge's menu bar. Then apply the applicable criteria and select Find. Bridge will display relevant images in the browser window. *Figure 2-41*

> *It's one thing to make unilateral editing decisions, and quite another when others are involved in the decision-making. It's not practical to provide RAW files to clients. (Most people wouldn't appreciate such large files that require special software anyway.) One of the easiest ways to share files for editing purposes is to create some sort of shared contact sheet. However you can use various Bridge and Photoshop automation tools to create a Web Photo Gallery, a printable Contact Sheet, or a PDF file that contains contact sheets. I'll show you a few ways to do this in Chapter 10.*

Renaming Files

There are many reasons to rename an image file. Digital cameras produce seemingly obscure strings of sequential numbers that have no relationship to the content of an image. Some photographers prefer adding some sort of descriptor to a particular set of images, which is very easy to do from within Bridge.

To rename a batch of image files:

1. From the Tools menu, select Batch > Rename. *Figure 2-42*

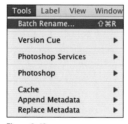

Figure 2-42

2. Under New Filenames, pick your criteria. For example, as you can see in here, I selected "text" from the pop-up menu. In the text field, I typed in "philips". Then, in the next criteria field, I selected "sequence number" from the popup menu. (There will be a next field only if you click the "+" icon.) I left "1" as my starting point and selected "Three Digits" from the adjacent pop-up menu. You can preview the changes at the bottom of the Batch Rename window. *Figure 2-43*

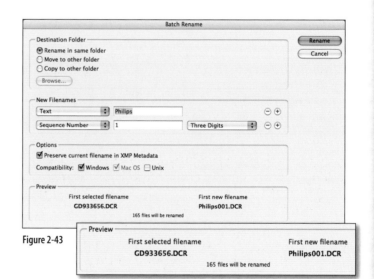

Figure 2-43

> Although it may seem like one at times, Bridge isn't technically an image asset manager on par with programs such as Extensis Portfolio, Canto Cumulus, ACDSee, iView, etc. Bridge doesn't create a separate image database and is therefore only capable of searching, organizing, and handling online image files. For more on handling your images with an asset management program, see The DAM Book: Digital Asset Management for Photographers by Peter Krogh (O'Reilly, 2005).

- If you want to retain a record of the original file name, under Options select "Preserve current file name in XMP Metadata". If you do this, you can always retrieve the data later by selecting "Preserved Filename" in the criteria pop-up window. Keep in mind that Bridge does its best to keep the *.xmp* file together with the original file, but if either file is moved, renamed, or opened by another application, the XMP data may be unreadable. If you want to use camera EXIF data—such as exposure time or focal length—simply select EXIF Metadata from the criteria pop-up window and then select your choice in the adjacent pop-up window. Again, you can preview the results in the Preview section of the Batch Rename window. *Figure 2-44*

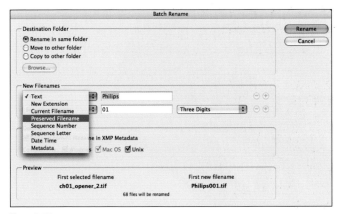

Figure 2-44

3. When you are done, select Rename. The time it takes for renaming depends on the number of files selected and whether you selected Copy to other folder, which makes a copy of the original and renames the copy. Copying obviously adds time to the process. *Figure 2-45*

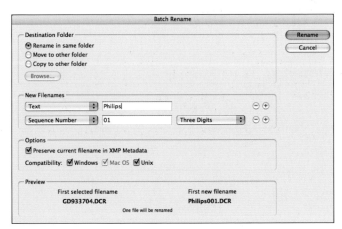

Figure 2-45

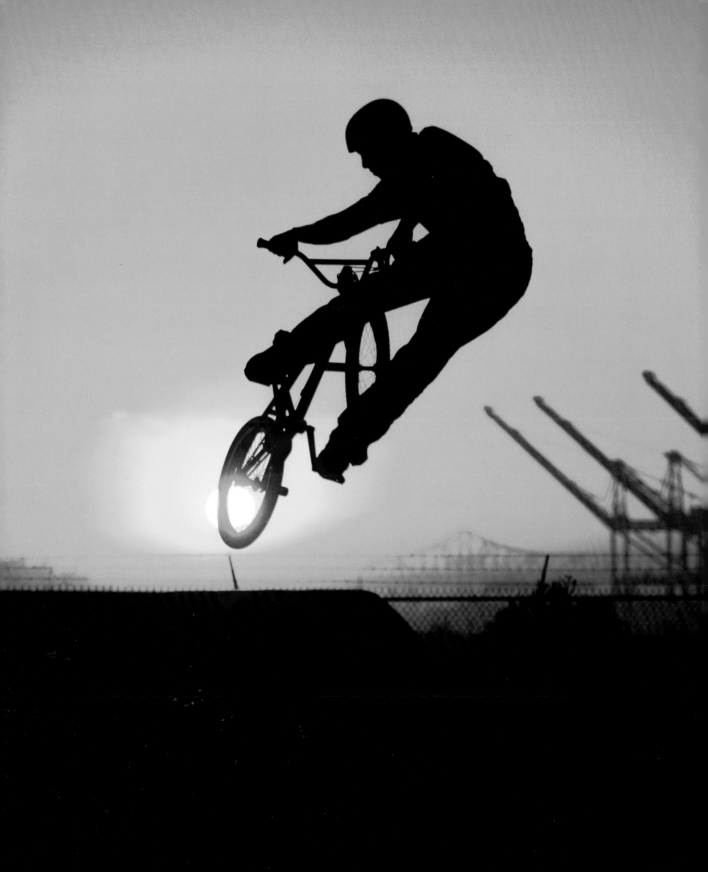

CHAPTER THREE

Using Adobe Camera Raw

The heart of CS2's RAW processing is the Adobe Camera RAW plug-in, developed and constantly updated by the eminent Thomas Knoll, one of the original creators of Photoshop. Camera Raw has come a long way in just a short time and has become the RAW processing tool for many photographers. Now in CS2, Camera Raw supports opening and viewing multiple images, making it not only an outstanding RAW processor but a viable editing environment as well. This chapter gives you a general overview of the basic controls and features of Camera Raw. Subsequent chapters expand into more detail on such subjects as tone mapping, white balance, sharpening, and reducing noise.

Chapter Contents

Updating Camera Raw

Workflow Options

Editing with Camera Raw

An Overview of Camera Raw Tools

Camera Raw Preview and Analysis Tools

Camera Raw Tabs

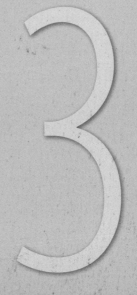

Updating Camera Raw

Before you do anything, you'll want to have the most recent version of Camera Raw. Note that the Adobe Camera Raw plug-in is a work in progress. Every few months or so, it is updated to support new digital cameras that come online. Minor, behind the scenes improvements, are also sometimes made. It's therefore best to periodically check the Adobe web site and download the latest version of Camera Raw. It's free.

At the Adobe site, you can also sign up to receive email notices informing you when new versions of Camera Raw (and the Adobe DNG Converter) become available. You can sign up at various locations on the Adobe site. Use the Adobe Search option and enter the keywords: notify camera raw updates. *Figure 3-1*

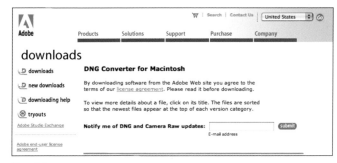

Figure 3-1

You can tell which version of Camera Raw you are using by selecting Photoshop > About Plug-In > Camera Raw... from the main Photoshop menu. In Windows, the "About Plug-In" location is under the Help menu. A dialog box containing the version number will appear. *Figure 3-2*

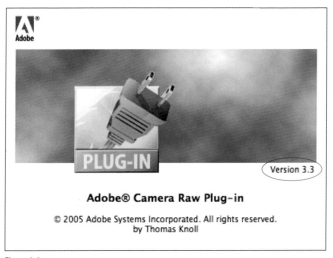

Figure 3-2

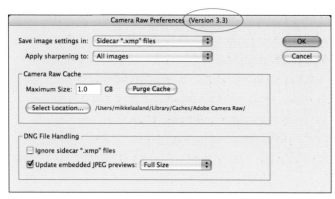

Figure 3-3

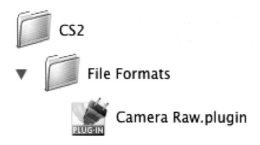

Figure 3-4

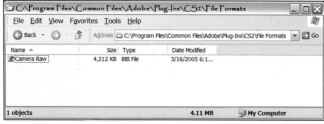

Figure 3-5

From Bridge, you can find the Camera Raw version number by selecting Bridge > Camera Raw Preferences from the main menu bar. (With Windows, Camera Raw Preferences are under the Edit menu.) The version number will be at the top of the Preferences dialog box. *Figure 3-3*

After you download the Camera Raw plug-in file from the Adobe site, do the following:

1. Close Photoshop.

2. On a Mac, go to the Finder, in Windows open My Computer and double-click Local Disk (C).

3. On a Mac, navigate to Library/ Application Support/Adobe/Plug-Ins/ CS2/File Formats. *Figure 3-4*
   In Windows, navigate to Program Files\ Common Files\Adobe\Plug-Ins\CS2\ File Formats. *Figure 3-5*

4. Move the existing plug-in to another location. Keep this version in case you need to revert.

5. Place the Camera Raw plug-in from the download into the same folder as in Step 3.

The next time you fire up Photoshop or Bridge, the new version will become available. It's not necessary—or desirable—to replace or throw away any Camera Raw cache folders. Just replace the plug-in itself.

Workflow Options

At the bottom of the Camera Raw workspace is a Show Workflow Options check box. It's easy to overlook the options provided here—Space, Depth, Size, and Resolution—but they are key to getting the most out of your RAW images. (Note that Chapter 10 will specifically address the issues of workflow and processing multiple RAW images with Camera Raw, Bridge, and Photoshop.)

When you select Show Workflow Options, a small portion of your bottom viewing area is used to present various options. Let's take a look at each one. *Figure 3-6*

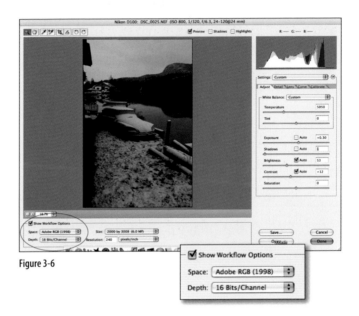

Space

Here you can choose from a variety of color spaces, including the ones you see here. *Figure 3-7* In Chapter 4, I'll go over the arguments for choosing each; for now, just keep in mind that since we are working with RAW files, you can apply any color space of choice (at any time) without actually changing the underlying image data.

Figure 3-6

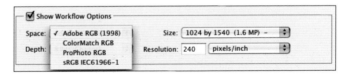

Figure 3-7

Depth

In Camera Raw, you can choose between two depths: 8 Bits/Channel and 16 Bits/Channel. *Figure 3-8*

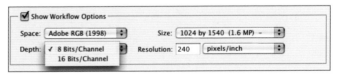

Figure 3-8

Most digital cameras save approximately 12 Bits/Channel of color data. To get the most out the RAW data when it is opened from Camera Raw into Photoshop, I work with 16 Bits/Channel for as long as possible, even though it results in larger file sizes. (As you will see in Chapter 10, if you are working on multiple RAW images, there may be times when 8 Bits/Channel is more efficient.)

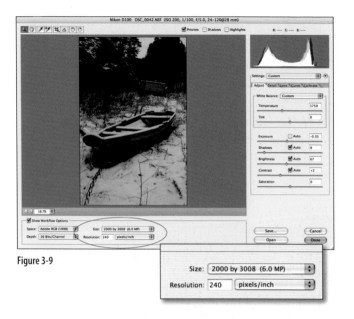

Figure 3-9

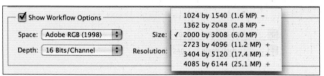

Figure 3-10

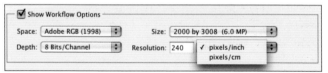

Figure 3-11

Size

Your digital camera is capable of a specific maximum image size. You can either reduce that size via camera settings or better yet, do it later in Camera Raw and Photoshop. *Figure 3-9*

Any size under the actual set by your camera is marked with a minus sign at the end. Any size over the actual size is marked with a plus sign at the end. *Figure 3-10* The actual size of your camera has no markings at the end. When should you go over or under the native size set by your camera? The fact is, this setting doesn't actually "resize" the RAW file. It only tells Photoshop how to size the RAW file when it's opened. I'll get into more detail about resizing in Chapter 10, but in short, I generally recommend resizing incrementally in Photoshop when quality is an issue, and using the different Camera Raw Size settings if they are appropriate and a speedy workflow is the main concern.

Resolution

The resolution value is relevant only when it comes time to print your image. It's a value used by a printer driver to determine how many pixels to print per inch/or centimeter. *Figure 3-11* The default of 240 pixels/inch is generally considered a suitable number for most desktop printers. You can set any number you want. It doesn't change the number of total pixels in your image, only the distribution of those pixels when it comes time to print. Again, I want to emphasize that changing any of these workflow settings doesn't do anything to the actual RAW file. It only creates a Camera Raw setting that is applied when the RAW file is opened in Photoshop, and the settings can be changed at any time.

Editing with Camera Raw

In the previous chapter we saw how to edit, select, and tag RAW files in Adobe Bridge. We also saw that Bridge has its limitations. Magnifying an image large enough to examine for noise and sharpness, for example, is not really a viable option in Bridge. Now that Camera Raw is capable of opening more than one image at a time, it has become a workable editing environment and a good adjunct to Bridge.

Using Camera Raw to Edit a Photo Shoot

Photographer Martin Sundberg, for example, uses Camera Raw to edit his photo shoots. Martin is best known as a photographer specializing in extreme outdoor sports. His subjects often move fast—very fast—and Martin often shoots several frames per second to maximize the chances of getting the perfect frame. However, shooting this way also increases the chances of an image being out of focus or blurred from camera or subject movement. One frame may be perfectly sharp and the next not. Examining for sharpness is therefore a critical component in Martin's editing process. In this section, we'll join Martin as he imports and edits a freestyle biking shoot.

To Edit a photo shoot in Camera Raw, Martin performs some preliminary steps:

1. Import the RAW files from the memory card into Bridge. Here Martin imports the shots from his Canon 1D Mark II. *Figure 3-12*

2. Next, select all the images in Bridge (Command/Ctrl+A). (If no images are selected, Bridge assumes all visible images are to be renamed.) Then apply a Batch Rename using Tools > Batch Rename from the menu bar. Martin creates a starting numerical identifier and the descriptive text: bike_ramp. *Figure 3-13*

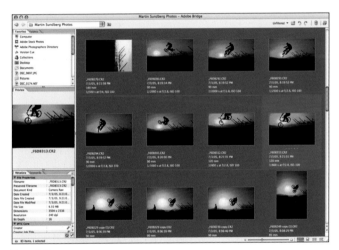

Figure 3-12

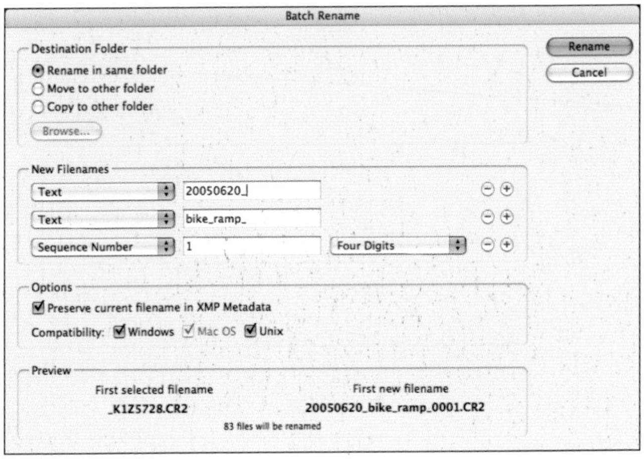

Figure 3-13

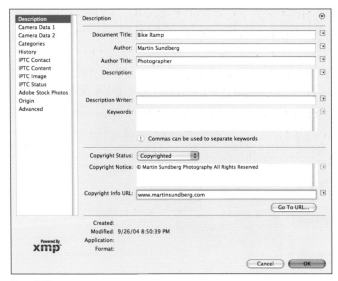

Figure 3-14

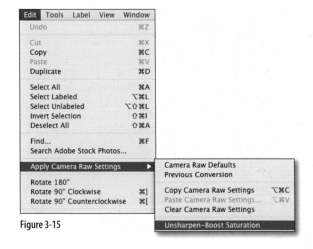

Figure 3-15

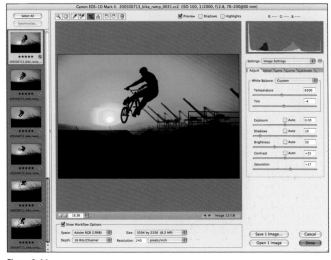

Figure 3-16

3. After batch renaming, select all the files again. Now use File Info (File > File Info) to apply a copyright notice, your name, and URL. The data entered in File Info will apply to all the selected images. *Figure 3-14*

4. At this point, in Bridge, select all your files. Then you can apply a custom Camera Raw setting to all the images. Martin has created a setting he calls Unsharpen-Boost Saturation. (Because he has the preset saved, he can use Edit > Apply Camera Raw Settings from the file menu. Right-clicking on an image brings up these options as well.) Martin's custom setting turns off sharpening in Camera Raw and boosts saturation by about 30 percent. (We'll go over creating and using custom Camera Raw settings in Chapter 10, but for now, just take note that this is a point where changes can be made to the whole collection of RAW files at once from within Bridge.) *Figure 3-15*

Whew! So much to do before actually editing! But everything Martin has done up to now is an integral part of any good workflow. Tagging images for copyright and ownership is critical for maintaining image integrity, and renaming files gives Martin hands-on control over critical image information. After all this, it's on to editing:

1. Open the selected files in Camera Raw by placing your cursor over one of the selected thumbs and double-clicking. After a while, the images appear in the Camera Raw window and look like this. *Figure 3-16* Note the image in the main window opens at 18.3 percent. Not a good size for determining sharpness. Also note the icon in the lower right

corner of each file's thumb. This signifies Camera Raw settings have been applied. Remember, in Martin's case, he applied the custom Camera Raw settings earlier, in Bridge.

2. Before magnifying the image to a desirable 100 percent, choose Select All from the top of the image window. Next, use the Zoom tools to magnify the image to 100 percent. (The keyboard command Command/Ctrl+Option/Alt+0 also sets an image to 100 percent.) Now all the images will appear at 100 percent, and you don't have to stop and change the zoom level each time. *Figure 3-17*

3. To quickly cycle through the images, use the keyboard up and down arrow keys. At 100 percent magnification, Martin can quickly see which images are sharp and which aren't.

Deleting and Assigning Ratings in Camera Raw

One of the great things about editing in Bridge is the ability to quickly trash, prioritize, and sort images. Well, you can do the same in Camera Raw (albeit without the sorting ability), but with the advantage of being able to enlarge and analyze images more fully than you could in Bridge.

To delete an image, select the image you wish to delete. Select the Trashcan in the tool bar at the top of the Camera Raw window. To deselect images marked for deletion, simply click the trash icon again. *Figure 3-18* You can also delete/undelete by using the delete keyboard command. (The Trashcan icon will appear in Camera Raw only when multiple RAW files are open.)

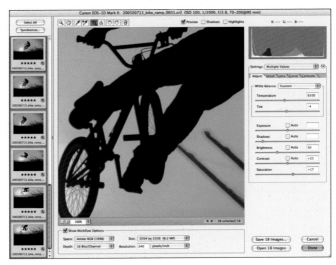

Figure 3-17

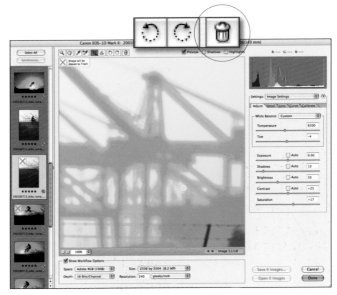

Figure 3-18

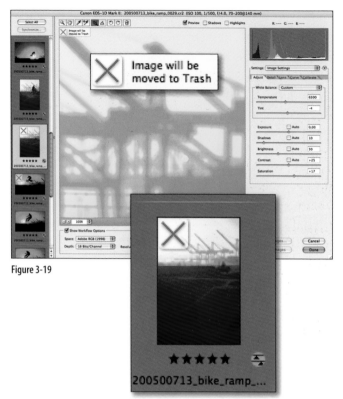

Figure 3-19

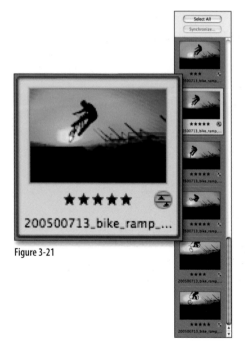

Figure 3-20

Figure 3-21

This reminder will appear in the image window. *Figure 3-19*

In the filmstrip view, the image icon will have a reminder as well, this time in the form of an X. *Figure 3-20*

When you exit Camera Raw the images marked for deletion will automatically move to the trash or recycle bin.

You can also assign your ratings here.

This is what Martin's thumbnails look like in Camera Raw after he assigns ratings. *Figure 3-21*

Camera Raw can't sort images by priority, so Martin saves this as a last step, in Bridge.

After editing and tagging your images, select Done. This doesn't open the images in Photoshop. That's not what you want—at least not at this time. Selecting Done closes the Camera Raw window and assigns a XMP sidecar file to each image that contains the tagging information. (Or, depending on how Camera Raw Preferences are set, it saves the information in a Camera Raw database.) Later, in Bridge, as a final editing step, you can sort your images according to rating and make a new folder to hold the cream of the crop (View > Sort > By Rating).

An Overview of Camera Raw Tools

Many Camera Raw tools will seem familiar to seasoned Photoshop users. There are navigation tools, zoom tools, color sample tools, and a crop tool, to name a few. In this section, we'll take a brief overlook at all of them. I think you'll find it particularly interesting to see how the Crop tool can be used creatively to make large-scale panoramas.

Zoom and Hand Tools

Some processing decisions—such as color and exposure corrections—are more easily made when the entire image is visible in the viewing area. Other tasks, such as sharpening and noise reduction, benefit from enlarging or magnifying an image so details are readily discernable. The key to getting the views you want is knowing how to use the Zoom and Hand tools.

To select the zoom level in Camera Raw:

1. Click on the pop-up window on the lower left side of the viewing area. *Figure 3-22*

2. Choose Fit in View to make the entire image visible in the viewing area. (The Fit in View option will set different files to different zoom amounts, depending on the original file size.) Double-clicking on the Hand tool (found in the toolbar at the top of the viewing area) also makes the entire image visible in the viewing area. The keyboard command Cmd/Ctrl-0 will also set the image to Fit in Window size. Use higher magnification percentages to zoom in. You can also use the Cmd/Ctrl-(+) and Cmd/Ctrl-(–) keystrokes to zoom in or out. Standard Photoshop magnifying keyboard commands also work. Place your cursor over the area you wish centered and then Cmd/Ctrl-click to zoom in, or Cmd/Ctrl+Option/Alt-click to zoom out.

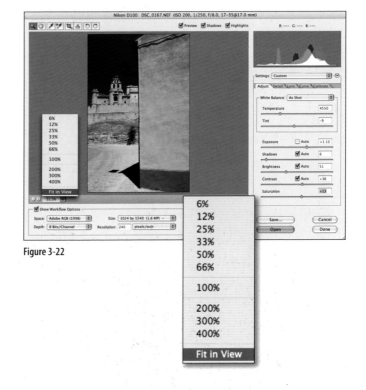

Figure 3-22

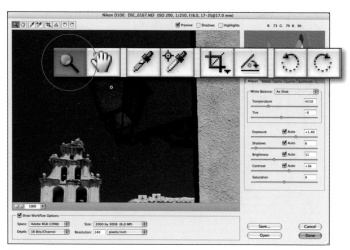

Figure 3-23

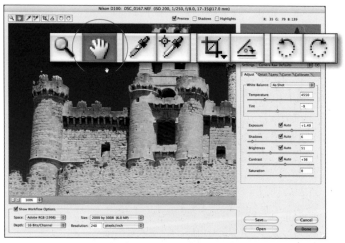

Figure 3-24

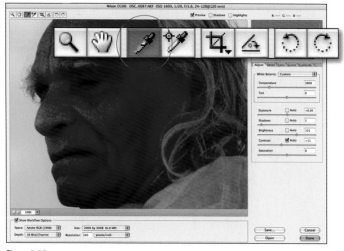

Figure 3-25

3. You can also use the Zoom tool (found in the toolbox at the top of the viewing area). Select it by clicking on the icon, or using the keyboard Cmd/Ctrl-Z. Hold your cursor over the area you wish to zoom in or zoom out. Use Option/Alt-click to zoom out, or just click if you want to zoom in. You can also simply drag the cursor over the area of interest and release to zoom in. *Figure 3-23*

To navigate a zoomed image with the Hand tool:

1. Click on the Hand tool icon (found at the top of the viewing area) or use the shortcut Cmd/Ctrl-H. *Figure 3-24*

2. Place your cursor over the image area, and click/hold and drag the image into position. The open hand becomes a clenched fist until your release your mouse.

3. Select the Hand tool at any time by holding the space bar. Your cursor will change to a hand.

White Balance Tool

The White Balance tool, located in the toolbar next to the Hand tool, can be used to automatically set the white balance based on a selected area of your image. (You can also set white balance manually using the Temperature and Tint Sliders in the Adjust tab.) I'll get into more detail on using this tool in Chapter 4, but it's very easy to use: simply select the tool and click on an area of your image that should be neutral gray or white. Then view the results. *Figure 3-25*

Color Sampler Tool

The Color Sampler tool is also located in the toolbar, next to the White Balance tool. You can use the tool to take up to nine static color samples from the preview image. (These sample points will update in real-time to reflect any color or tonal adjustments.) *Figure 3-26*

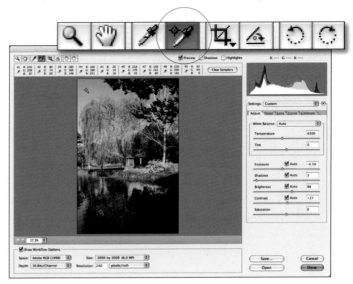

Figure 3-26

The values appear as RGB values above the preview image and can be cleared by clicking Clear Samplers. *Figure 3-27*

You can also get a real-time RGB readout by moving the Zoom tool, Hand tool, White Balance tool, Color Sampler tool, Crop tool, or Straighten tool anywhere over the preview image. The RGB values of the areas under the cursor will appear, in the upper right corner of the dialog box over the histogram.

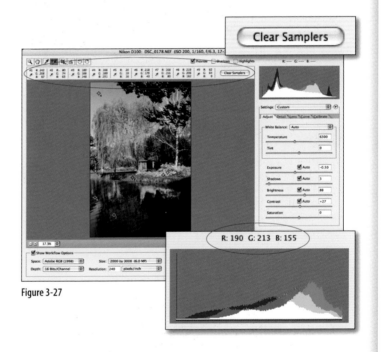

Figure 3-27

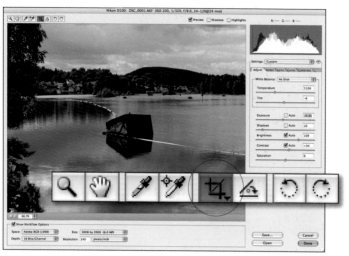

Figure 3-28

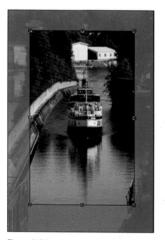

Figure 3-29

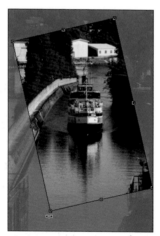

Figure 3-30

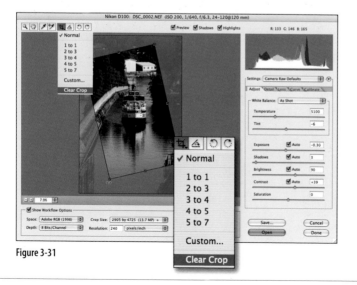

Figure 3-31

Crop Tool

Cropping is used to remove unwanted objects, to create a specific size images for printing, and to improve composition. Camera Raw's Crop tool is located in the toolbar shown here. *Figure 3-28*

Camera Raw's crop tool works pretty much the same as the one in Photoshop does. Either select the Crop icon in the tool bar, or use the keystroke "C". Click on the image window and drag to the desired size. Once you release the mouse, a rectangular box with bounding bars at the edges appears. *Figure 3-29* You can adjust the size of the crop at any time or click and drag the crop into place. If you have multiple images open in Camera Raw, you can apply a similar crop to all the images by using the Select All button.

You can even rotate the crop to any angle you wish. To do this, place the cursor slightly outside one of the bounding boxes. The cursor will turn into a curved arrow. Click/Rotate to the desired angle. *Figure 3-30*

To clear a crop, use the pop-up menu that appears when you click/hold on the Crop tool, or simply use the keyboard delete key. *Figure 3-31* The main difference between Camera Raw's Crop tool and Photoshop's is that once you are finished cropping in Camera Raw you don't really crop or throw away any data. The crop is honored by Photoshop when you open the RAW file in that application, and when you reopen the RAW file in Camera Raw, the crop mark remains. However, it will be completely changeable or removable.

Also, when you use the crop tool in Camera Raw, all you see is a grayed-out area designating the area to be cropped. *Figure 3-32* You have to use your imagination a little to visualize the final cropped image. You can get around this by opening multiple images. When you do this, the thumbnail version reflects the actual crop or rotation. (The Bridge thumbnail will also contain a crop icon, indicting a crop has been made.)

Camera Raw also includes useful presets and customable crop settings. Click on the Crop icon arrow and a drop-down menu appears.

If you select Custom, you will get the dialog box shown here. *Figure 3-33*

And if you click on Crop, you get the options shown here. *Figure 3-34*

Choose Ratio and you can type in custom ratio values. Chose Pixels, Inches, or cm, and select an exact crop dimension, much like you can in Photoshop's Crop option bar.

Creating a Panorama with Custom Crop

The Crop Custom settings can be very useful. For example, photographer Martin Sundberg (featured earlier for his action shots) discovered a clever way of quickly turning a normal image into a ready-to-print panorama.

This is what to do:

1. Select the Crop tool.

2. Selects Custom from the drop down menu. Martin chooses Ratio, and types in a 6 to 17 ratio. *Figure 3-35*

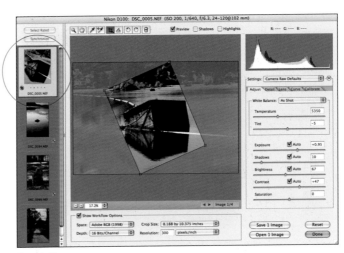

Figure 3-32

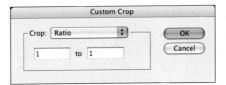

Figure 3-33

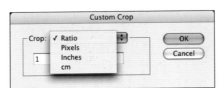

Figure 3-34

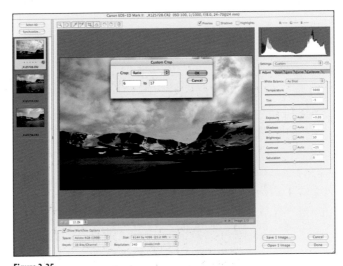

Figure 3-35

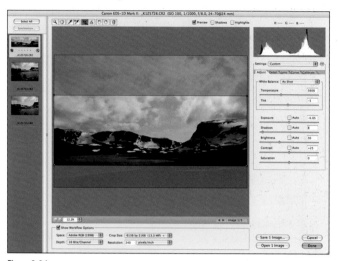

Figure 3-36

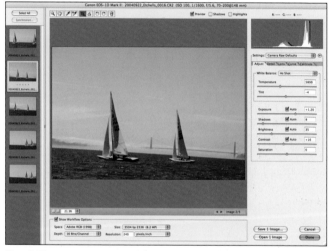

Figure 3-37

Figure 3-38

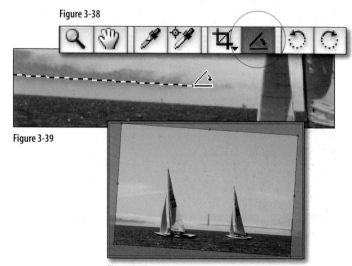

Figure 3-39

Figure 3-40

3. Click and drag the custom shape into place. *Figure 3-36*

4. Next, at the bottom of the Camera Raw window, select the crop size. Martin chooses a Crop Size of 6144 by 2168 (13.3MP). Now when he opens the file in Photoshop, it will automatically interpolate up to a printable size worthy of the panorama.

Straighten Tool

Sometimes you just want things to be perfect, even if they aren't shot that way. Take Martin's example shown here. *Figure 3-37* As mentioned earlier, Martin specializes in fast moving action, and it's not always possible for him to frame a shot perfectly. In this shot, Martin wanted to straighten the horizon. With Camera Raw's new Straighten tool, it's easy to get shots like this one right.

Here is what to do to fix a shot like this in Camera Raw:

1. Select the Straighten Tool in the toolbar at the top of Camera Raw window. (You can simply type "A" to select the tool.) *Figure 3-38*

2. Click/drag and follow the slant of the horizon line. *Figure 3-39*

3. That's all. When you release the mouse, Camera Raw does the rest, calculating the correct angle and adjusting the image to make up the difference. You can see the results in the viewing window, with crop marks. The area that won't be deleted is grayed out. When you select Done and open the file in Photoshop, it will be cropped and straight. *Figure 3-40*

If you find it hard to visualize what the final image will look like in Camera Raw without opening the image in Photoshop, there is a workaround. You'll need to start by opening at least two RAW files in Camera Raw, including the one you wish to fix. Because Camera Raw creates thumbnails of the multiple images, you can actually see the effects of the Straighten tool on the thumbnail. It's not a perfect solution, but it works. *Figure 3-41*

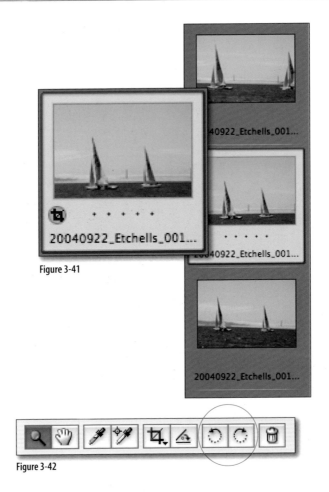

Figure 3-41

Image Orientation

Camera Raw offers a couple of ways to rotate images to their proper orientation::

1. Click on an appropriate arrow key found in the toolbox. *Figure 3-42*

2. Use the keystroke R to rotate right (clockwise) or Shift-R (clockwise) and L (or Shift-L) to rotate left.

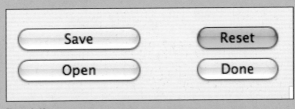

Figure 3-42

What to Do When You Mess Up?

There are couple ways to undo unwanted operations in Camera Raw. Of course, there is the standard Undo command. You an also hold the Option key and Cancel changes to Reset. Click Reset and your image will remain open in Camera Raw but revert to the settings that were applied with the image first opened in Camera Raw. (From Bridge you can also use Edit > Apply Camera Raw Settings > Clear Camera Raw Settings to do this on one or more selected thumbs.) Figure 3-43

Save	Reset
Open	Done

Figure 3-43

Before you manipulate a RAW image, you need to take moment to analyze what needs to be done. First, Camera Raw generates a large preview reflecting the current Camera Raw settings. It also provides other ways to analyze an image, including a histogram and Shadow/Highlights warnings. Let's take a look at these features.

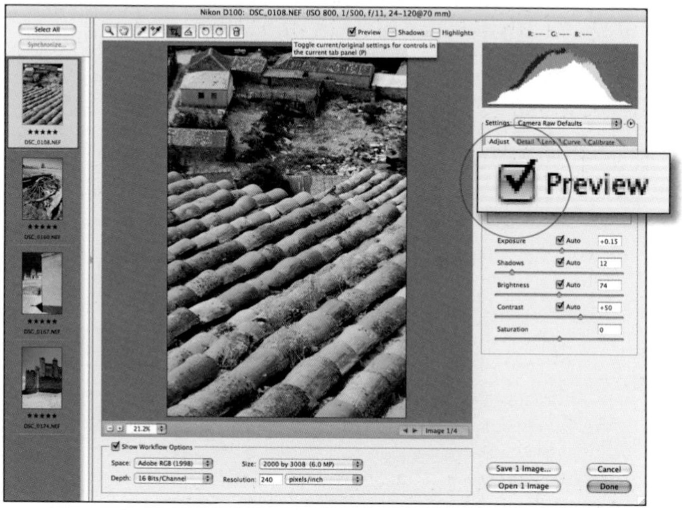

Camera Raw Preview and Analysis Tools

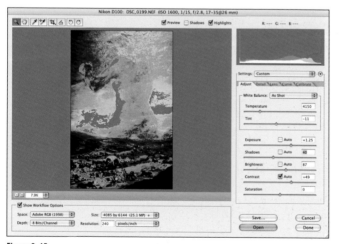

Figure 3-44

Preview Option

At the top of the Camera Raw window is a Preview check box. *Figure 3-44* Use this to toggle between current and original Camera Raw settings. Unchecked means you are viewing your image at original Camera Raw settings, checked means you are viewing the image with current settings. (Toggle the keystroke "P" for checked and unchecked.)

If you haven't touched any of the Camera Raw controls, the Preview checked version will look exactly like the Preview unchecked version.

Shadow & Highlight Clipping Warnings

New to the latest version of Camera Raw are easy-to-find-and-use Shadow and Highlight clipping warnings. (In earlier versions, you had to use a keyboard command while selecting the Exposure and Shadow controls.) These warnings take any tonal or color adjustments you make in Camera Raw into consideration, so the RAW file itself might be fine, but show clipping warnings after an adjustment.

If you select Highlight, anything that falls beyond the range of 255, or pure white, is shown in red. *Figure 3-45* You can also use the keystroke "O".

Figure 3-45

If you select Shadow, anything that falls below the range of 0, or pure black, is shown in purple. *Figure 3-46* You can also use the keystroke "U".

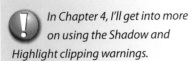 *In Chapter 4, I'll get into more on using the Shadow and Highlight clipping warnings.*

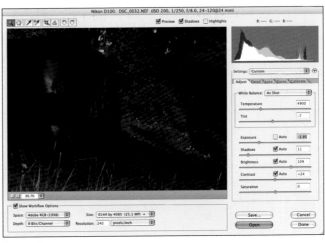

Figure 3-46

Color Histogram

The histogram found in the top right of the Camera Raw window displays red, green, and blue values visually. As you change Adjust settings, the histogram adjusts accordingly. I use the histogram more in Chapter 4.

Figure 3-47

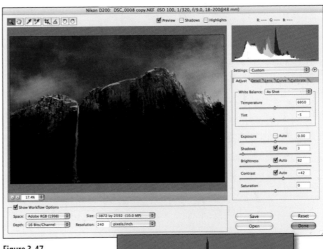

Figure 3-47

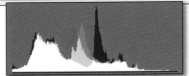

Camera Raw has five tabs, and each tab is a gateway to controlling the look and feel of your RAW image. Under the Adjust and Curve tabs, for example, you can control the way the tonal values are mapped and how the white balance is set. Under the Detail and Lens tabs, you can control how much sharpening is applied and correct any image anomalies. The Calibrate tab provides fine-tuning over the way color is interpreted. Let's look at the tabs, one by one.

Camera Raw Tabs

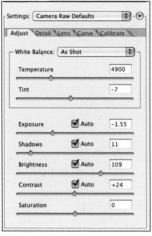

Figure 3-48

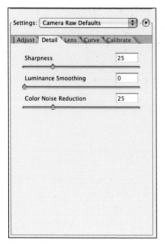

Figure 3-49

Adjust Tab

The Adjust controls, found under the Adjust tab, control white balance, tint, Exposure, Shadows, Brightness, Contrast, and Saturation. By default, the Auto checkboxes are selected. *Figure 3-48* As I mentioned in the previous chapter, you may want to change the default so the Use Auto Adjustments setting isn't automatically applied. (Thumbs created for Bridge may be misleading if Use Auto Adjustments is selected.) You can do this via the pop-up menu (found by clicking on the arrow to the right of the Settings options). Deselect Use Auto Adjustments or use the keyboard shortcut Cmd/Ctrl-U. You may want to set it permanently off by deselecting Use Auto Adjustments and then selecting Save New Camera Raw Defaults.

I'll get into the proper use of these Adjust tab settings in Chapter 4.

Detail Tab

Detail controls, found under the Detail tab, control Sharpness, Luminance Smoothing, and Color Noise Reduction. Chapter 6 is devoted to using Sharpness controls, and in Chapter 7, I discuss how to use the Luminance Smoothing and Color Noise Reduction controls. *Figure 3-49*

Lens Tab

The Lens controls, found under the Lens tab, provide tools to overcome Chromatic Aberrations and Vignetting. I go into great detail on this subject in Chapter 7.

Figure 3-50

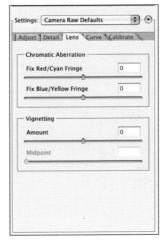

Figure 3-50

Curve Tab

New to Camera Raw is the Curve control, found under the Curve tab. Like Exposure in the Adjust tab, Curve lets you adjust the entire tonal range of an image. However, with Curve, you adjust up to 14 different points throughout an image's tonal range (from shadows to highlights). You can also save Curve settings for use in another image. I'll get into using Curve controls in more detail in Chapter 4. *Figure 3-51*

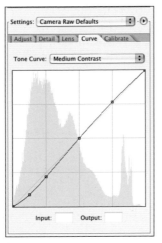

Figure 3-51

Calibrate Tab

You can use the Calibrate controls found under the Calibrate tab to improve the color accuracy of your RAW files. You can also use these controls to create special effects and create grayscale images from RGB. I go into the use of Calibrate for fine-tuning the behavior of Camera Raw's built-in camera profiles in Chapter 4. I cover using the Calibrate controls for special effects and the creation of grayscale images in Chapter 8. *Figure 3-52*

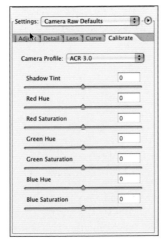

Figure 3-52

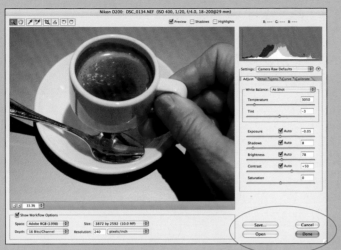

Figure 3-53

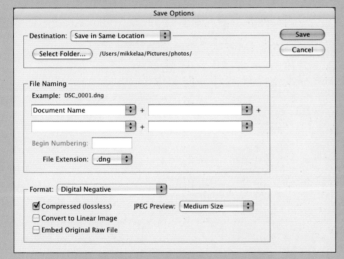

Figure 3-54

What to Do
When You Are Done?

You have several options when you are finished adjusting and working on your image in Camera Raw. Figure 3-53

- *Save when you want to convert your RAW file (or files) into a TIFF, JPEG, PSD, or DNG file. When you select Save, you get this dialog box. Figure 3-54*

- *Open when you want to open your RAW file as-is in Photoshop.*

- *Cancel if you want to exit Camera Raw with no new settings applied.*

- *Done applies your current settings, exits Camera Raw, and returns you to Bridge or Photoshop (depending on which application is host to Camera Raw) without opening the file.*

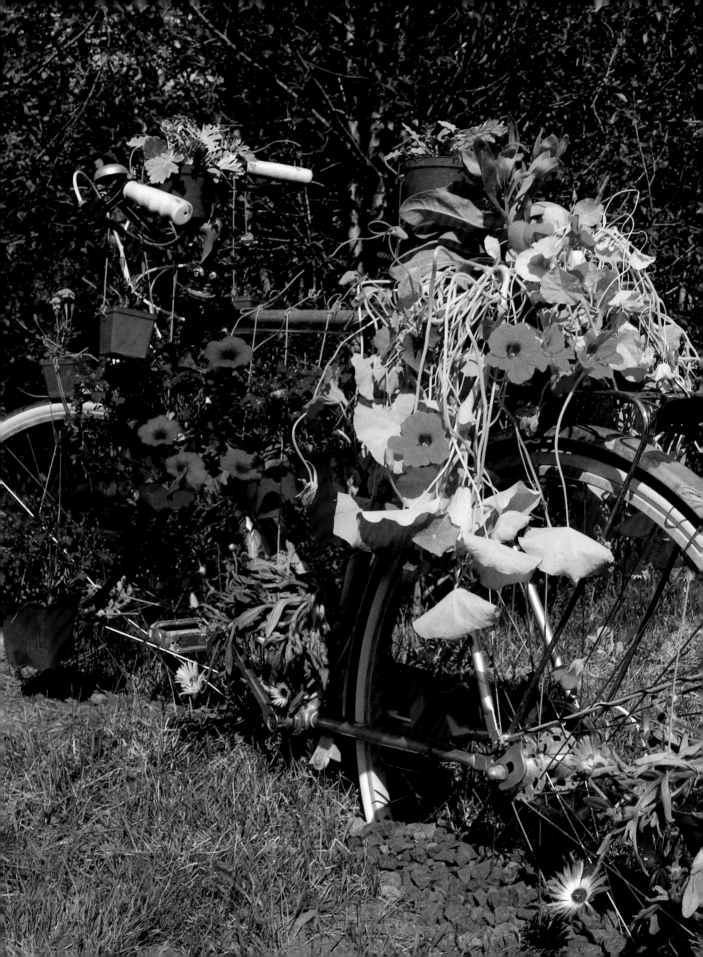

CHAPTER FOUR

Using Camera Raw Adjust & Curve Controls

All RAW files require extensive processing to produce an image pleasing to the eye. As we saw in the previous chapter, Adobe Camera Raw provides many ways to do this. You can use the Adjust or Curve tab controls to automatically set the look and feel of a particular image. Or, if you prefer, you can manually change the white balance or tweak the Adjust or Curve tab controls to make an image more contrasty, cooler, or more saturated. Some of these same controls can also be used to redistribute tonal values to compensate for a less-than-perfect exposure. I'll cover all these topics in detail and more in this chapter.

Chapter Contents

Using Camera Raw Auto Adjustments

Customizing Camera Raw Default

Evaluating an Image in Camera Raw

Manually Adjusting White Balance

Manually Mapping Tone

Using Camera Raw Curve for More Control

Useful Keyboard Commands for Adjust & Curve Tabs

Creating Custom Camera Profiles with the Calibrate Tab

Finishing Up Adjustments with Photoshop

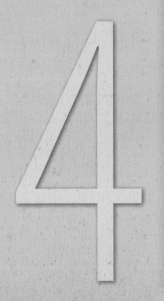

Using Camera Raw Auto Adjustments

When you open a RAW file in Camera Raw for the first time—and your Settings menu is set to out-of-the box Camera Raw Defaults—use Auto Adjustments is enabled and all the Auto checkboxes in the Adjust tab are checked.

With Use Auto Adjustments enabled, Camera Raw applies a made-to-order tone map based on the individual characteristics of a particular image. This often produces satisfactory results, and it's a good place to start. *Figure 4-1*

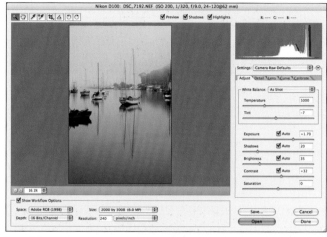

Figure 4-1

When Use Auto Adjustments is deselected, the preview window shows a behind-the-scene interpretation of the RAW data determined by image data, camera model, and camera white balance settings, without any attempt to "optimize" the tonal map. *Figure 4-2*

You can easily turn auto settings off by deselecting Use Auto Adjustments in the Settings pop-up menu. To toggle Use Auto Adjustments on and off, you can use the keyboard shortcut Cmd/Ctrl-U. (You can also create a custom Camera Raw Default with Use Auto Adjustments deselected. See the following section, "Customizing Camera Raw Default.")

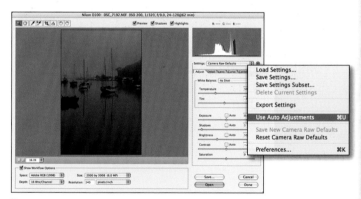

Figure 4-2

The auto adjustments work well for many images, but not all. The earlier photo in Figure 4-1, for example, was shot under even lighting conditions and the auto adjustments worked very well. This example, however, shows an image shot under strong backlit conditions. Here it is with Auto Adjustments off. *Figure 4-3*

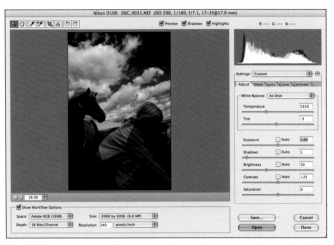

Figure 4-3

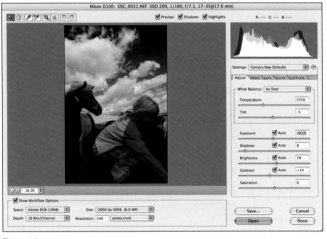

Figure 4-4

In this case, auto adjustments improved things slightly, but didn't go far enough to open the darker areas in the foreground. *Figure 4-4*

Actually, this image is a perfect candidate for manual tweaking of the Adjust tonal controls, which I'll get into shortly.

> *As I said in Chapter 2, selecting Use Auto Adjustments as part of your Camera Raw Default setting can cause confusion when you use Bridge to view and edit images. Say you shot one image frame at f/5.6 and another of the same scene at f/8 using the same shutter speed. Clearly there should be tonal differences between the two shots, and these differences should be reflected in Bridge's thumbnails. However, if Use Auto Adjustments is selected in Camera Raw, the two Bridge thumbnails will likely look the same because Camera Raw generates the thumbs and auto adjustments will make each thumb look the same or very similar.*

Customizing Camera Raw Default

If you consistently don't like the way the Camera Raw Default setting makes your images look, or if you don't want Use Auto Adjustments as part of the Camera Raw Default, you can easily customize the default setting.

The Camera Raw Default setting is always applied when you open a RAW image for the first time in Camera Raw. To change the Camera Raw Default so that Use Auto Adjustments is deselected, and to generally make your images say, more saturated and "Fujichrome film-like:"

1. Open a RAW file in Camera Raw.

2. Deselect Use Auto Adjustments.
   Figure 4-5

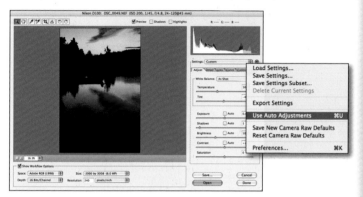

Figure 4-5

3. Slightly increase the saturation values with the Saturation slider, to taste.
   Figure 4-6

> *If you make any changes to an image in Camera Raw, and select Open or Done from the bottom of the Camera Raw window, the next time you open the RAW file, the Settings menu will display Image Settings and the saved settings will be applied. The settings are also reflected in the Bridge thumbnails. You can always revert to the factory Camera Raw Default in the Settings menu.*

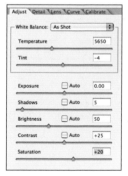

Figure 4-6

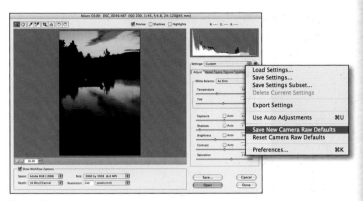

Figure 4-7

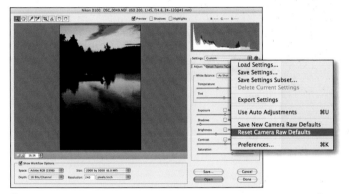

Figure 4-8

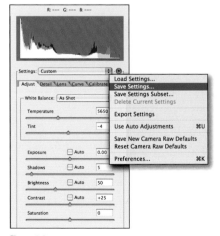

Figure 4-9

4. Select Save New Camera Raw Defaults from the pop-up menu. *Figure 4-7*

The next time you open an image and Camera Raw Default is displayed in the Settings menu, your altered default settings will apply. To revert back to the original, out-of-the-box Camera Raw Defaults, select Reset Camera Raw Defaults from the pop-up menu. *Figure 4-8*

Of course, this is a very simple example of what you can do. In fact, you can use any of Camera Raw's controls to create a quite different Camera Raw Default. In many cases, however, it might be more useful to simply make a user-defined custom setting instead of radically changing your Camera Raw Default. For example, you might make a custom setting that applies only to files from one particular digital camera, or that applies to indoor images, or to backlit images, etc.

Basically, you do this by:

1. Making the appropriate Camera Raw adjustments.

2. Instead of selecting Save New Camera Raw Defaults, select Save Settings from the pop up menu. (Template custom settings are also available by selecting Save Settings Subset... from the pop-up menu.) *Figure 4-9*

3. Name your new setting. *Figure 4-10*

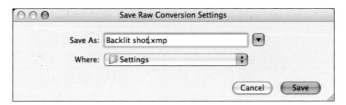

Figure 4-10

Your custom-named setting will now appear under the Settings menu, where it must be selected. *Figure 4-11* The setting will also appear as an option in the Bridge menu (e.g. Edit > Apply Camera Raw Settings > Backlit shot) *Figure 4-12* so you can apply the custom setting to one or multiple images without opening Camera Raw.

For the ultimate fine-tuning of your Camera Raw Default setting, you might consider the very comprehensive, but labor intensive, calibration controls found under the Camera Raw calibrate tab. I'll get into more on this later in the chapter.

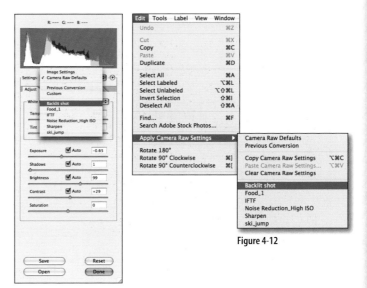

Figure 4-12

Figure 4-11

This discussion on changing default and creating custom settings emphasizes one of the more compelling reasons to shoot RAW. In the past, you'd have to switch films to get this kind of user control over the look and feel of your images. Kodachrome was known for one kind of look, and Ektachrome or Fujichrome were known for another. *Figure 4-13* Photographers would pick the appropriate film based on personal taste or shooting conditions and subject matter. Now you can create a look and feel on an image-by-image basis, and change your mind back again with no permanent consequences.

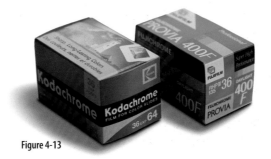

Figure 4-13

How do you know if or when an image is adjusted correctly? From a technical point of view, just looking at Camera Raw's preview window can be deceptive, even if your monitor is perfectly calibrated. Our visual system is extremely adaptive, and what may look good on screen may in fact have serious technical shortfalls which will become especially evident when you click Camera Raw's Open or Done buttons, render the RAW file, and go to print.

Evaluating an Image in Camera Raw

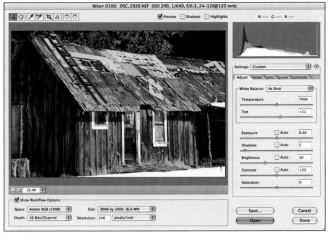

Figure 4-14

Let's take a look at how this deception can occur. For example, this image may look fine at first glance. *Figure 4-14*

> **!** *While an image preview is being generated, a yellow caution icon appears in the preview window. Wait until the caution is gone before evaluating the image.*

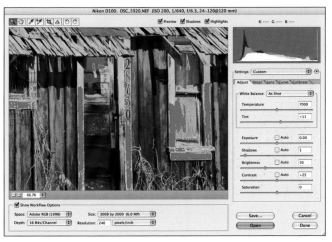

Figure 4-15

But click on the boxes at the top of the image window to activate Camera Raw's Shadows and Highlights warnings, and you'll see several highlight areas lacking in detail, which are represented in red. (Shadow areas lacking detail—which this particular image doesn't have—would be represented in blue.) *Figure 4-15*

Normally, it's not useful to rely on just one or even two tools or methods when evaluating an image. For example, the Shadows and Highlights warnings in the previous image can be confirmed by looking at the histogram or by using Camera Raw's Exposure and Shadows clipping display. I'll explain both in more detail shortly.

Here is an evaluation procedure that'll highlight most of Camera Raw's evaluation tools and give you a good grip on the state of a particular image, such as the one shown here.
Figure 4-16

Once you've determined what needs to be done—if indeed anything needs to be done at all—you can then proceed to apply the necessary changes using Camera Raw's Adjust or Curve controls. (The procedure, as written, may seem laborious, but stretching it out this way, gives me a chance to delve into Camera Raw features that are useful for you to know.)

Think of an evaluation procedure like the process of selecting fruit from a farmer's market. Pick up the fruit, examine it, touch it, squeeze it gently, and smell it. Take everything into account before you buy and eat it.

Ok, let's start:

1. Open the RAW file. Note whether the Adjust tab auto boxes are selected. As mentioned earlier, Use Auto Adjustments is set for the original Camera Raw Default, but many photographers create a new Camera Raw default with Use Auto Adjustments deselected. This way, their Bridge previews will accurately reflect differences in exposure.
    Figure 4-17

2. Note the Work Flow settings; you can choose your color space here. *Figure 4-18* The relevant settings depend on the final destination of your image. (See the sidebar "Choosing a Color Space".)

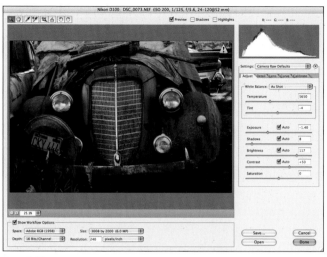

Figure 4-16

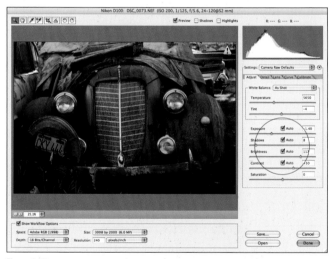

Figure 4-17

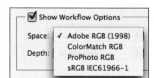

Figure 4-18

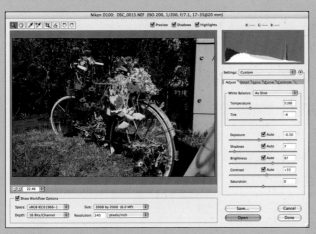

Figure 4-19

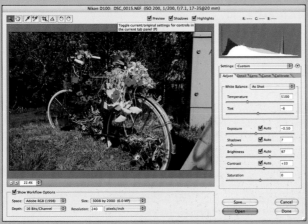

Figure 4-20

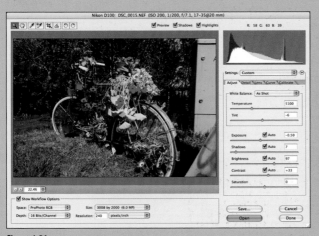

Figure 4-21

Choosing a Color Space

Color space mathematically defines the boundaries of color. Think of color space in terms of relative size. A small color space limits colors to a relatively small space—or technically, a smaller gamut. A large color space creates a large room capable of holding more colors, i.e., a larger gamut. sRGB is often described as smaller color space. Adobe RGB is larger (ColorMatch RGB is a slight variation on Adobe RGB). The largest color space available in Camera Raw is ProPhoto RGB.

You can easily see what I mean by simply looking at Camera Raw's histogram as you change color spaces. The top example shows the histogram for my image using sRGB. Figure 4-19 Note the clipping on both the shadow and highlight sides of the histogram, as indicated by the abrupt vertical lines on either end of the graph.

Next is the same image using Adobe RGB. There's still some clipping. Figure 4-20 Finally, you see the image using ProPhoto RGB. Note all clipping is gone. Figure 4-21

Which space you use depends on your goal and the color space you are used to working in. If you have no plans to further process your image outside of Camera Raw, and your destination is a display monitor or low-end desktop printer, sRGB may be your best option. If you plan on editing your images further in Photoshop, use the color space with the widest possible gamut. (Keep in mind that ProPhoto is a less supported color space than Adobe RGB, and ProPhoto images can look really bad if viewed in a non-color managed application.)

3. Set your preview to Fit in View. You'll want to magnify your image when it comes time to evaluate sharpness, luminance smoothing, color noise reduction, vignetting and chromatic aberrations, but when it comes to checking white balance and tonal distribution, it's best to have the whole picture in view. The exception to this, as you'll see, is when you use the Exposure or Shadows clipping display when 100% or higher magnification makes the warnings more discernable. *Figure 4-22*

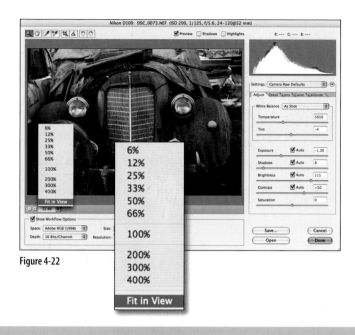

Figure 4-22

Using the Color Sampler Tool

Camera Raw provides a couple of ways to precisely measure color. One way is to simply move your cursor—be it the Zoom tool, Hand tool, White Balance tool, Color Sampler tool, Crop tool, or Straighten tool—over the preview image, and the RGB values of the area below the cursor will appear in the upper-right corner of the dialog box over the histogram. Figure 4-23

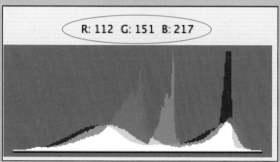

Figure 4-23

Or, you can select the Color Sampler tool, and place up to nine color samplers in the preview image as shown here. Clear the color samplers by clicking Clear Samplers. Figure 4-24

Color sampling is particularly useful if you have included a quantifiable color target in your image, or if you can find an area in your image that should be close to neutral. In that case, you can determine color cast by comparing the R, G, and B values.

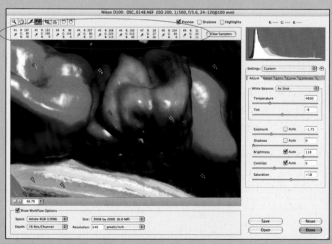

Figure 4-24

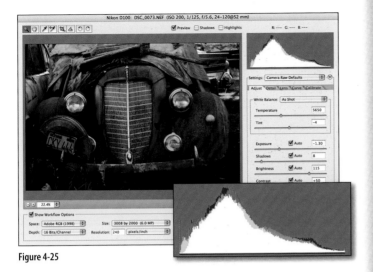

Figure 4-25

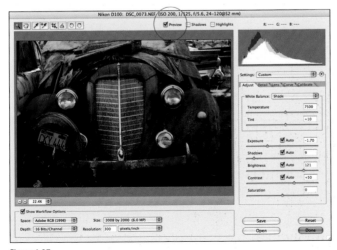

Figure 4-26

Figure 4-27

4. Note the histogram. This is your road map to proper distribution of tonal values. (See sidebar "Interpreting the Histogram.") *Figure 4-25*

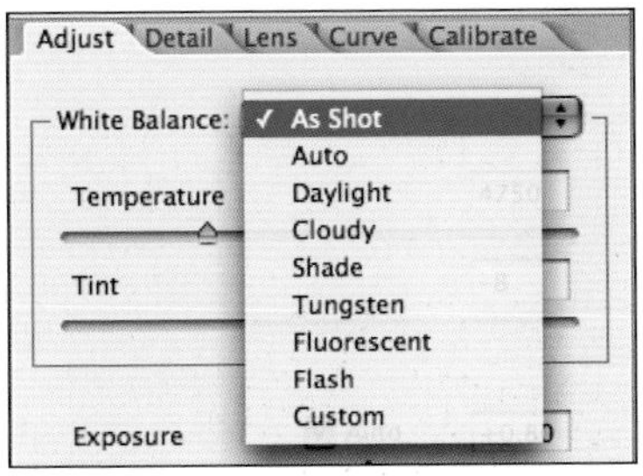

5. Check white balance. At this preliminary stage, I switch between As Shot and the other presets, observing the effects. *Figure 4-26* I leave fine tuning via Camera Raw's Temperature and Tint sliders for later, when I'm actually doing the work on the image. (If you really need to know precisely what is going on with the color, you can use the Color Sampler tool. See the sidebar "Using the Color Sampler.")

6. Toggle auto setting off and on and observe changes. Do this by using the keyboard Cmd/Ctrl-U, or going to the Camera Raw pop-up menu described earlier and selecting/deselecting Use Auto Adjustments. You can also toggle the Preview check box at the top of the Camera Raw window. *Figure 4-27* When selected, the Preview reflects any setting changes made in the current tab, along with settings in the hidden tabs. Deselecting the Preview check box displays the image with the original settings when you first opened the image. (You can create a side-by-side image comparison environment. See the sidebar "Side-by-Side Comparisons".)

Interpreting the Histogram

Camera Raw's histogram graphically displays the 8–bit Red, Green, and Blue (RGB) values of your image. The histogram is not a reflection of the actual RAW data (which is grayscale and linear), but a reflection of the processed RGB data with non-linear tone mapping applied. The histogram updates in real time to reflect changes you make in color space, white balance, or tone mapping. The Camera Raw histogram is much more accurate than the one associated with your digital camera, so don't be surprised to see a difference.
Figure 4-28

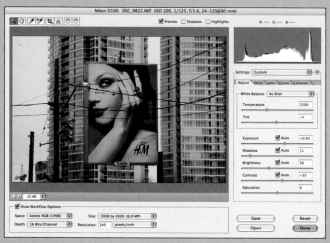

Figure 4-28

Note the colors in this histogram. Figure 4-29 It's fairly intuitive to figure out what they represent. White represents pixels in all three channels: red, green, and blue. Red represents red pixels, green represents green pixels, and blue represents blue pixels. Cyan represents pixels in both the green and blue channels. Magenta represents pixels in both the red and blue channels. Yellow represents pixels in the red and green channels.The sharp lines on either end of the histogram indicate clipping. The height of the line in indicative of the degree of clipping: higher lines represent more clipping, lower lines indicate less clipping. White lines represent clipping in all three color channels. The color of the line tells you which color is actually clipped, and in this example, you can see no highlight clipping, and shadow clipping mostly in the blue channel.

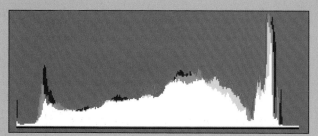

Figure 4-29

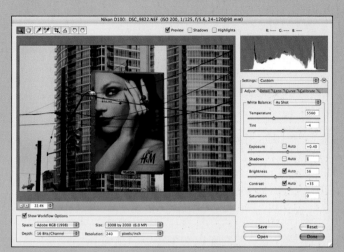

Figure 4-30

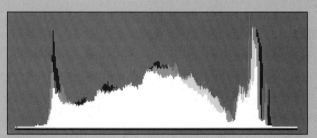

Figure 4-31

The next histogram displays the tonal values of the same image, but with different Adjust settings. *Figure 4-30* (I'll show you exactly how I adjusted the image in the section titled "Manually Mapping Tone".) Now the clipping is gone and the values are distributed more evenly over a narrower space. This histogram also indicates that the opposite of clipping has occurred: there are zero white (or near-white) pixels, and zero black (or near-black) pixels. This may or may not be desirable depending on what is done later with this image. *Figure 4-31*

Every image—and every tonal or color change—to that image will produce a different histogram. As you'll see in subsequent sections, the goal is to produce a distribution of tonal values based on both subjective response and quantifiable criteria (such as highlight or shadow clipping). The histogram is not the final judge, but it's an indispensable tool for getting you the image you want or need.

7. Observe the Exposure—or more accurately, highlight—clipping display. Do this by holding down the Option/Alt key while clicking on the Exposure slider. (As you change the values by sliding the slider, the clipping display updates in real time). Best to view the results at 100% or higher zoom levels. Black represents unclipped pixels, red represents red channel clipping, green represents green channel clipping, and blue represents blue channel clipping. Yellow represents clipping in red and green channels, magenta represents clipping in red and blue channels, and cyan represents clipping in the green and blue channels. White represents all three RGB channels clipped.
   Figure 4-32

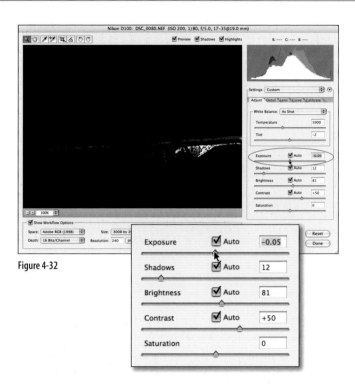

Figure 4-32

8. Observe the Shadows clipping display. Do this by holding down the option key while clicking on the Shadows slider. (As you change the values by sliding, the clipping display updates in real time.) Again, the display is best viewed at 100% or higher zoom levels. White represents unclipped pixels. Red pixels display clipping in the green and blue channels, while green displays clipping in the red and blue channels. Blue displays clipping in the red and green channels. Cyan represents red channel clipping, magenta represents green channel clipping, and yellow represents blue channel clipping.
   Figure 4-33

9. Finally, if I have the luxury of time, I turn my attention away from the image. Even a few minutes away from the image is helpful. That way I come back to work on it with fresh eyes.

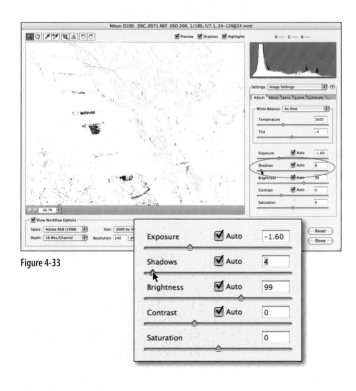

Figure 4-33

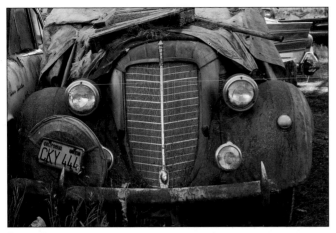

Figure 4-34

Of course, I also have to emphasize the best photograph is not always the one that is technically perfect. A successful image can be taken apart and criticized for not containing enough detail in the highlights or for having shadows that are blocked up. The colors may not be exactly as the scene warranted. However, any evaluation of an image should take the emotional content into consideration. *Figure 4-34*

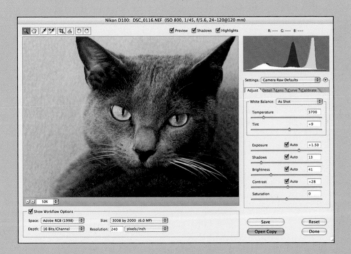

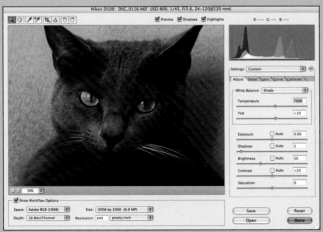

Figure 4-35

Side-by-Side Comparisons

Side-by-side image comparisons are handy when you want to quickly evaluate changes to one image with the original. There is no simple way to do this in Camera Raw, but there is a roundabout way. It requires you to first open your RAW file in Camera Raw with Photoshop as Camera Raw's host, and then, back in Bridge, open another version of your RAW file with Bridge as Camera Raw's host. (You need to start with Photoshop as host—otherwise you won't be able to got back to Bridge and open the second screen.) You'll end up with two Camera Raw windows. If you have enough screen space (or two monitors), you can position them to make side-by-side image comparisons. Figure 4-35 (To open a RAW file with Photoshop as host, assuming Bridge preferences are set to default: Cmd/Ctrl-O and click on the Bridge thumb. To open a Raw file with Bridge as host: Cmd/Ctrl-R and click on the Bridge thumb.)

Manually Adjusting White Balance

I begin my work on an image by setting white balance. Some may find issue with this order and suggest doing tonal corrections first, but both affect each other. Regardless of which you do first, you may want to go back and fine-tune either adjustment. I use a couple approaches to manually adjusting white balance.

In the White Balance pop-up menu, you have the following choices: As Shot, Auto, Daylight, Cloudy, Shade, Tungsten, Fluorescent, Flash, and Custom. You also have a Temperature and Tint slider for fine-tuning. *Figure 4-36*

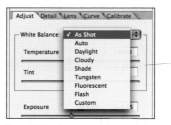

Figure 4-36

If you select As Shot, Camera Raw will apply the white balance setting that was recorded at the time of exposure. In my experience, when lighting conditions are simple—i.e. light comes from a single light source—I am generally happy with the As Shot preset. *Figure 4-37*

This assumes that the camera does a good job determining white balance in the first place—and nowadays most prosumer cameras do. It also assumes Camera Raw is capable of reading the camera white balance data—which is sometimes encrypted. If Camera Raw can't read the camera white balance setting, then As Shot will not appear (but the Auto option will).

In situations where the light comes from multiple sources, correct white balance becomes more problematic. For example, in this shot, the light comes from both natural light and an incandescent bulb. In this case, there is a strong magenta tint. *Figure 4-38*

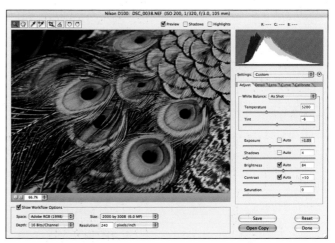

Figure 4-37

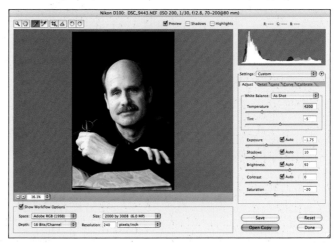

Figure 4-38

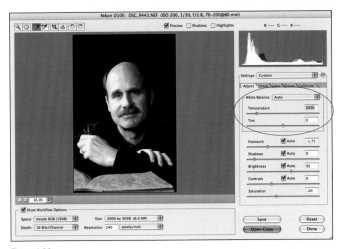

Figure 4-39

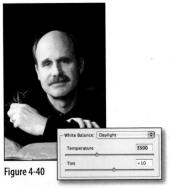

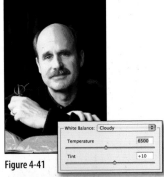

Figure 4-40

Figure 4-41

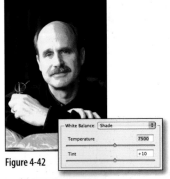

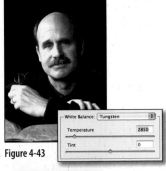

Figure 4-42

Figure 4-43

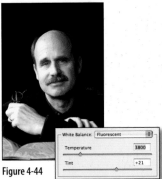

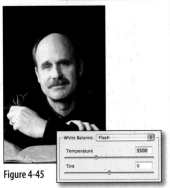

Figure 4-44

Figure 4-45

White Balance Presets

If you are not satisfied with the As Shot setting, you can try the other settings from the pop-up menu. Start with Auto. Camera Raw reads the image data and automatically attempts to adjust the white balance. Auto often works fine. However, Auto gives our example image a bluish cast. *Figure 4-39*

Select the other presets and observe the changes in your image. Shown are the effects of the various presets on my sample image. As you can see, none of the presets do the trick:

Daylight *Figure 4-40*
Cloudy *Figure 4-41*
Shade *Figure 4-42*
Tungsten *Figure 4-43*
Fluorescent *Figure 4-44*
Flash *Figure 4-45*

> *The presets are also available by selecting the White Balance tool from the menu bar, placing your cursor over the image area, and right-clicking (Control-click for one button Mac users).*

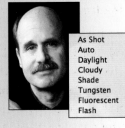

White Balance Tool

You can also select and use the White Balance tool from the Camera Raw tool bar to set white balance. (Alternately, you can hold the Shift key and the cursor becomes the White Balance tool.) Select the tool and click in an area of the image that should be gray, neutral, or white. The White Balance tool then attempts to make the color exactly neutral. The changes are reflected in the Temperature and Tint sliders. You'll also notice a change in the histogram. Sometimes this works, sometimes it doesn't. I tried using the White Balance tool in tour sample image, with no luck. First I got this warning. *Figure 4-46* Then I poked around more, but never found a satisfactory target to take a reading from.

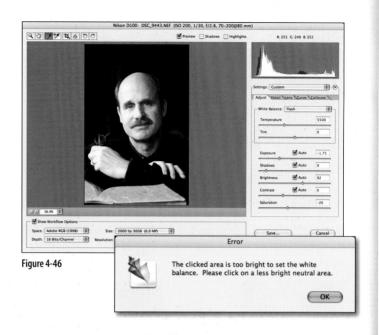

Figure 4-46

Temperature and Tint Controls

Below the White Balance pop-up menu are two sliders—Temperature and Tint—that can be used to fine-tune the white balance, or produce creative effects. If you move the Temperature slider to the left, colors will appear bluer (or cooler). Move the slider to the right, and the colors appear more yellow (warmer). If you move the Tint slider to the left (negative values), you'll add green to your image. Move it to the right (positive values) and you'll add magenta. (Moving either slider will change the White Balance pop-up menu setting to Custom.) By using the Tint slider and moving it –35 to the left, I finally removed the magenta tint and achieved a satisfactory result. *Figure 4-47*

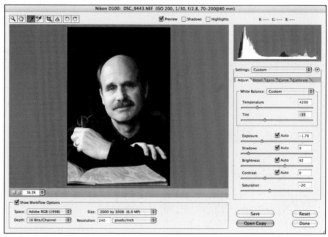

Figure 4-47

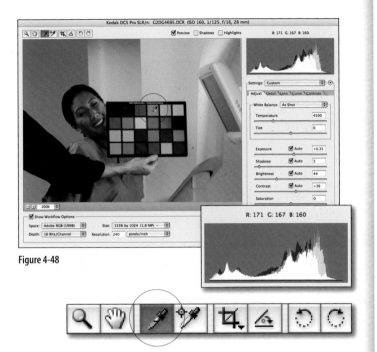

Figure 4-48

Determining White Balance from a Target

Unless you include a quantifiable target in your shot, it's difficult, if not impossible, to know if your white balance is perfectly correct. I find it very useful to include a GretagMacbeth color test chart in a shot whenever possible. (A common, less-expensive, 18% gray card also works fine, but I like the added bonus of the reference colors.) Then I simply select and position my White Balance tool over the target (a neutral square in this example) in the Camera Raw preview window. If my exposure is in the ballpark, the R, G, and B numbers over the histogram should be close, but not necessarily the same. *Figure 4-48*

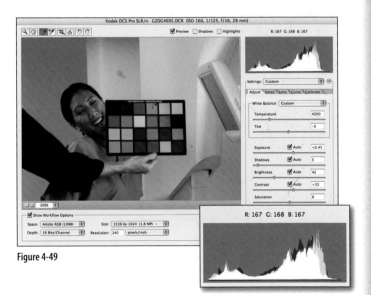

Figure 4-49

I then click on the target and the numbers become exactly the same, or neutral, and the changes in the white balance are reflected in the image and in the histogram. *Figure 4-49* I use this setting as a basis for all the shots taken with the same lighting conditions. (I go into the details on how to do this in Chapter 10.)

Manually Mapping Tone

If the auto or default settings aren't producing the image you want, you should manually adjust the Adjust tab tone settings. As a general rule of thumb, this is done after setting white balance, as white balance adjustments alter tonal distribution and before tweaking the curve control found under the Curve tab. (It's also true that changing tonal distribution affects white balance settings, so this is one of those rules you can argue both ways),

Briefly, in as non-technical terms as I can get for a very technical subject, the list to the right shows what the various tonal control sliders do. *Figure 4-50*

Looking at these tonal controls—or reading about them—may make some photographers feel like they just slipped into the cockpit of a 747. Fortunately, if you select the wrong controls, or sequence, you won't crash. However, there are consequences to blindly sliding any of the controls and you can easily make a moderately problematic image worse.

> ! *Setting a white point establishes a cut-off point from which pixels with lighter values are clipped, or, in other words, set to pure white. Other pixel values are adjusted relative to the new highlight values. Setting a black point establishes a cut-off point from which pixels with darker values are clipped, or set to pure black. Other pixel values are adjusted relative to the new shadow values.*

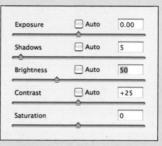

Figure 4-50

Tonal Control Sliders

Exposure: Positive values (over 0) brighten an image and set a white clipping point. Negative values darken an image, while attempting to maintain detail in the highlight areas. Default non-auto setting is 0.

Shadows: Darkens the darkest part of the image (setting a black clipping point), while mostly leaving the rest of the image alone. Default non-auto setting is 5.

Brightness: Similar to Exposure, but redistributes the tonal values in a linear adjustment. While positive Exposure settings often clip highlights—moving the Brightness slider to the right doesn't result in highlight clipping—it compresses the highlights and opens up the shadow areas. Conversely, moving the slider to the left darkens an image by compressing the shadow areas and opening up the highlights. (Observe this by watching the histogram as you move the Brightness slider.) Default non-auto setting is 50.

Contrast: Works in conjunction with the Brightness setting, applying a S-curve that results in either increased or decreased contrast, while leaving the extremes alone. (Again, you can easily observe this by watching the histogram as you move the Contrast slider.) Default non-auto setting is +25.

Saturation: Increases the strength of colors. (In the histogram you'll see individual colors become more pronounced.) Default setting is 0.

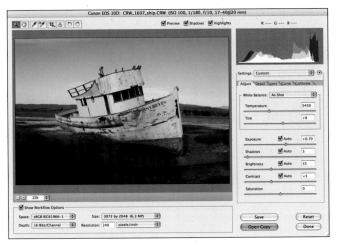

Figure 4-51

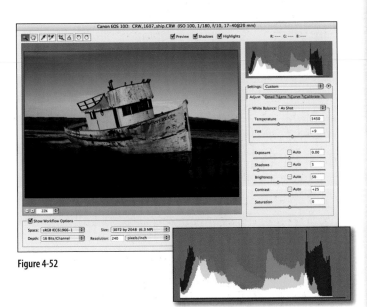

Figure 4-52

Simplifying the Process

I'm going to try and simplify the process of using these controls as much as possible—and give you a semblance of procedure you can follow that will be useful for many images. I'll leave the more advanced Curve discussion for the next section.

Let's start with the work of photographer Derrick Story. (I'll follow up with a couple other step-by-step examples using some my own images that should further convey my point how all these controls are interrelated.) *Figure 4-51*

Derrick begins by following an evaluation procedure much like the one I outlined earlier. He turns global auto settings on and off using the Cmd/Ctrl-U shortcut. He leaves the Shadows and Highlights warning on, but as you'll see, he only considers the warnings as rough guides. He always keeps a close eye on the histogram throughout his editing process. *Figure 4-52*

Note that Derrick works in the sRGB color space. This is a very conscious and deliberate decision on his part. Derrick's images often end up on the web, and he has set up his whole workflow based on that color space. Like most photographers, he sets his Depth to 16 Bits/Channel, and drops down to 8 Bits/Channel later (in Photoshop), after he has confirmed a final destination.

Let's follow the next steps of Derrick's workflow:

1. Turn auto settings off, one at a time, starting with the Exposure slider. In this case, Derrick quickly notices that deselecting the Exposure Auto setting doesn't improve the image. In fact, having Auto selected works fine for Exposure, so he reselects it. Using his original histogram, he sees the problems lie mostly in the shadow areas, so he deselects the Shadows Auto setting and starts work there. *Figure 4-53*

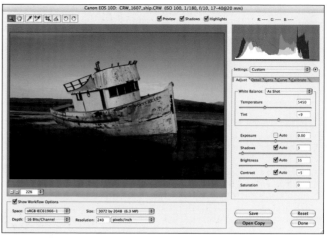

Figure 4-53

2. Slide the Shadows slider completely to the right, to a value of 100. In Derrick's image, his Shadows warning is going crazy, and the histogram confirms shadows clipping. *Figure 4-54*

3. Hold the Alt/Option key while clicking on the Shadows slider arrow to bring up the Shadows Clipping display, which gives a color-by-color clue to the clipping. *Figure 4-55*

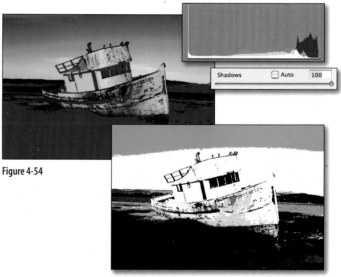

Figure 4-54

Figure 4-55

4. Sliding the Shadows value back to 0 is too much the other way. The image looks a bit flat without solid blacks. *Figure 4-56*

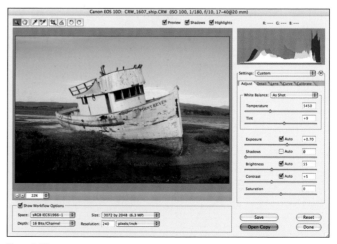

Figure 4-56

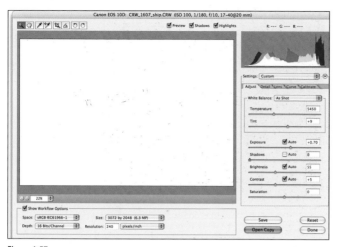

Figure 4-57

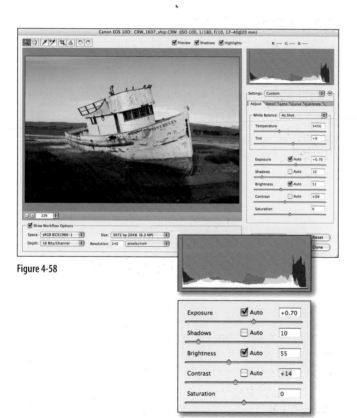

Figure 4-58

5. Holding the Alt/Option key while clicking on the Shadows slider arrow brings up the Shadows Clipping display, which gives a color-by-color clue to the clipping. Clearly, most of the clipping is gone. *Figure 4-57*

6. Finally, sliding the Shadows to 10 produces some clipping in the dark areas and gives the image more depth. Increasing the Contrast slider slightly (to a value of +14) helps too. (Because of the relationship between the Contrast control and the Exposure, Shadows, and Brightness tonal controls, it's generally best to adjust the Contrast setting last.) *Figure 4-58*

> *Camera Raw Exposure settings are often compared to lens f-stops, where each f-stop lets in twice (or half) as much light as the next. If this analogy helps you figure out the relationship between Camera Raw Exposure settings and the actual effect on your image, great. However, for some, using f-stops as analogy can be confusing, especially when the results have very little to do with the results you'd get if you changed stops on a camera—via aperture or shutter speed or ISO controls. F-stops and shutter speeds control the amount of light striking a sensor. ISO determines the sensitivity of a sensor to light. If you change an f-stop, you also change the depth-of-field. If you change shutter speeds you can add or stop motion. F-stops and shutter speeds work together to determine the quantity of light striking a sensor. When you use the Exposure setting in Camera Raw on a RAW file, the tonal information is either there or not. You don't add new information. You change the emphasis of the information by changing its distribution.*

Here is another example, one my own, which we saw previously. With all the Auto settings selected, the image looks a little punchy for my taste, and there is obvious clipping in the highlights and shadow areas. (I know "punchy" isn't a technical term, but so much of what we are doing here is subjective—and a matter of personal taste.) *Figure 4-59*

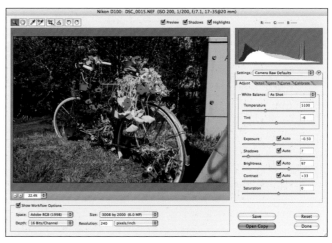

Figure 4-59

With the Auto settings off, it looks like this. *Figure 4-60* As you can see—and as is confirmed by the histogram shift to the left—the image is now darker, too dark for my taste.

Here is what I did to this image, which loosely follows what I do to other problematic images.

1. Toggle auto settings off (Cmd/Ctrl-U).

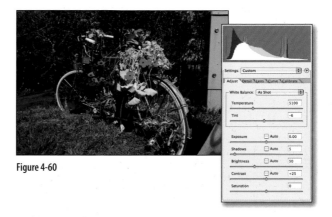

Figure 4-60

2. Start with the Exposure slider. Because there is clipping in the highlights, I decreased the setting to about 50, which makes the image look too dark, but I plan to brighten it up later with the Brightness slider. *Figure 4-61*

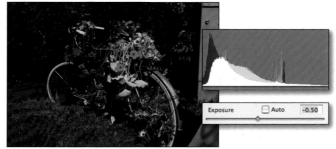

Figure 4-61

3. Next, I turned to the Shadows. Even when I set the Shadows to 0, the clipping remains. Increasing Brightness helps a little. *Figure 4-62*

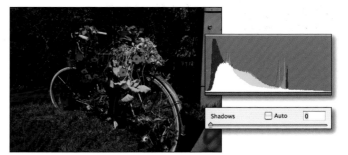

Figure 4-62

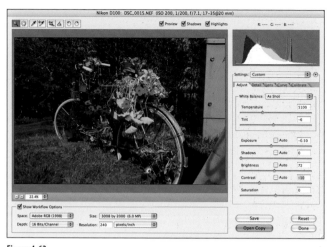

Figure 4-63

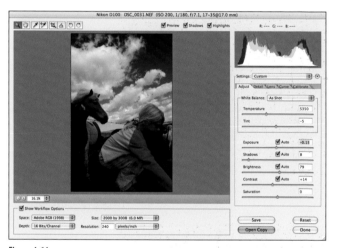

Figure 4-64

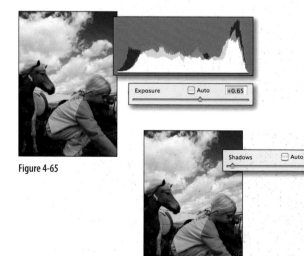

Figure 4-65

Figure 4-66

4. To brighten the image, and move the histogram to the right and open up the shadows, I slid the Brightness slider to 72, which shifted the histogram nicely to the right. As a final step, I decreased my Contrast setting to –10. *Figure 4-63*

I could have completely removed the shadow clipping by changing from Adobe RGB color space to ProPhoto RGB color space, but since I'm set up for Adobe RGB, I was satisfied to stop here.

As a last example, let's look at another one of my previously used images. *Figure 4-64* It's the one from the beginning of the chapter, where Auto settings helped a bit, but were not wholly effective. This time, I'll manually adjust some of the Adjust tone controls to fine tune it. As you will see, tweaking it helps, but to get the final image, I need to bring it into Photoshop and apply localized adjustments with an adjustment layer. (I'll get into how I do that at the end of the chapter.)

To tweak the Auto adjusted image:

1. Open up the highlights with the Exposure control, pushing the histogram as far to right as possible without clipping the highlights. (Remember, it's always best to start your adjustments with the Exposure control.) *Figure 4-65*

2. Adjust the Shadows slider slightly to open the shadow areas. *Figure 4-66*

The background now appears too light, but as you'll see later, I was able to work Photoshop magic and get things right because there still is detail in the highlights. I did try using the Camera Raw curve control—which I'll get into next—but the contrast between the foreground and background was too extreme.

Using Camera Raw Curve for More Control

As we just learned, the tonal controls of Camera Raw's Adjust tab redistribute linear RAW data produced by digital camera into a form pleasing to the eye. You can get even more control over how this data is mapped with the Camera Raw curve, found by selecting the Curve tab. It's generally recommended that you first do your major editing in the Adjust tab, then use the Camera Raw tone curve for fine tuning.

For photographers familiar with using Photoshop curves, the graph that appears when you select the Camera Raw Curve tab will seem very familiar. *Figure 4-67* The horizontal axis represents the original intensity values of the pixels, and the vertical axis represents the new tonal values. You can adjust up to 14 different points throughout an image's tonal range, which is represented by a diagonal line. (With Adjust tab controls you effectively only control 5 points on a tone curve.) Many of the methods for applying and manipulating these points are the same as those in the familiar Photoshop Curves dialog box. Custom curves can be saved and applied to other images.

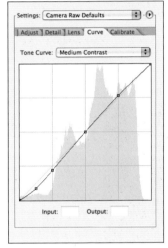

Figure 4-67

Some photographers may find the added control offered by Camera Raw's tone curve daunting. For these photographers, the easy-to-apply Tone Curve presets might suffice. Let's go over these presets— which are found in the pop-up menu next to Tone Curve— first, then move on to actually working on the curve itself.

Tone Curve Presets

The default Tone Curve preset is Medium Contrast. As you can see, four points have been added to the diagonal line and input/output levels were adjusted to slightly increase contrast.

Figure 4-68

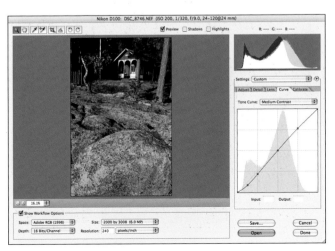

Figure 4-68

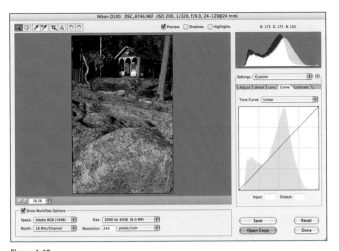

Figure 4-69

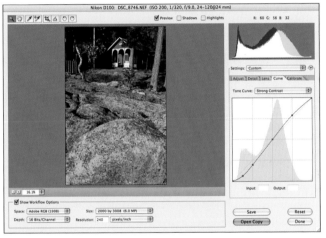

Figure 4-70

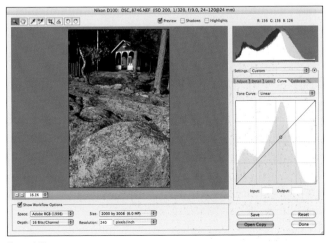

Figure 4-71

(It may not be so obvious here, in print, but this illustrates how even very slight changes in the tonal curve can appreciably affect an image.)

The Linear preset creates a perfectly straight diagonal line in the tonal curve graph. This results in an image with no change from input to output, effectively ceding all control to the Adjust tab tonal settings. *Figure 4-69*

Strong Contrast creates a Curve shown here. Four points are set and manipulated to increase contrast. (Again, the manipulation is very slight, but effective.) *Figure 4-70*

> If you press the Delete key without selecting a point on the curve, Camera Raw assumes you want to trash your current file and a warning will appear. If this occurs, simply press the Delete key again and the warning will disappear.

Creating a Custom Curve

To create a custom tonal curve, start with the Linear Tone Curve Setting. Add a point along the straight diagonal line by either clicking directly on the line or right-clicking on a pixel in the Camera Raw image preview window. *Figure 4-71*

You can add up to 16 control points to the curve. To remove a point from the tonal curve, do one of the following:

- Drag it off the graph
- Select it and press Delete
- Cmd/Ctrl-click the control point

There is no way I can go into all the details required to fully explain how to use curves—and still have room for the other subjects in this book! However, from a very basic point of view, changing the shape of the curve alters the tonal distribution. Bowing the curve upward or downward will cause the image to lighten or darken. (I've lightened the image by placing a single point in the middle and bowing the curve upwards.) *Figure 4-72*

Steeper sections of the tonal curve represent areas of more contrast, and flatter sections of the tonal curve represent areas of lower contrast. Any points you placed on the curve will remain anchored and you can make an adjustment in one tonal area while other areas remain unaffected.

The Custom selection appears in the Tone Curve pop-up window whenever you manually manipulate the tonal curve. If you save a custom setting properly, it will also appear in the Curve Settings pop-up menu. It's best to save your Curve setting as a subset. (Save Subset Settings from the Settings pop-up menu, which appears next to the Settings arrow.) That way, it will be automatically saved in the Curves folder as long as the subset contains only a Curve custom setting. You can also save a Curve setting by selecting Save Setting from the Settings pop-up menu appearing next to the Settings arrow. Just keep in mind this also saves all other Camera Raw settings, which may or may not be intended. Name the setting appropriately and be sure to save the new setting in the Camera Raw Curves folder; otherwise it won't appear in the Curve Tone Curve pop-up menu. In this image, I've turned the image into a negative by inverting the histogram and saved it as a custom setting. *Figure 4-73*

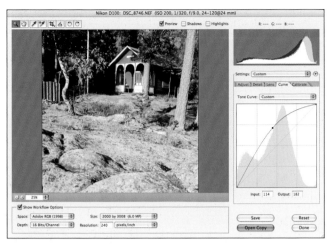

Figure 4-72

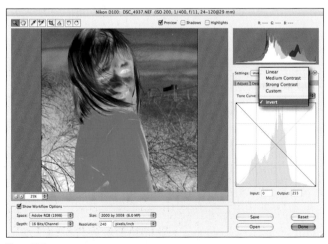

Figure 4-73

Useful Keyboard Commands for Adjust & Curve Tabs

Here is a sampling of general keyboard commands you can use to streamline your work while in the Adjust and Curve tabs. I've already mentioned some of them in the relevant sections.

- ***Cmd/Ctrl-U** toggles Use Auto Adjustments off and on.*

- ***Tab** cycles through the Adjust controls.*

- ***Cmd/Ctrl+0** automatically reverts the preview window to Fit in View.*

- ***Down/Up Arrow keys** move the Adjust values incrementally. Shift+Down/Up Arrow keys increase the incremental values.*

- ***Esc** is for when you are totally frustrated and want to get out of Camera Raw as fast as possible. None of your changes are saved.*

In addition to the keyboard key shortcuts, Camera Raw uses scrubbers. To use scrubbers, place your cursor over one of the sliders. The cursor should change to a double-ended arrow such as the one shown here. If you click and drag to the left, the numeric entry will decrease; if you drag to the right, it will increase. Figure 4-74

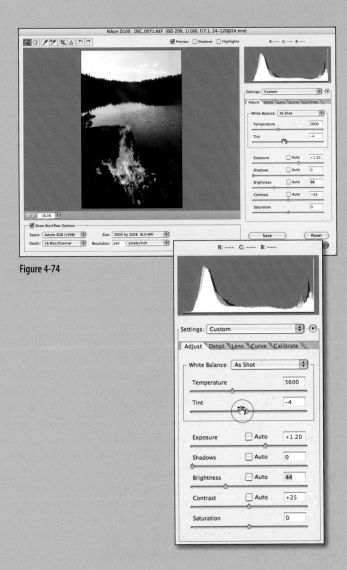

Figure 4-74

Creating Custom Camera Profiles with the Calibrate Tab

If you really want to fine-tune a Camera Raw default setting—or a custom setting—to compensate for the difference between the actual behavior of your digital camera and Camera Raw's interpretation of it, use the Calibrate Tab. Figure 4-75

There is nothing simple about using the Calibrate controls to do this. You must first systematically and carefully create a controlled shooting environment, use a calibrated color target, and spend a lot of time building a new profile which will only be good for one particular camera. The upside: images exactly the way you like them.

Instead of walking you through this laborious process, I'm going to refer you to the work of Thomas Fors, who has created an awesome Photoshop script for automating much of the calibration process. His script, and a lot of supporting text, is available at http://fors.net/scripts/ACR-Calibrator/.

(You can also use Calibrate controls to convert images to black and white and for other creative purposes as well. For more on this, refer to Chapter 8.)

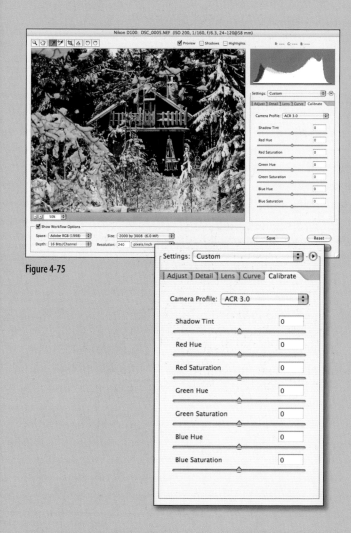

Figure 4-75

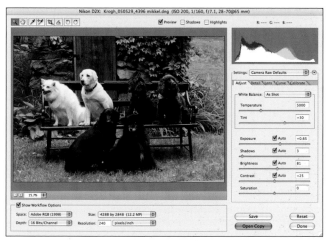

Figure 4-76

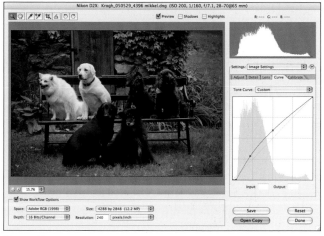

Figure 4-77

Here's a real-world example of using Camera Raw tonal curve to get an effect that wasn't possible with the Adjust controls alone. The photo was shot by photographer and author Peter Krogh. *Figure 4-76* As you can see in the histogram, the shadow areas are heavily clipped.

Peter did what he could using the Adjust tonal controls, but finally resorted to using the Camera Raw curve tonal control. He's found the Curve tab very useful for adding contrast in the darks, without blowing out the highlights. Look at Peter's tonal curve, and you'll see the simple adjustment made by adding two points on the curve and extending the shadow "toe." This method is simple but effective. (Why black and white? Peter just liked how it worked for this particular image. He simply set the Adjust tab Saturation setting to 0.)

Figure 4-77

To delete custom settings from the Tone Curve pop-up menu, you'll need to go to the Camera Raw/ Curves folder found on your desktop. (Location of this folder varies between platforms. Best to search with the words "Camera Raw Curves" to determine the exact location.) Here you will find .xmp files. Select the one(s) you want to delete and drag them to the trash. The next time you open Camera Raw they will not appear.

This list shows some other useful Curve dialog box keyboard shortcuts. *Figure 4-78*

 To Undo a previous action, use the keyboard shortcut Cmd/Ctrl-Z. To revert, use the same shortcut again.

- *Shift-click points on the curve to select multiple points. Selected points are filled with black.*
- *Press arrow keys to move selected points on the curve.*
- *Press Cmd/Ctrl-Tab to move forward through control points on the curve.*
- *Press Shift-Cmd/Ctrl-Tab to move backward through control points on the curve.*

Figure 4-78

Reverting and Undoing

There are a couple ways to revert to the Camera Raw default settings or undo actions you have taken in Camera Raw.

To revert to the original Camera Raw default:

1. *Select Camera Raw default from the Settings menu.*

2. *Hold the Option/Alt key and Cancel changes to Reset.*

3. *To view the original Camera Raw default settings (or the settings applied when you first opened a RAW file in Camera Raw), deselect the Preview check box at the top of the display window. Figure 4-79*

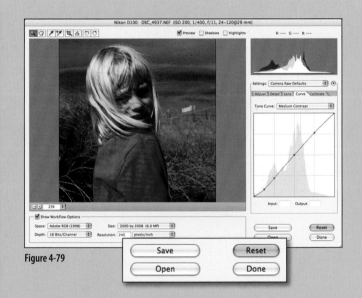

Figure 4-79

Camera Raw applies adjustments globally to the entire image. If you want specific control over specific parts of an image, you'll need to convert your RAW file with Camera Raw and open it in Photoshop. Once in Photoshop, you'll have a wide range of familiar tools to work with—including masks and adjustment layers—that'll enable you to apply tonal corrections to some areas of an image, and not others.

Finishing Up Adjustments with Photoshop

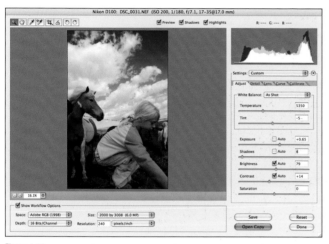

Figure 4-80

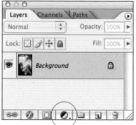

Figure 4-81

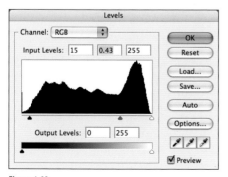

Figure 4-82

Let me illustrate this by returning once again to an earlier image. In Camera Raw, I was able to improve the foreground, but only at the cost of making the background look washed out in the preview window. However, the Camera Raw histogram indicated no clipping in the highlights, so I was fairly confident detail remained. *Figure 4-80*

Here is a fairly simple way to use Photoshop to improve images like this one:

1. Open the image from Camera Raw into Photoshop (From the bottom right of Camera Raw, select Open.)

2. Create a Levels (or, if you prefer, Curves) adjustment layer. (Layer > New Adjustment Layer > Levels. Or click on the adjustments layer icon at the bottom of the layer palette.) *Figure 4-81*

3. Apply Levels adjustment until background is correct. The foreground is now too dark, but we'll fix it shortly. *Figure 4-82*

Even though the clouds originally looked blown out on my monitor, I knew from Camera Raw's histogram that there was no highlight clipping. This was confirmed when I was able to successfully use the Levels to correct the background. *Figure 4-83*

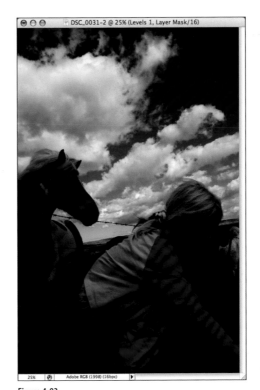

Figure 4-83

4. Select the Adjustment layer and select the Brush tool from the toolbar. Make sure the foreground swatch at the bottom of the tool bar is set to black. (The keystroke X will switch the background and foreground colors alternatively. Keyboard command "D" will make sure default colors are selected.) *Figure 4-84*

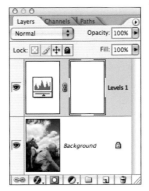

Figure 4-84

5. With the brush tool and an appropriate-size brush, "paint" or "mask" the foreground area of the image, leaving the effect of the Levels adjustment only on the background. (Use the bracket keys to increase or decrease the size of the brush.) *Figure 4-85*

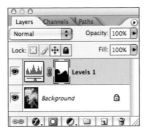

Figure 4-85

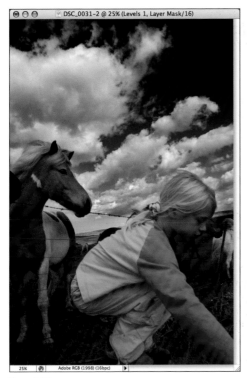

Figure 4-86

6. The final image is shown here.

Figure 4-86

There are other Photoshop techniques similar to this one that will apply specific corrections to specific parts of an image. In the next chapter, I will go into more detail, but this is a subject for a book unto itself—and several good books offer good techniques on this subject. I especially recommend Martin Evening's *Photoshop CS2 for Digital Photographers.*

I want to emphasize an earlier point: if you plan on doing any editing in Photoshop, bring in as much data as you can. Use the appropriate color space—usually Adobe RGB—and start with 16-bit depth. Also, get your white balance—or color—as close as possible in Camera Raw. You may have more control over specific colors in Photoshop, but you will always pay a price in the form of image degradation.

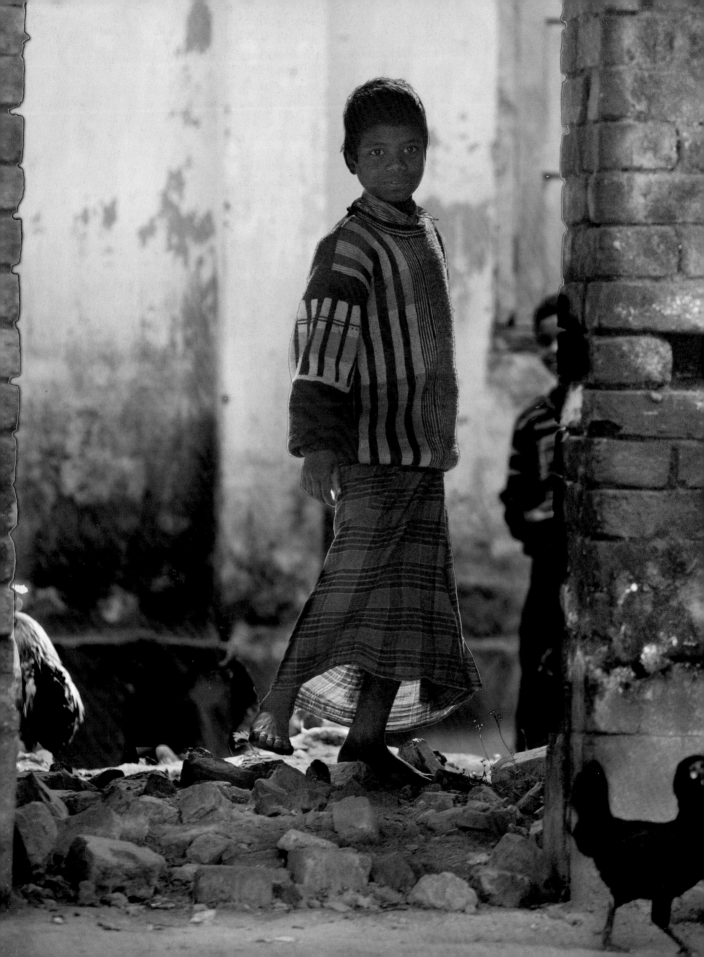

Advanced Tonal Control

In the previous chapter, we learned basic Camera Raw
techniques for distributing tonal values of your RAW files.
In this chapter, I'll show you a more advanced technique
that takes a bit more work but often produces dramatic
results. The technique uses Camera Raw to create two
or more versions of the same image with different
distribution of tonal values. Then, in Photoshop, the
different versions are merged into one image that
displays or prints an amazingly wide range of shadow and
highlight detail. I'll also show you how to use Photoshop's
new Merge to HDR feature to combine multiple RAW
images into one with high dynamic range.

Chapter Contents

Advanced Tonal Control with Camera Raw and Photoshop

Creating Multiple Versions of the Same RAW File

Part One: Blending in Photoshop

Part Two: Extending Dynamic Range

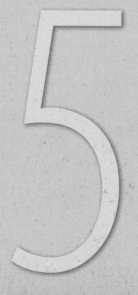

Advanced Tonal Control with Camera Raw and Photoshop

Some RAW images need more work than others to make them display properly on a typical monitor, or print correctly on a printer with limited dynamic range. Let's look at an advanced technique that'll come in handy with images containing extreme highlight and shadow tonal values.

To illustrate this technique, I'm going to use the work of photographer and eminent digital photography educator, Michael Reichmann. Michael took this shot with a Canon EOS 1DS Mark II. *Figure 5-1* As confirmed by Camera Raw's histogram, the camera captured details in both the highlight and shadow areas for a RAW image with superb dynamic range. However to prepare this image for optimal viewing or printing, I'll need to selectively compress the dynamic range.

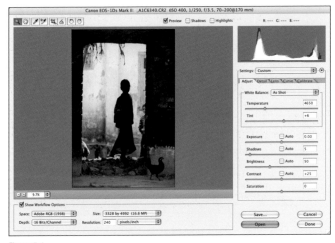

Figure 5-1

Simply using Camera Raw Adjust controls doesn't do the trick, as you can see here. Even though the background is better, detail is still lacking in the foreground. (Using the Curve controls didn't help much either.) *Figure 5-2*

To solve this problem, I'll present here what I did to Michael's image, step-by-step. I'll break the process into two main parts: Part One shows a couple ways to create multiple versions of the same RAW file in Bridge and Camera Raw and open them in Photoshop. Part Two shows a couple ways to use Photoshop to selectively merge the different versions into one.

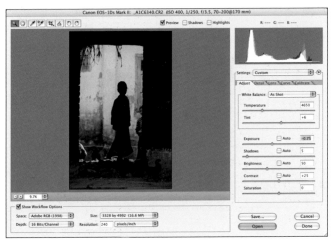

Figure 5-2

Let's look at two ways to create multiple versions of the same RAW file with Camera Raw. The first way requires you to make one or more duplicate RAW files in Bridge, then open them in Camera Raw. The other technique uses the Place command, and takes advantage of a new addition to Photoshop CS2, Smart Objects.

Part One: Creating Multiple Versions of the Same RAW File

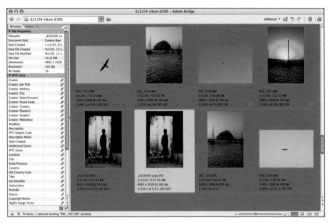

Figure 5-3

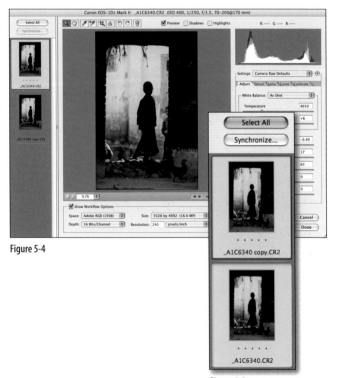

Figure 5-4

Figure 5-5

Creating Duplicates in Bridge

1. Starting in Bridge, make a duplicate (or duplicates) of the RAW file. To duplicate an image in Bridge, with the image selected choose Edit > Duplicate from the menu bar, or Cmd/Ctrl-D *Figure 5-3*

2. While still in Bridge, select both the original and the copy. (Hold the Cmd/Ctrl key while clicking on different thumbnails to select multiple, adjacent or non-adjacent, files one-by-one.) Open both files in Camera Raw (File > Open in Camera Raw).

3. As you can see here on the left, the two versions of the same image are open in the Camera Raw's Filmstrip View. *Figure 5-4*

4. Next, click on Select All. Now any change you make to one image is applied to the other. *Figure 5-5*

5. In this case, while the two images were selected, I tweaked the white balance and slightly increased sharpening.

6. Select one of the two images in the Filmstrip. (Click on the one you want to remain selected. It doesn't matter which one you select first.)

7. Adjust the exposure setting for the selected image. In Michael's image, the background is correct but, as indicated by the blue shadow clipping warning, the shadow areas in the foreground are lacking detail. *Figure 5-6*

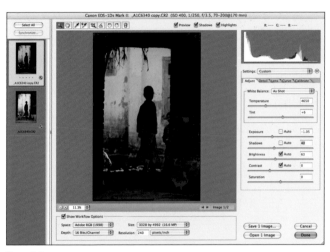

Figure 5-6

8. Next, select the second image and adjust the exposure so the shadow areas are correct. Now Michael's background is blown out, as depicted by the red highlight warning. I quickly noticed that opening up the shadow areas revealed a lot of image noise. At this stage of the process, I ignored this obvious distraction, choosing to fix it later with Photoshop's new Reduce Noise filter. (For more on using this filter see Chapter 7.) *Figure 5-7*

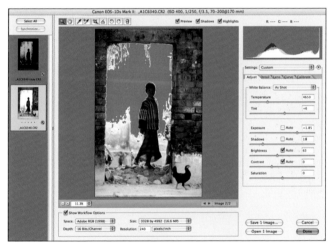

Figure 5-7

9. Open both images in Photoshop. (Choose Select All, and note that the buttons on the bottom right of the Camera Raw window reflect the number of images you select. Click on Open X Images to open images in Photoshop) *Figure 5-8*

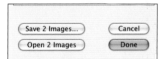

Figure 5-8

10. You'll now have at least two images open in Photoshop. You'll need to copy and paste them into one multi-layered document. With both images open in Photoshop, select and copy one of the versions (Cmd/Ctrl-A, then Cmd/Ctrl-C). It doesn't matter which one. Select

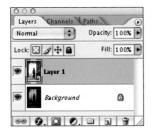

Figure 5-9

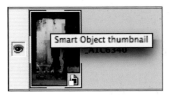

Figure 5-10

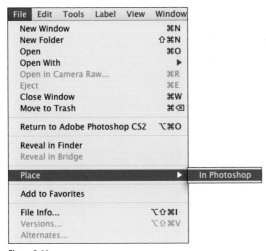

Figure 5-11

the other image, and then paste your selection onto it (Cmd/Ctrl-V). The Layer Palette I created with Michael's image is shown here. *Figure 5-9*

Now you are ready to blend the images. I'll get into that shortly, after showing you another way to open multi-versions of the same image in Photoshop.

> *At this point, the original RAW file and duplicate(s) are taking up at least twice as much space on a hard drive. When I was finished with Michael's image in Camera Raw, I went back to Bridge and deleted the duplicate image.*

Using Place in Photoshop

Using this method you won't have to make a duplicate of your original RAW file; instead, you'll rely on a new feature of Photoshop, Smart Objects. A Smart Object, once embedded in a Photoshop file, retains its original characteristics and remains fully editable. In the case of this example, the RAW file can be reopened at any time in Camera Raw and edited. *Figure 5-10*

1. Open your original RAW file from within Bridge into Camera Raw. No need to duplicate it, as we did in the previous method.

2. In Camera Raw, adjust your exposure values to optimize either highlights or shadows, as described earlier.

3. Open the RAW file from Camera Raw into Photoshop by clicking on Open in the Camera Raw window.

4. Back in Bridge, make sure your original RAW file is selected. Select File > Place > In Photoshop from the Bridge menu. *Figure 5-11*

5. When Camera Raw appears, choose an exposure value that complements your earlier correction. (If you adjusted for highlights earlier, adjust now for shadows.) You can perform these adjustments now, or later, after the file is placed in Photoshop as a Smart Object. Select Open from the Camera Raw window.

6. The second version will open in Photoshop and be pasted into the original one as a Smart Object as shown here. It'll have a large X across the image. *Figure 5-12*

> ! *As an alternative to the methods described here, try Dr. Brown's Place-A-Matic script. The free, downloadable script, automatically places multiple photo exposures from Adobe Bridge into a single Photoshop document as Smart Objects.The script is available on the Adobe site and at* http://www.russellbrown.com/tips_tech.html.

7. Select the Commit button from the Options bar. *Figure 5-13*

8. Now your Layer palette will look like this. Because the layer contains a Smart Object, it means you can always go back to Camera Raw and change settings. To do this, simply double-click the Smart Object icon in the Layer palette. *Figure 5-14*

Next, you'll need to blend the layers together. I'll show you a couple ways to do this in the following section.

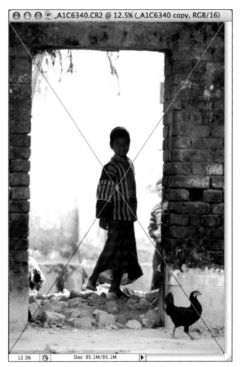

Figure 5-12

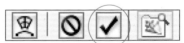

Figure 5-13

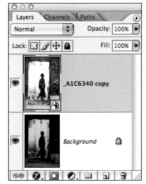

Figure 5-14

OK, up to now things have been fairly straightforward. Instead of trying to come up with a compromised exposure value, I was able to focus on specific areas of Michael's image and adjust the exposure without regard to other areas. I could, of course, have created three or four or five versions of the same image, if the image warranted it. Now comes the tricky part, blending the different versions into one.

Part Two: Blending in Photoshop

Blending Two or More Copies of an Image

There are actually several ways to do this. I'll show you two variations, one based on using a layer mask, the other on using Layer Blending Options. (The layer mask technique is similar to the one I used at the end of the previous chapter.)

CREATING A MASK

The goal is to leave the correct parts of one image and delete the others. To do this:

1. Select the layer you wish to mask. Shown here are two Layer palettes, one with a Smart Object layer (right), the other without. (left) *Figure 5-15*

2. Use the Color Range selection tool to select the shadow areas your wish to keep intact. (Select > Color Range from the menu bar.) Note that Color Range selection works with a Smart Object Layer. With some images, it's easier to select the highlight areas with the Color Range selection tool. If you do this, you won't need to invert the selection, as described in Step 4. Note how I choose Quick Mask as a Selection Preview in the Color Range dialog box. I find it makes it easier to see my selection, but experiment for yourself and see which option works best for you. *Figure 5-16*

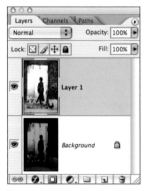 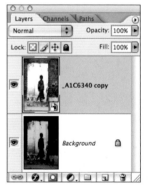

Figure 5-15

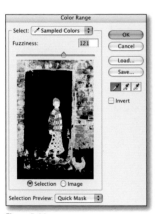

Figure 5-16

12. Invert your selection (Selection > Inverse) and turn your selection into a mask by clicking on the Create Layer Mask icon found at the bottom of the Layer palette. *Figure 5-17*

13. With the Layer Mask selected, use the Brush tool to add and subtract from the mask, revealing or hiding parts of the layer accordingly.

> *Using Masks is a subject unto itself. For more on this, I suggest you use the excellent Adobe Help tool found in the menu bar or check out Deke McClelland's* Adobe Photoshop CS2 One-on-One *(O'Reilly, 2005).*

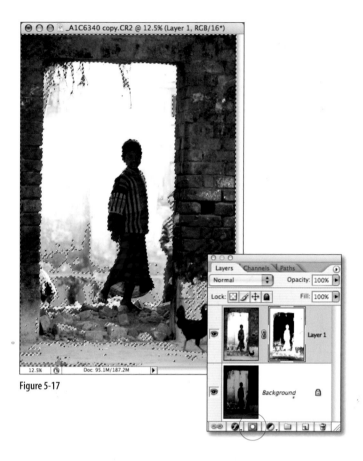

Figure 5-17

14. The final image is shown here. *Figure 5-18*

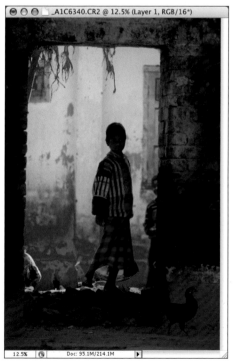

Figure 5-18

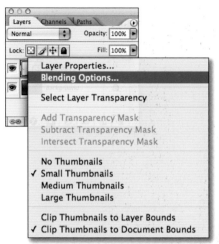

Figure 5-19

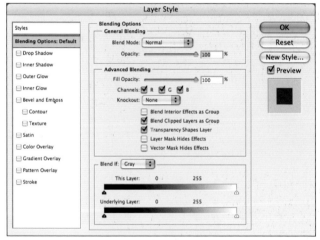

Figure 5-20

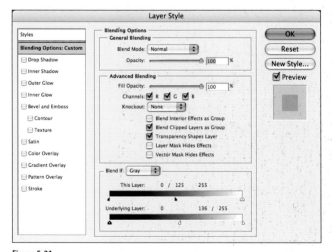

Figure 5-21

Using Photoshop's Blending Options

This method, using the Blending Options in Photoshop, is fast and doesn't rely on masking techniques, but it doesn't work well on all images. (Case in point: It didn't work on the previous example.) It can be used on Smart Object layers. To use it:

1. After pasting or placing the duplicate layer, right-click on a layer thumbnail. Choose Blending Options. *Figure 5-19*

2. This brings up the Layer Style dialog box. *Figure 5-20*

3. Use the Blend If sliders at the bottom of the dialog box to control the relationship between layers. If you hold Opt/Alt while clicking anywhere on the This Layer slider, it will automatically spilt the values. Try doing the same with the Underlying Layer slider. The result may be adequate. If not, tweak the sliders to get the blend just right. *Figure 5-21*

Extending Dynamic Range

A brightly lit scene can contain an infinite number of tonal values. Our vision system ingeniously adapts to such conditions; however, no camera—digital or otherwise—is capable of recording the entire tonal range of such a scene in a single shot. In this section, I'll show you how to use Photoshop's new Merge to HDR filter to create digital images with incredible dynamic range.

Let me show you what I mean by limited dynamic range. If you look at this test image, which was taken with a Nikon D200 digital camera, the histogram indicates that the details in the highlight areas of the image are clipped or missing. *Figure 5-22*

There isn't much I can do with Camera Raw's Adjust controls to fix this image, because the data just isn't there to work with. In this section, I'll show you an how to create an image with great dynamic range. Short of buying another digital camera, it's the best possible solution.

> ![!] *Some digital cameras, such as the Fuji FinePix S3, boast improved dynamic range capabilities, and it is safe to say in a matter of time digital capture will surpass the capabilities of print film. Even when this occurs, the various techniques outlined in this chapter will be useful for those who want the ultimate control of the tonal range of their images.*

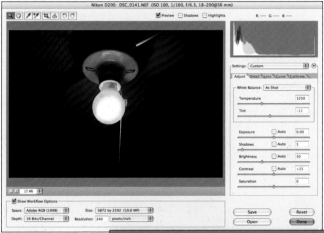

Figure 5-22

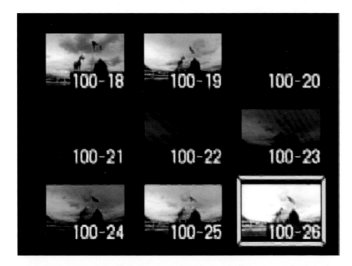

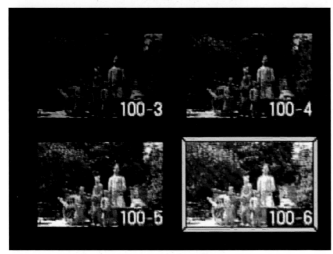

Figure 5-23

Using Merge to HDR

One of the newest additions to Photoshop is Merge to HDR (High Dynamic Range). Created by John Petersen, the same brilliant engineer responsible for Photomerge, Merge to HDR allows you to blend or merge three or more files taken of the same scene with different exposures and create a new file capable of storing an almost infinite number of tonal values. *Figure 5-23*

Few displays—and no printers—are capable of utilizing all this data. You'll need to rely on another new Photoshop feature, HDR Conversion, created by Chris Cox. HDR Conversion automatically appears when you change modes to a lower bit rate and provides a variety of ways to squeeze the dynamic data into a useable form.

The advantage of using Merge to HDR is obvious: by using different multiple shots at different exposures, you can extend your dynamic range much greater than is possible with a single shot.

There are obvious limitations to the multiple shooting technique often referred to as "bracketing." First, it's most effective with static scenes. Second, it works best if you carefully frame each shot, preferably using a tripod. Third, it uses up more memory both in the camera and on the hard drive. As you'll see, it also takes some effort to properly use HDR Conversion and get optimal results.

Shooting for HDR

Merge to HDR will work a lot better if you shoot with it in mind from the start:

- Use a tripod for consistent results. You can get decent results hand holding your camera, but it becomes hit or miss.

- Don't use your digital camera's autofocus! Even the slightest change in focus affects results and autofocus systems are notoriously imprecise.

- Vary your exposure by changing the shutter speed using your camera's manual or Aperture Preferred Mode. *Figure 5-24* Changing the f-stop would alter the depth of focus and quality would suffer. Don't change ISO between shots either. If you use a flash, use it consistently between frames.

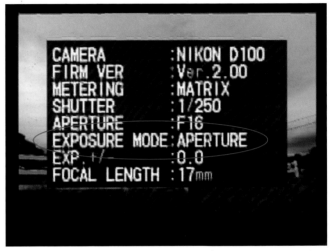

Figure 5-24

- Vary your exposure by at least one stop between frames. (Adobe actually recommends 2 stops between shots; that's fine but it really depends on the capabilities of your camera. Some digital cameras capture less dynamic range than others, and I like to err on the safe side.) *Figure 5-25* The bottom line is, if the exposure values are too close, Merge to HDR won't have much effect and if they are too far apart the final image will become posterized. HDR can handle such an extreme range that you can basically shoot from complete black to complete white. (One photographer told me he successfully used 26 images, shot 2 stops apart!)

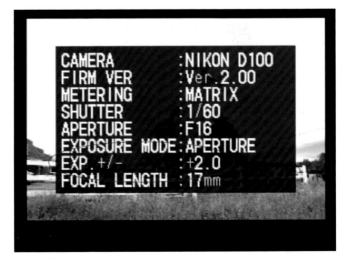

Figure 5-25

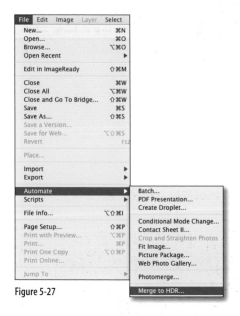

Figure 5-26

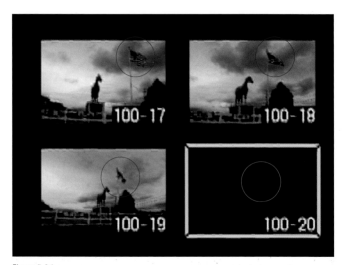

Figure 5-27

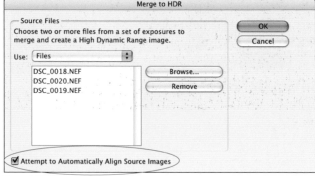

Figure 5-28

- Don't rely on automatic exposure bracketing. Many cameras offer this feature, however the range is usually limited, typically 2–3 stops plus and 2–3 stops minus. I use my camera's +/- exposure controls instead. Refer to your camera manual if you don't know how to set your camera to over- or underexpose.

- If you are shooting outdoor scenics, take the shots in rapid sequence. Clouds move, trees and flags wave in the wind, and every change between frames will affect the final image. *Figure 5-26*

Merging with HDR

Ok, you've got your shots. Here you go.

1. Select File > Automate > Merge to HDR. Browse to your images. (You can also access Merge to HDR directly from Bridge. Just select the files you wish to merge, hold the Shift or Cmd/Ctrl keys to select multiple files, then Select Tools > Photoshop > Merge to HDR.) *Figure 5-27*

    If your images were shot without benefit of a tripod, be sure to select Attempt to Automatically Align Source Images.

    Figure 5-28 If you are working from Bridge, you don't have a choice: your images will open without benefit of auto alignment. This is fine if your images were shot using a tripod, but it'll be a problem if they were not.(Officially, you are required to use multiple photos shot with different exposure values. However you can fool Merge to HDR if you strip the EXIF information from your single RAW file.

    It can take some time for the images to open in the Merge to HDR window, especially if you have selected Attempt to Automatically Align Source Images. How long it takes depends on the number of images you selected, the resolution, and of course, the processing speed of your computer. *Figure 5-29* Keep in mind that Merge to HDR uses Camera Raw to convert RAW files. However, it overrides Camera Raw's exposure, shadow, brightness, and contrast controls and relies instead on the camera's EXIF data for these values. It also converts the RAW data to 8 Bits/Pixel. If you change other Camera Raw parameters (such as Sharpen) be sure to do the same for all RAW files. Otherwise, quality may suffer.

2. Preview the results of your merge. Use typical navigation keyboard shortcuts, or control the viewable size by selecting from the percentage values at the bottom of the window. However, since most monitors are capable of displaying only 8 Bits/Channel of color data, you are only seeing a slice of the full HDR range. You can use the slider under the Set White Point Preview to vary the visible slice. This doesn't do anything to the HDR data; it just controls the preview. *Figure 5-30*

3. Adjust the effects of the merge by deselecting images and removing them one at a time. *Figure 5-31* To do this, un-check the box below the thumbnail image. Each time you deselect an image, the process of recreating a new merged image takes time, as indicated by the status bar at the bottom left of the window.

4. When you are ready, you can select OK, or choose a bit depth. I suggest for now you just select OK, and save the full 32-bit HDR data. You can select a lower bit depth later, if that is what you want.

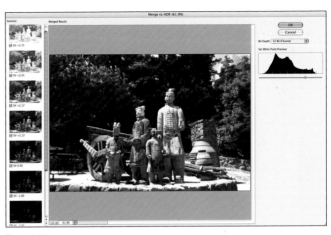

Figure 5-29

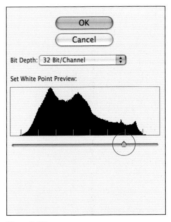

Figure 5-30

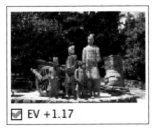

Figure 5-31

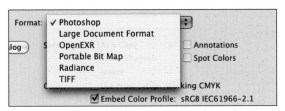

Figure 5-32

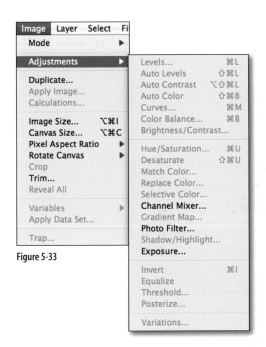

Figure 5-33

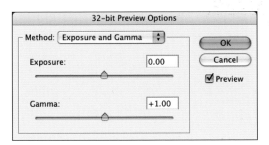

Figure 5-34

Saving Your HDR File

You can save the HDR file in any file format capable of retaining floating point data, which includes: Photoshop (*.psd*), Portable Bitmap (*.pfm*), TIFF (*.tif*) and OpenEXR (*.exr*). *Figure 5-32* You can't save a HDR file as a JPEG unless you convert it first to 8 Bits/Pixel, but then it won't be HDR anymore. Remember HDR files are quite large. For example, an HDR file created by merging images from my 6MP camera weighed in at 68.8MB.

Working with HDR Files in Photoshop

If you wish to work on the HDR file in Photoshop, you'll find the tools limited at this time. The Histogram palette is not functional, although the Info palette is. Levels and Curves aren't an option, but Channel Mixer, Photo Filter, and Exposure are. *Figure 5-33* Multiple layers are not an option, but the History Brush and Clone Stamp tools are. You can crop and resize and change the canvas size. You can apply arbitrary rotations and flips, as well as free transform and warps. Many filters are available, including Gaussian Blur, Unsharp Mask, Smart Sharpen, and Add Noise. You may find it easier to simply convert your HDR file to a lower bit range and do your serious editing then. If you thought Smart Sharpen was slow on a 16-bit file, just try it on a HDR file!

Changing the Preview for Your HDR File

You can change the preview to reflect different exposure and gamma settings without affecting the underlying data. Select View > 32-bit Preview Options from the main menu bar and this dialog box will appear. *Figure 5-34*

You can compare multiple versions of the same image by choosing Window > Arrange > New Window from the Photoshop menu. Then use the 32-Bit Exposure slider found at the bottom left of the image window to preview different settings for different windows and do a side-by-side comparison. *Figure 5-35*

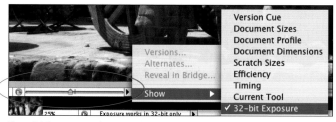

Figure 5-35

Converting HDR Files to a Useable Form

For all practical purposes, you'll want to convert your HDR files to a usable tonal distribution and practical bit depth. The way you squeeze all that data into a more limited space is critical, and sometimes it takes a bit of work to get it right.

To convert your file:

1. With your HDR file open, select Image > Mode > 16 Bits/Channel or 8 Bits/Channel. (Choosing Grayscale only discards color values and doesn't reduce the bit value.)

2. When you do this, you'll get this dialog box. This is where you'll make all the hard choices. *Figure 5-36*

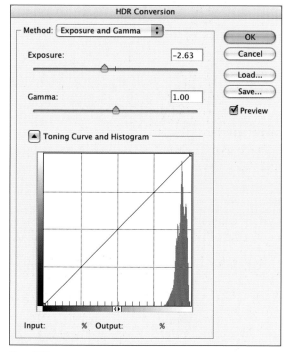

Figure 5-36

Your options are found in the Method pop-up menu. They include Exposure and Gamma, Highlight Compression, Equalize Histogram, and Local Adaptation. *Figure 5-37*

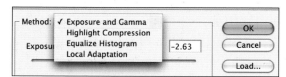

Figure 5-37

Exposure and Gamma, as the name implies, gives you straightforward control over brightness and contrast. Don't be mislead by the Toning Curve and Histogram. The histogram displays the inherent values, but the Toning Curve isn't functional. (It's functional only when you select Local Adaptation.)

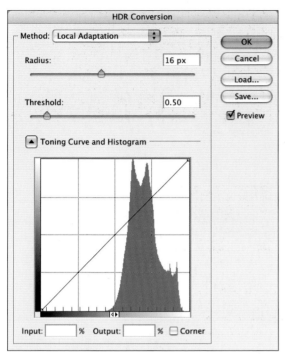

Figure 5-38

Highlight Compression and Equalize Histogram apply preset equations that may or may not be appropriate. There are no user controls for these options. I've found the Equalize Histogram works reasonably well on some merged images, but I've haven't had much luck with Highlight Compression. Try for yourself.

Use Local Adaptation to gain real control. Local Adaptation and Photoshop's Shadows/Highlight image adjustment command work similarly: they both attempt to lighten or darken an image, based on surrounding pixels. With a localized approach, it is possible to lighten a dark area (or darken an area that's too light) without affecting other areas of the image. *Figure 5-38*

In the case of Local Adaptation, this is achieved using a combination of Radius, Threshold, and Toning Curve controls. There are no fast rules on how to use these controls. What you do depends on the content of the image, resolution, and tonal range.

As a very general rule of thumb:

• *Pay particular attention to areas of detail and extreme tonal range as you adjust Radius and Threshold controls. Standard keyboard navigation commands are available. The Histogram palette isn't functional, but you can use the Eyedropper tool and Info palette to confirm your highlights and shadow areas are within range.*

• *A high resolution image with fine detail requires an increased Radius setting. A low resolution image with little detail requires a very low radius setting. Keep in mind, higher Radius values require more processing power, and it'll take longer for your image to convert. (Simply put, Radius controls edge detail.)*

• *An image with high tonal values will require a higher Threshold setting. (The most useful Threshold settings, however, range from .5 to 2. Higher values really don't do much for the majority of HDR images.)*

• *Set your Radius and Threshold values first, then adjust the Toning Curve. (Some images benefit from a further tweaking of Radius and Threshold values after applying a new Toning Curve.)*

Here are three different versions of the same image. For the first two images, I adjusted the Radius and Threshold controls to extremes, with just a slight adjustment of the Toning Curve.

The first image is "flat" and very soft. *Figure 5-39*

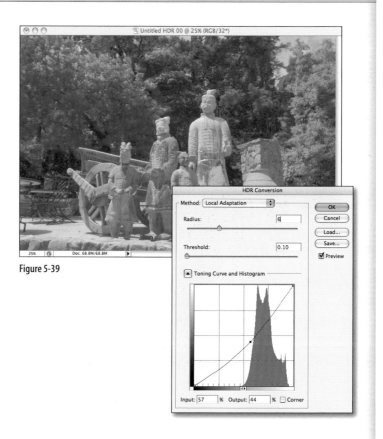

Figure 5-39

The second image has more contrast and detail, but the highlights are actually blown out. *Figure 5-40*

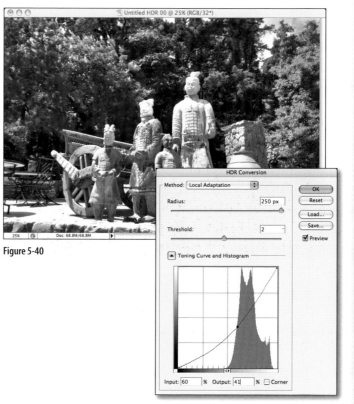

Figure 5-40

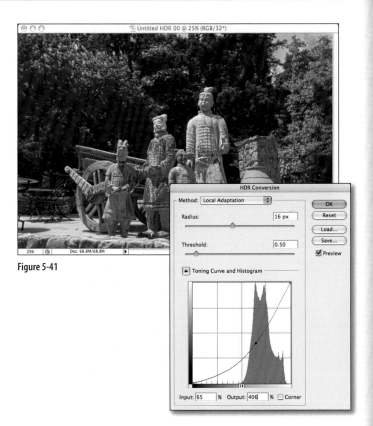

Figure 5-41

The third image demonstrates the effect of the default Radius and Threshold settings, with just a slight tweaking of the Toning Curve. It is a nice compromise. *Figure 5-41*

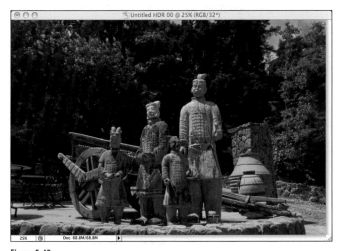

Figure 5-42

Note that the 68.8MB HDR file was created with a Nikon D100 6MP camera, mounted on a tripod *Figure 5-42* (8 shots, 1 stop apart, merged using Merge to HDR.)

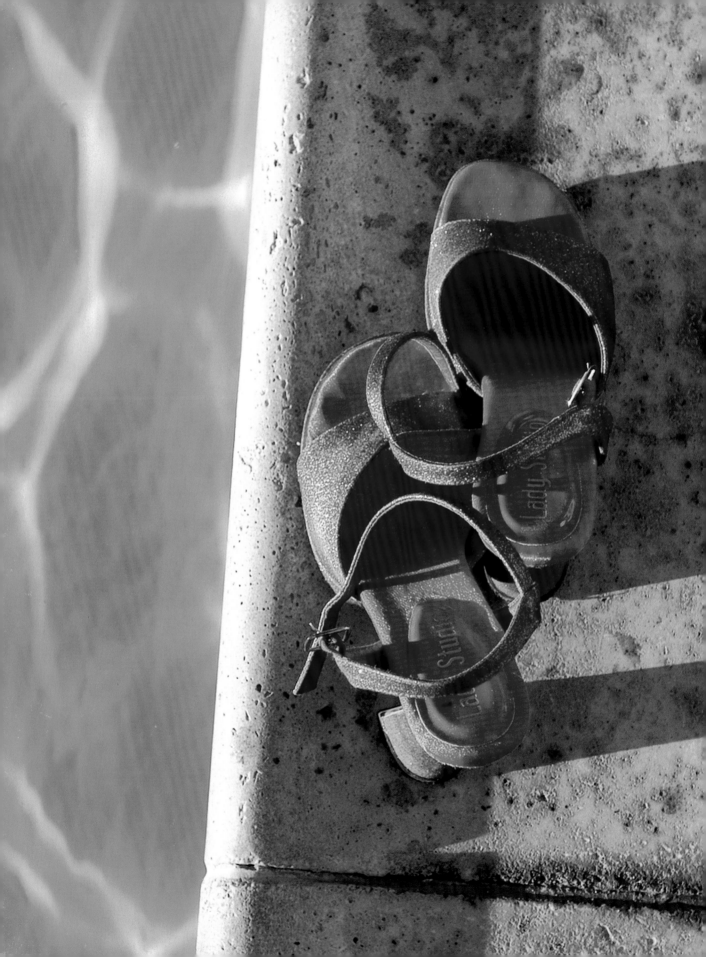

CHAPTER SIX

Sharpening RAW Smartly

Almost every RAW file requires some degree of sharpening to counter the effect of blurring that occurs at some stage of image capture or image processing. But when do you apply the sharpening? In Camera Raw, or later, in Photoshop? The answer isn't as straightforward as you might think. The fact is, there are compelling reasons to apply some sharpening to your RAW file using Camera Raw. There are also compelling reasons to turn sharpening off in Camera Raw, wait until your RAW file is open in Photoshop, and then apply sharpening via the new Smart Sharpen filter or one of the many third-party sharpening tools. As you'll learn in this chapter, it really depends on what you want: optimal workflow or ultimate flexibility and user control. This chapter will also hone your sharpening skills and teach you how to produce the best possible image.

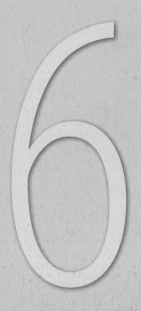

Chapter Contents

Raw Sharpening 101

Camera Raw, Smart Sharpen, or Other?

Sharpening with Adobe Camera Raw

What's with the Number 25?

Fixing the Effects of Over Sharpening

Using Photoshop's Smart Sharpen

Sharpening High ISO Images with Reduce Noise

RAW
Sharpening 101

The goal of sharpening is to produce an image with crisp, clearly defined edge detail, devoid of color fringing and extraneous noise. The challenge is to apply just the right amount of sharpening, without introducing distracting noise or artifacts to other areas.

The right amount of sharpening allows you to see all the detail in this image.

Figure 6-1

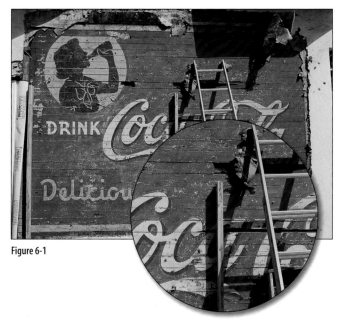

Figure 6-1

Whereas in this image, detail is actually lost from over-sharpening.

Figure 6-2

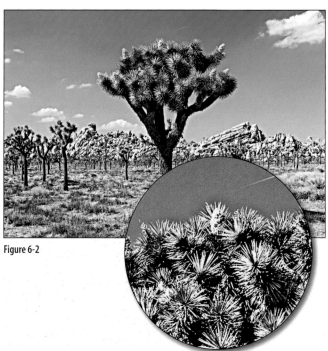

Figure 6-2

When to Apply Sharpening

There is a lot of misunderstanding about when and how to apply sharpening. I find it useful to break sharpening down into three general categories, applied sequentially in the order listed here:

1. Capture sharpening: sharpening that compensates for purposeful blurring at either the camera level or during raw conversion.

2. Cosmetic sharpening: sharpening applied to a specific part of an image and not another, i.e., eyes, but not blemishes. *Figure 6-3*

3. Print or output sharpening: final sharpening based on a specific size and destination of an image.

Since this is a book on processing RAW files, I'm going to emphasize capture sharpening, and just lightly touch the other two types of sharpening—which are huge subjects in and of themselves. (Applying correct output sharpening, for example, depends on a myriad of factors including the type of printer, ink, and media, not to mention image size.)

Capture sharpening is best understood by looking at an image with no sharpening applied. For example, look at this closeup of the same image shown earlier. *Figure 6-4* The photo was taken with a Fuji FinePix S3 Pro SLR using a very high-end Nikon lens for optimal sharpness. It was shot at f/8 at 1/250th of second and carefully focused.

I used the Camera Raw sharpening slider to turn sharpening completely off, and the resulting image is not an accurate representation of the scene as I shot it. It also doesn't do the equipment I used justice.

Ok, so we agree this image requires sharpening, but what's the best way to do it?

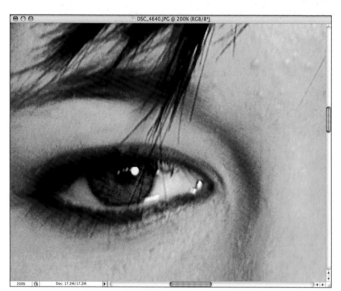
Figure 6-3

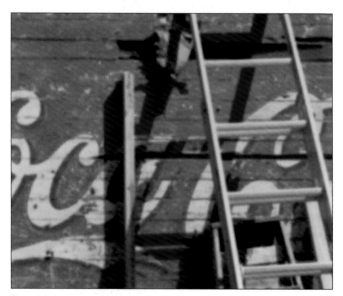
Figure 6-4

Camera Raw, Smart Sharpen, or Other?

I recommend using the sharpen feature in Camera Raw whenever you are processing large numbers of RAW files, or when speed is an issue and you simply want to create an image that appears sharp on a monitor. Figure 6-5 I say this knowing full well that you'll likely need to use other sharpening methods to apply Cosmetic or Output sharpening at a later point.

I recommend using the Smart Sharpen feature in Photoshop when you have a problematic image that Adobe Camera Raw sharpening doesn't do justice, or if you have the time and desire to perfect a particularly special image. The Photoshop Smart Sharpen filter can also be used effectively for both Cosmetic and Output sharpening. Figure 6-6

There are several other third-party sharpen options. My favorites include Nik Sharpener Pro, PhotoKit Sharpener, and FocalBlade. These commercial products all streamline workflow by offering various sharpening presets appropriate to different stages of sharpening.

I can't end this discussion without bringing up Photoshop's Unsharp Mask filter, which has been part of Photoshop since Version 1. Figure 6-7 Some of you may have finally mastered this filter and find comfort in using the familiar. But I highly recommend trying some of the other options described above. Unsharp Mask relies on fairly old technology, now largely replaced by space-age edge detection methodology.

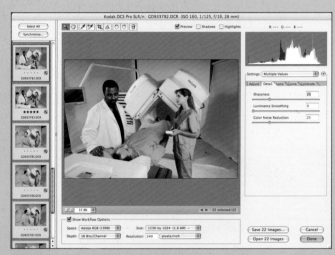

Figure 6-5

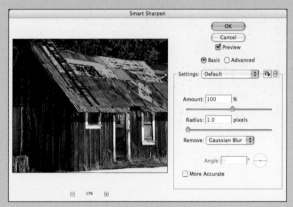

Figure 6-6

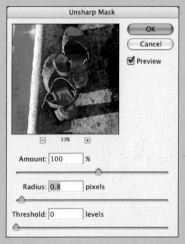

Figure 6-7

A sharpening value is automatically applied to a RAW file when you open it in Camera Raw for the first time . More often than not, the default Camera Raw sharpen setting works pretty darn well. There are good reasons for this. First, Camera Raw automatically applies a sharpening factor based on relevant data specific to a particular digital camera. Second, sharpening occurs only in the luminous channel, thereby reducing the chance of unwanted artifacts. Third, Thomas Knoll, a certified genius, built the Camera RAW sharpen algorithm from scratch.

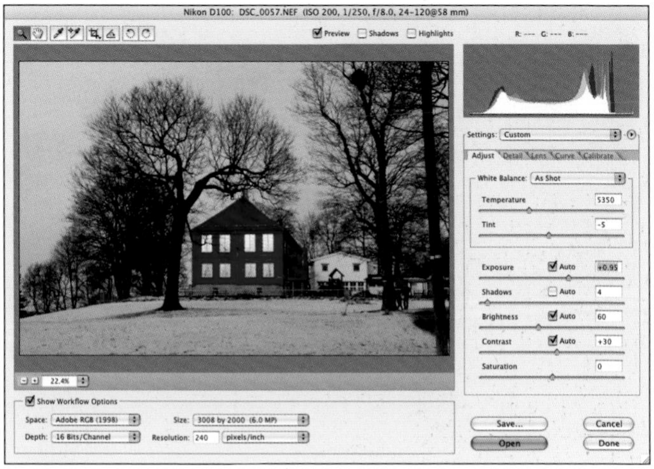

Sharpening with Adobe Camera Raw

Of course, if you have the time or inclination, you can tweak the Camera Raw sharpen settings and apply your custom settings to other images taken with the same digital camera.

For an example of how to adjust the sharpness setting, I'll use an image with a combination of detail (trees) and continuous tone (sky). I want sharp, clearly defined branches, but I also want to avoid adding noise or artifacts to the sky. *Figure 6-8*

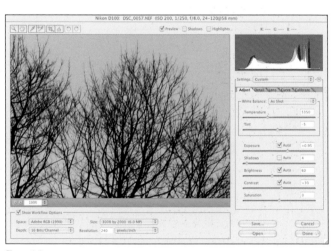

Figure 6-8

1. First, I set the white balance and exposure controls (see Chapter Four). In this case, the Auto settings are fine. I check these settings first because it's easier to judge detail appearances when the colors and exposure are correct.

2. Then, I identify a representative area of the image that contains both detail and continuous tone. *Figure 6-9* Using Camera Raw Magnify tools—either the Zoom tool or the Zoom level controls— I enlarge the image at least 100% and use the Hand tool to position the area I wish to observe in the middle of the Camera Raw window.

Figure 6-9

3. I select the Detail tab in the Camera
    Raw controls. *Figure 6-10*

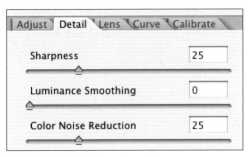

Figure 6-10

4. Unless you changed the number
    previously, the sharpening setting is
    always 25, regardless of what digital
    camera you use. (See sidebar: "What's
    with the number 25?".) I find it useful to
    start by sliding the slider to 0 and then
    examining the image to establish a
    baseline for future sharpening.
    Figure 6-11 Keep in mind; the effect of
    no sharpening will vary from camera to
    camera. With some digital cameras, the
    effect is barely noticeable. With others,
    it'll appear extremely noticeable.
    For an explanation, see sidebar: "No
    Sharpening is not always equal".

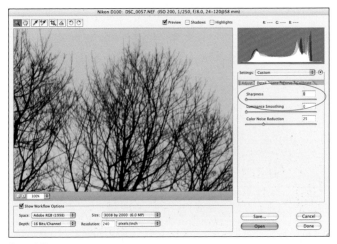

Figure 6-11

> ! Remember, when Preview is
> deselected you see a
> representation of your image determined
> by Camera Raw settings applied when the
> file first opened and before you changed
> anything. This means if Sharpening
> is set to 25 at Camera Raw startup,
> when preview is deselected you are
> actually viewing your image with some
> sharpening applied. *Figure 6-12*

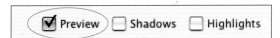

Figure 6-12

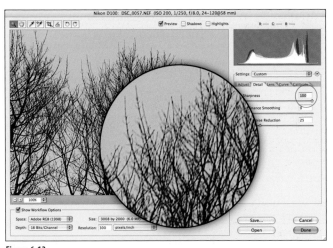

Figure 6-13

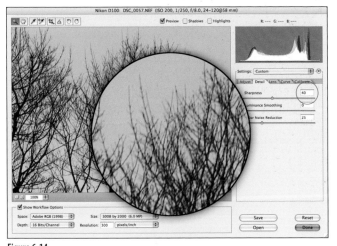

Figure 6-14

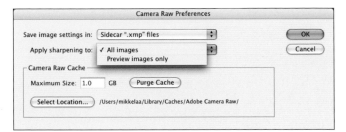

Figure 6-15

5. Next, move the slider to 100%, which obviously is way off. *Figure 6-13* Again, I'm going to the extreme to get a sense of the range I have to work with.

6. Through trial and error, I finally come up with the number 40. *Figure 6-14* Now I have the right balance between sharpness of the branches, with no noticeable noise added to the sky. In general, don't go to far with sharpening. It's always best to err on the side of caution. If you overdo it, future Cosmetic or Output sharpening will suffer.

Apply Sharpening to Preview Images Only

You can set Camera Raw to apply sharpening to the preview images only. However, when you open the image in Photoshop, the image will open with no sharpening applied. This allows you to see the effects of sharpening on your other Camera Raw adjustments.

To do this:

1. Select Preferences from the Settings flyout menu or from Camera Raw Preferences in Bridge.

2. Then select Apply sharpening to Preview images only from the Preferences dialog box. *Figure 6-15*

What's with the Number 25?

When you open a RAW file in Adobe Camera Raw, you'll notice the sharpening is set to 25, regardless of which digital camera you use. *Figure 6-16* Why this number and what does it mean? You need to know how Camera Raw works. Every RAW file is subject to a demosaicing algorithm that includes purposeful blurring. This blurring helps prevents color fringing by slightly blending adjacent pixels. Every digital camera model requires a different amount of blurring. The exact amount depends on many factors, including the size and characteristics of the camera sensor. Smaller sensors with many pixels typically produce a lot of "noise" and require more blurring during the RAW conversion in order to prevent the halo effect.

Camera Raw uses information specific to a particular camera model to process a RAW file and determine how much blurring to apply. Since it knows how much blurring has been applied, it also knows how much sharpening is needed to compensate for that blurring. The number 25 represents the optimal sharpening strength for a particular camera. For example, 25 for a RAW file produced with the Sony 828, which uses a relatively small sensor, will represent more sharpening than say a 25 for a RAW file produced by Nikon D70 with its larger sensor. *Figure 6-17*

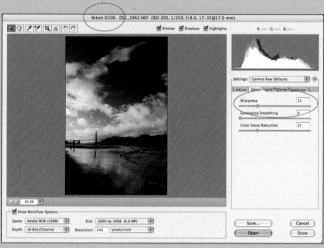

Figure 6-16

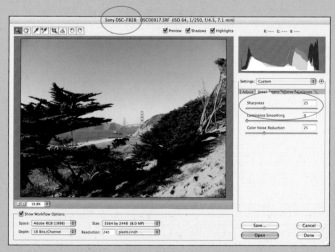

Figure 6-17

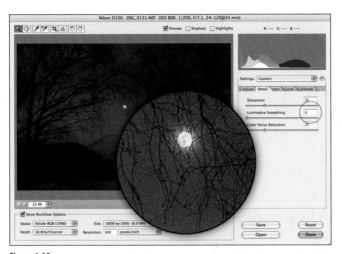

Figure 6-18

Fixing the Effects of Over Sharpening

For some images, such as the moonscape shown here, you can use Camera Raw's Luminance Smoothing controls to diminish artifacts caused by over sharpening, or, as in this case, a combination of sharpening and a high 800 ISO. *Figure 6-18*

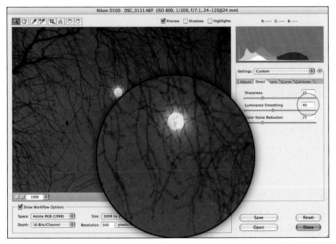

Figure 6-19

To do this:

1. Enlarge your image using magnification controls.

2. Select the Detail tab.

3. Find the optimal sharpening using the Sharpness slider.

4. Increase the Luminance Smoothing slider slowly, observing the effects. Stop when you achieve a balance between edge sharpness and diminished noise or artifacts in the continuous tone areas. In this example, 40 worked. *Figure 6-19*

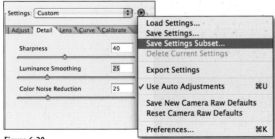

Figure 6-20

Save Your Detail Tab Settings

To specifically save Sharpness, Luminance Smoothing, and Color Noise Reduction settings;

1. Select Save Settings Subset from the flyout menu. *Figure 6-20*

2. In the Save Settings Subset dialog window, select Details from the Subset pop-up menu. (Or deselect all the settings except those you want to save.) *Figure 6-21*

3. Select Save. Name your setting and make sure it is saved in the default Settings folder. Otherwise, it won't show up in the Settings pop-up menu or in Bridge's Apply Camera Raw Settings menu.

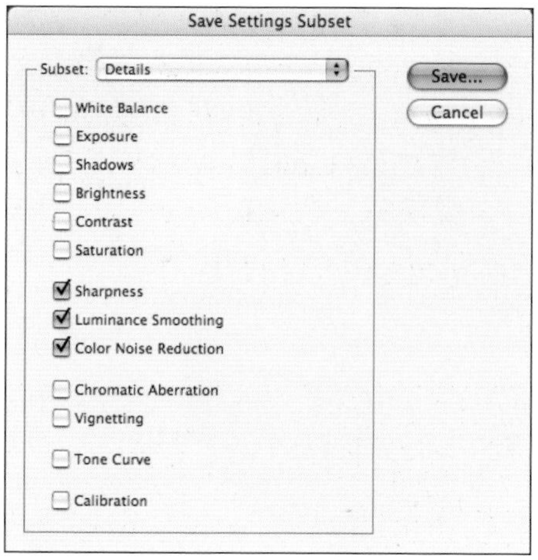

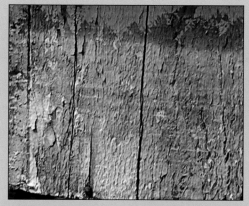

Figure 6-21

"No Sharpen" Isn't Always Equal

I opened a NEF RAW file in Nikon Capture Editor and turned sharpening off by deselecting Unsharp Mask. Then I converted the NEF RAW file to a TIFF file and opened it in Photoshop. Figure 6-22 Next, I took that same NEF RAW file and opened it in Camera Raw. I turned off sharpening and opened the image in Photoshop. Figure 6-23 When you compare the two images, you'll see that the one processed using the Nikon software is sharper than the one processed with Camera Raw, even though both had sharpening turned off in the RAW conversion. Why? Different applications process the same RAW data differently. In this case, I suspect that the Nikon software didn't apply as much softening to compensate for antialiasing, therefore resulting in a sharper image—even though sharpening was turned off.

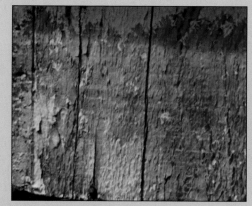

Figure 6-22

Figure 6-23

Using Photoshop's Smart Sharpen

It's called Smart Sharpen, and in Advanced More Accurate mode it uses state-of-the-art edge detection algorithms and a sophisticated deconvolving method to remove blur. In plain language, deconvolving means reverse—it attempts to identify the root cause of the blur and "reverses" the effect.) It also takes "smarts" to use Smart Sharpen properly.

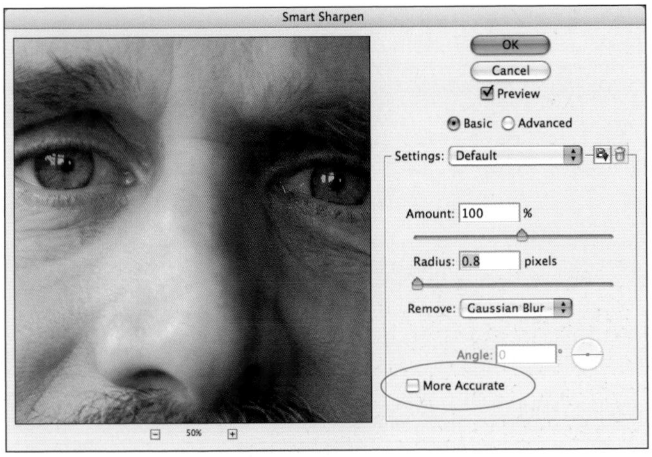

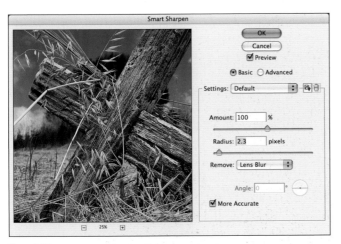

Figure 6-24

Figure 6-25

Fast sharpening or quality sharpening?

Smart Sharpen has two speeds: relatively fast and slow. When you deselect More Accurate you are basically crippling some of Smart Sharpen's most compelling technology, but things really speed up. *Figure 6-24* From a technical point of view, the results are on par with what you'd get if you used the good old fashioned Unsharp Mask, especially if you choose Gaussian blur as your Remove option.

With advanced settings selected, you also gain control over highlight and shadow sharpening, which is something you don't get with Unsharp mask.

It's your choice, but since I'm advocating Smart Sharpen for those special images— the ones that deserve a lot of your time and attention—I recommend using Smart Sharpen in More Accurate mode. *Figure 6-25*

Even if you decide not to use More Accurate, all the following information on using the filter applies. Just keep in mind the required Amount percentage values will need to be slightly higher if you turn More Accurate off.

Ok, now let's throttle this baby to full power and see how to use it.

> *If you are working with multiple layers, be sure to make the layer you want active before selecting the Smart Sharpen filter.*

Gaussian Blur or Lens Blur?

Several things cause image blur. It can be caused by a Gaussian blur applied during the assembly of the RAW data. Camera Raw and other RAW processing applications do this to some degree for every RAW file. It can also be caused by poor camera optics, or simply by poor focus. Figure 6-26 It can be caused by tiny micro lenses placed over digital camera sensors to minimize aliasing and color fringing. It might be caused by a subject or camera moving while the image is captured. Figure 6-27 The more you know about the source of image blurring, the better your chances of effectively undoing or removing the blur. This is where the different choices in Smart Sharpen come in. Unfortunately, image blurs are often caused by a combination of factors, so fixing them is not always that simple. You may find that, for some of your RAW images, the Gaussian blur option (with More Accurate selected) is the way to go. (Gaussian blur also processes much faster than Lens blur.) Other images may benefit from the Lens blur option. You just have to experiment to get it right. Remember, once you have found the optimal choice, save your settings for future images taken under similar conditions with the same camera.

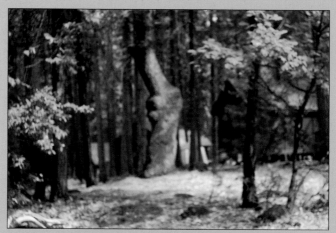

Figure 6-26

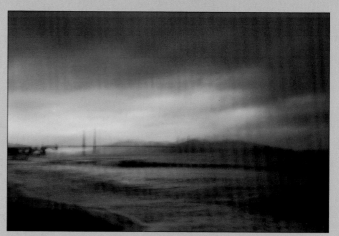

Figure 6-27

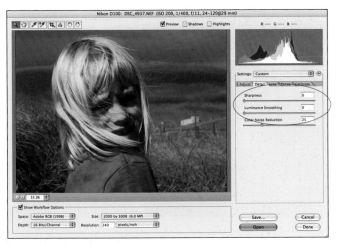

Figure 6-28

Selecting Proper Smart Sharpen Settings

Let's walk through how to use the filter:

1. Use Camera Raw to process your RAW data. Be sure to turn off all sharpening by sliding the Camera Raw Sharpness slider to 0. Leave the Camera Raw Luminous Smoothing setting on 0 as well. For best results, keep your Depth set to 16 Bits/Channel. *Figure 6-28*

2. Click Open.

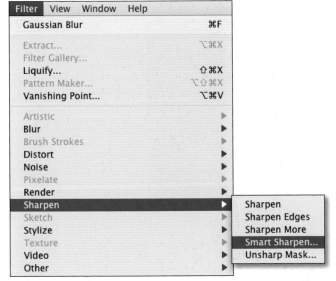

Figure 6-29

3. Select the Smart Sharpen filter (Filter > Sharpen > Smart Sharpen) from the Photoshop menu bar. *Figure 6-29*

4. With the filter open, select More Accurate for optimal quality. When you select More Accurate, the "intelligence" of Smart Sharpen is ramped up. As the engineers who wrote the software code explained to me, "you go from the capabilities of a 3rd grader to those of a college grad."

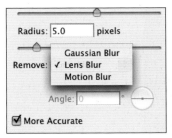

Figure 6-30

5. Next to "Remove", choose between Gaussian Blur and Lens Blur. (See sidebar "Gaussian Blur or Lens Blur?") Motion Blur, which is another Remove option, should be used only when the blur is caused by camera or motion blur, and isn't relevant to our discussion.) *Figure 6-30*

1. Enlarge your image using the + and -
   controls at the bottom of the preview
   window. Use your cursor—which turns
   into a Hand icon when placed over the
   preview window—to navigate to an
   area of your image that contains both
   edge detail and continuous tones.
   Figure 6-31

2. Make your adjustments according to
   the characteristics and resolution of
   your image. Images with fine detail
   and average resolution generally take
   a Radius of approximately 0.9–2.0.
   Change the Radius value by sliding
   the slider or typing directly in the box.
   Higher resolution images require higher
   Radius values. Your changes are reflected
   in the image preview window. You
   can compare the new values with the
   original unsharpened image by placing
   your mouse over the preview window
   and clicking and holding. As soon as you
   release the mouse, the preview changes
   to reflect the current settings.

   *Mac users: Don't forget to wait
   until the flashing bar at the
   bottom of the preview window disappears
   before deciding on the correct settings.
   (Window users should not experience a
   preview lag.) Figure 6-32*

3. Fine-tune the effect of the Radius
   settings with the Amount slider.
   Figure 6-33 Start at 100% and gradually
   increase the strength by moving the
   slider to the right (or by typing in a
   higher value). It's useful to go too far,
   to a point where noise appears in the
   continuous tone areas, and then
   back off.

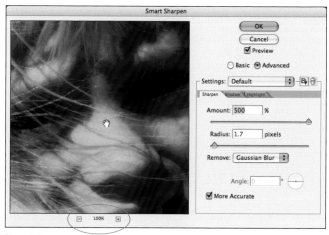

Figure 6-31

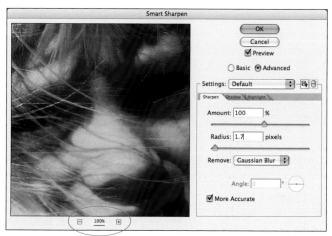

Figure 6-32

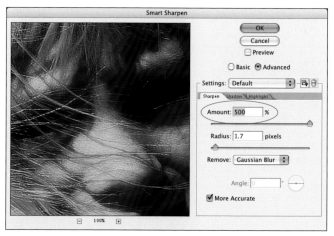

Figure 6-33

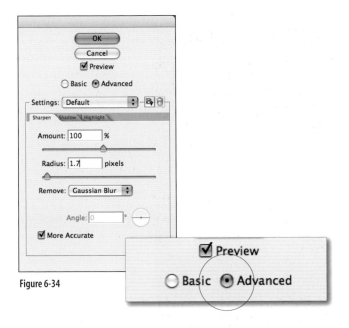

Figure 6-34

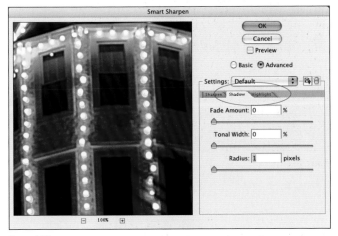

Figure 6-35

Advanced Smart Sharpen Settings

For the ultimate in control, select Advanced Settings. *Figure 6-34*

When you do this, tabs containing the words Shadow and Highlight appear. With these controls you can determine exactly how much sharpening is applied to areas of shadow and highlight. Commonly, these are areas that more readily exhibit sharpening artifacts.

The user controls for these Advanced Settings are a bit confusing, so bear with me as I walk you step-by-step through the process:

1. Start by using the Sharpen controls to get your edge details correct. You'll be working on removing the noise from shadows and highlight areas, so concentrate on edge detail and don't worry about the rest.

2. Select either the Shadow or Highlight tab. *Figure 6-35*

3. Navigate to the part of your image containing prominent shadows (or highlights, depending on which tab is selected).

> *If you previously used the Smart Sharpen filter and increased the Highlight and Shadow Fade Amount from 0 to a higher value in the Advanced mode, be aware! Values are sticky, meaning that whatever values you set last time will still apply the next time the filter is opened. If you increased the Fade Amount from 0 to a higher value, you may get unexpected results when you work in Sharpen mode. It's best to make sure the Fade Amount for both the Highlight and Shadow controls is set to 0—effectively turning these controls off—before working in Sharpen mode.*

4. Set the Fade Amount to 100%. This lets you readily see the effects of the Radius and Tonal Width. *Figure 6-36* You can always throttle the effects back later.

5. Pick a radius. This setting is determined by the nature of the shadow areas. Larger areas require larger radius. Smaller areas require a smaller radius. Throttle the Fade Amount back and forth from 0 to 100 % to see the effects of different Radius settings. *Figure 6-37*

6. The Tonal Width controls the diffusion of the tonal width as set by the Radius. The higher percentages spread the tonal borders. Smaller percentages shrink the tonal borders.

7. If necessary, repeat the above steps, using Highlight controls.

Saving Smart Sharpen Settings

Once you come up with an optimal setting, you can save your settings and later apply them to similar images.

To save a setting:

1. Click the disk icon, located near the Settings pop-up window. *Figure 6-38*

2. In the resulting New Filter Settings dialog box, give your setting a descriptive name and select OK. *Figure 6-39* The next time you go to the Setting pop-up menu, your setting will appear.

3. Save as many Settings as you wish. To remove a setting, select it and click the trashcan icon (it's next to the disk icon).

4. Share settings with others by making an Action, or sharing your entire Preset folder.

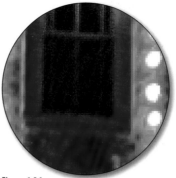

Figure 6-36

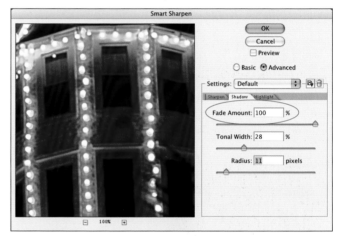

Figure 6-37

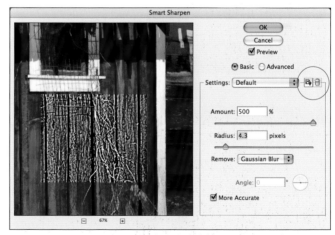

Figure 6-38

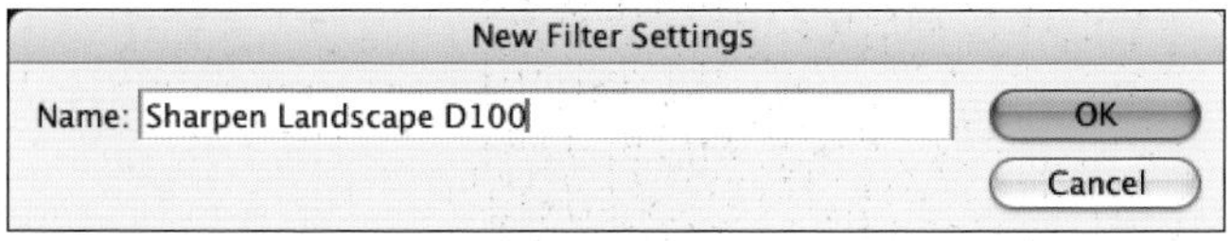

Figure 6-39

RAW images shot at a high ISO are problematic. Not only do they often need sharpening, but they also contain a lot of noise that is invariably boosted in the sharpening process.

Sharpening High ISO Images with Reduce Noise

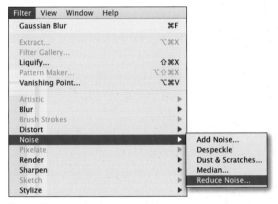

Figure 6-40

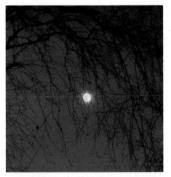

Figure 6-41

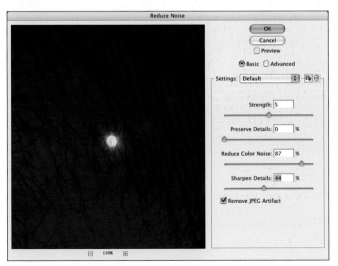

Figure 6-42

Reduce Noise is another new filter in Photoshop that effectively sharpens images and removes noise from images shot with a high ISO. *Figure 6-40* Like Smart Sharpen, it uses space-age inspired math to do the job. And, like Smart Sharpen, the intense math results in slow performance.

I go into great detail on using this filter in Chapter Seven: Noise Reduction & Correcting Chromatic Aberrations, but as you can see in the following before *Figure 6-41* and after *Figure 6-42* images, it is quite effective in sharpening as well as noise removal.

Although TIFF or PSD files converted from RAW don't usually contain JPEG artifacts, there are times when selecting this option helps. This is because some RAW data is actually compressed using a lossy, JPEG-like compression. With some digital cameras, this is a user option, but other times the compression is simply performed without the users knowledge.

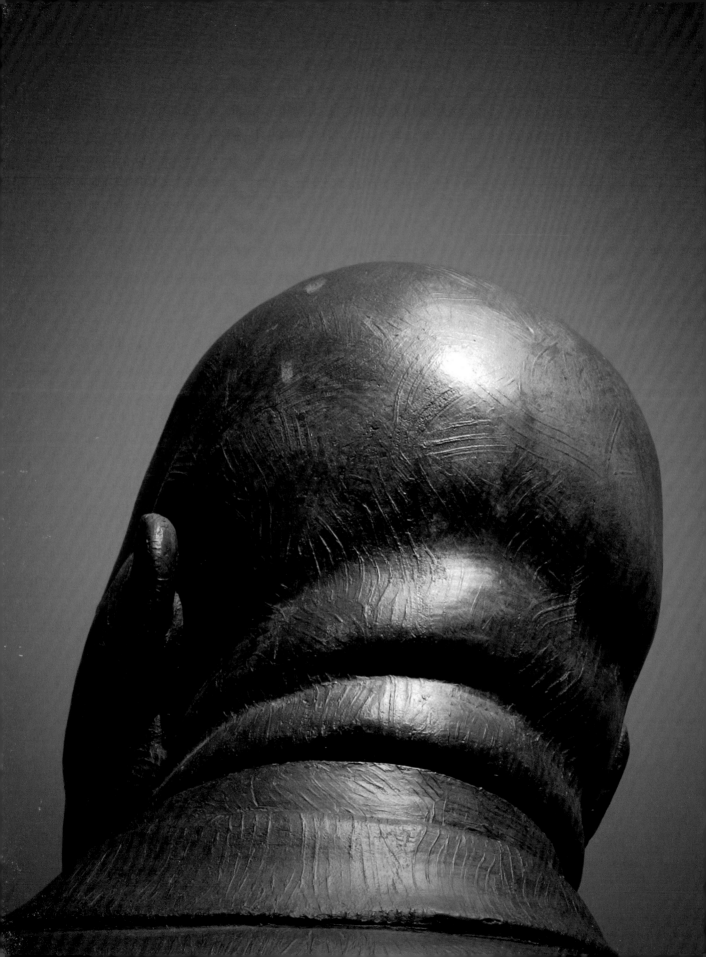

CHAPTER SEVEN

Reducing Noise, Correcting Chromatic Aberrations & Controlling Vignetting

With varying degrees, all digital cameras produce images with electronic noise, chromatic aberrations, and vignetting. Electronic noise shows up as extraneous pixels sprinkled throughout an image. Chromatic aberrations appear in transitional tonal areas as colored halos, color banding, or purple fringing (especially around backlit edges). Vignetting—darkening around image edges—occurs with a filter/lens/sensor mismatch. In this chapter, I'll cover how you can reduce the effects of these imperfections in your RAW files.

Chapter Contents

About Noise

Using Camera Raw to Reduce Noise

Using Photoshop's Reduce Noise Filter

About Chromatic Aberrations

Reducing Chromatic Aberrations with Photoshop's Lens Correction Filter

Diminishing or Adding Vignetting

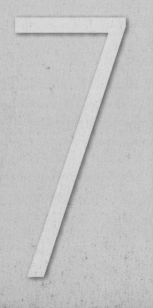

About Noise

Electronic noise is inherent to all RAW images, but its cause varies. It is more apparent is some images, and barely noticeable in others. Higher ISO values will enhance this effect, as will underexposure or long exposure. Process over-sharpening will also enhance electronic noise.

The noise in this detail, enlarged to 400%, for example, is a result of shooting at a high ISO setting. *Figure 7-1* Mark Richards captured this rare shot of the inside of San Quentin for *People* magazine by boosting the sensitivity of his Canon EOS 1Ds to 1600 ISO. He got the exposure settings he wanted, but obviously at a price in image quality.

On the other hand, the noise in this next detail (enlarged to 200%) taken at night at a normal ISO is due to a relatively long exposure (1/3 second) and it's mostly apparent in the dark sky. *Figure 7-2*

Of course, noise isn't necessarily bad. As Luis Delgado Qualtrough, a fine art photographer puts it, "Noise gives an image dimension—and authenticity." Luis came across this old painting hanging on the wall in a very dark room at an old hacienda in Mexico. Using a Canon Digital Rebel set to 1600 ISO, Luis managed to get the shot without a tripod. Luis chose to leave the noise in the image, to emphasize the impressionist style of the painting. The final shot hangs in a Danish museum. *Figure 7-3*

In any case, it's relatively easy to use Photoshop to remove or reduce the effect of electronic noise and—this is key—maintain image detail. You can either do this in Camera Raw, or after you open your file in Photoshop with the new Reduce Noise filter, which gives you much more options and frankly, in my opinion, better results. Once again, your choice of which to use will depend on what your want: speed and efficient workflow, or quality.

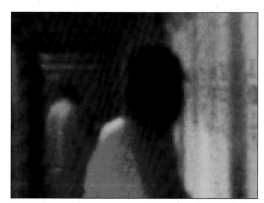

Figure 7-1

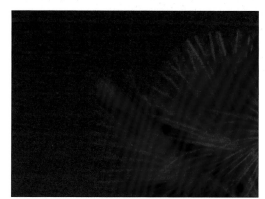

Figure 7-2

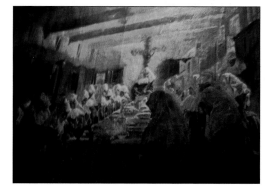

Figure 7-3

Noise isn't always apparent when you examine an image at a low magnification, as you can see in the first image below. If you use Camera Raw's magnifying tools to enlarge your image after applying Camera Raw exposure and color controls (but before applying additional sharpening), the noise will become apparent, as you'll see later in the section. Pay particular attention to areas of continuous tone, and shadow areas. Note the makeup of the noise. Does it look like a colored patchwork quilt? Or is the noise speckled and monochromatic?

Using Camera Raw to Reduce Noise

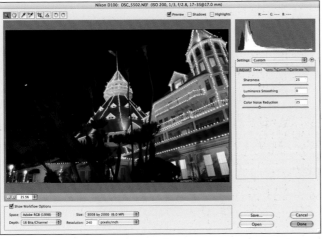

Figure 7-4

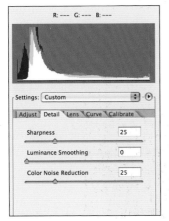

Figure 7-5

Some images actually contain a combination of chromatic (color) and luminance (monochromatic) noise. As you'll soon see, getting a handle on the type of noise will help determine which Camera Raw control—Luminance Smoothing, Color Reduction, or both—will be more effective. *Figure 7-4*

To begin the process:

1. Select the Detail tab. You'll notice right away the default Color Noise Reduction setting is 25, while Luminance Smoothing is set to 0. *Figure 7-5* Unlike the Sharpness setting, which is a relative value based on the type of camera you used, the Color Noise Reduction setting is an absolute value. This value is applied generically, and while it may or may not be right for your camera or image, it's almost always a good starting point.

2. Enlarge your image preview to at least 100%, preferably higher. Start by sliding the Color Noise Reduction slider to the left, down to 0. Next, move the slider incrementally to the right, increasing the value. *Figure 7-6* This affects the chromatic (color) noise and leaves details found in the Luminance (brightness) channel alone for the most part. If you go too far with the Color Noise Reduction setting, you won't lose detail per se, but you'll compromise color accuracy. (For the image shown here, a value of 50 is all it takes.) The chromatic noise is reduced without touching the Luminance Smoothing slider.

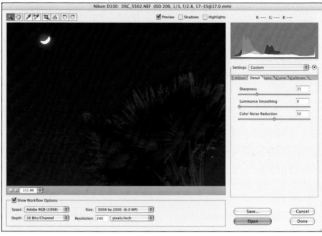

Figure 7-6

3. If increasing the Color Noise Reduction value doesn't do the trick—as in the next example—set it to zero and use Luminance Smoothing. *Figure 7-7*

   Go easy and increase the value incrementally.

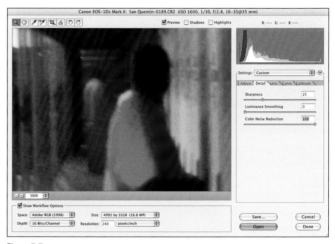

Figure 7-7

When working on the luminance channel, you can quickly compromise image detail. For this image, a Luminance value of 100 blurred it appreciably.

Figure 7-8

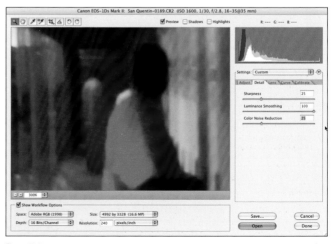

Figure 7-8

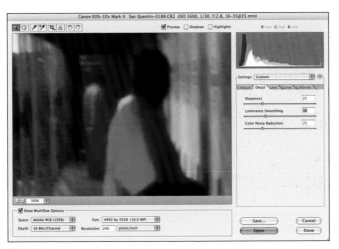

Figure 7-9

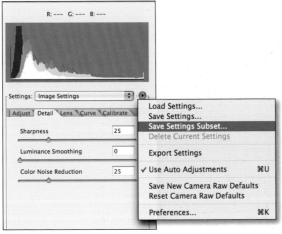

Figure 7-10

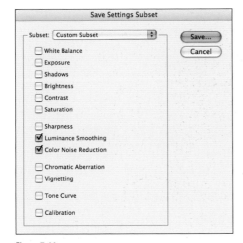

Figure 7-11

4. Sometimes a combination of Luminance Smoothing and Color Reduction produces the best result. You'll have to experiment to get the correct combination, as the correct values vary from image to image. Remember, the trick is to reduce noise without losing too much image detail. For this image, a Luminance Smoothing setting of 30 and a Color Noise Reduction setting of 25 worked best. *Figure 7-9*

Saving Noise Reduction Settings in Camera Raw

Once you find an optimal setting for your camera, at a frequently used ISO, you can save specifically those settings and apply them to other similar images.

To do this:

1. Select Save Settings Subset from the pop-up menu. *Figure 7-10*

2. In the Save Settings Subset dialog window, select Details from the Subset pop-up menu. Deselect Sharpness (or whichever settings you don't want to include) and the Details Subset becomes Custom Subset. *Figure 7-11*

3. Select Save. Name your setting and make sure it is saved in the default Settings folder. *Figure 7-12*

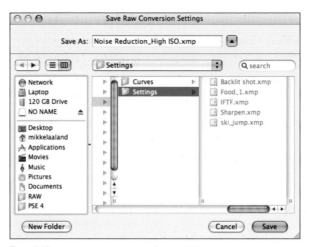

Figure 7-12

Otherwise, it won't show up in the Settings pop-up menu or in Bridge's Apply Camera Raw Settings menu. *Figure 7-13*

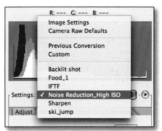

Figure 7-13

The Reduce Noise Filter is new to Photoshop CS2, and like the Smart Sharpen filter, it's based on some fancy state-of-the-art software coding. Frankly, I find this filter to be very effective and it often produces better results than I can get from the Camera Raw controls. Of course, the minute I call the filter "state-of-the-art" you likely suspect there is a downside, and there is. The user interface isn't very intuitive, and unless you are working on a very fast computer, it is slow.

Using Photoshop's Reduce Noise Filter

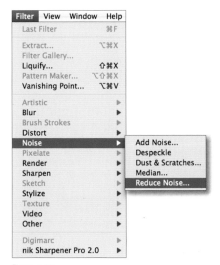

Figure 7-14

There are two modes to this filter: Basic and Advanced. I'll show you how to use both, although most users will find the Basic controls more than enough. Regardless of whether you use the Basic or Advanced settings, you'll need to run your RAW data through Camera Raw. Use Camera Raw to optimize your exposure and white balance settings, as explained in Chapter 4, but I suggest you turn Color Noise Reduction to 0 and leave Luminance Smoothing to 0 as well. *Figure 7-14*. The Reduce Noise filter works on 16-bit files, but performance is slowed.

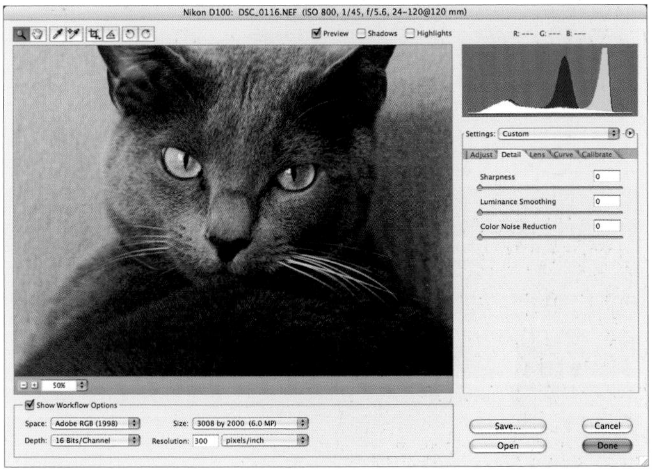

Basic Settings for Photoshop's Reduce Noise Filter

Let's start with the basic settings:

1. After preparing your RAW image in Camera Raw, select Open and bring it into Photoshop.

2. Select Filter > Noise > Reduce Noise from Photoshop's main menu. *Figure 7-15*.

Figure 7-15

3. Enlarge your preview to 100% or more. (Clicking on the percentage value at the bottom of the filter reverts it to 100%.) You can speed the efficiency of the filter up by making a small selection before you open the Reduce Noise filter. *Figure 7-16*

    Determine your Reduce Noise filter settings, then select OK and close the filter. Undo the effect of your filter on your selection (Cmd/Ctrl-Z), then deselect your selection, (Cmd/Ctrl-D). Select Filter > Reduce Noise (Cmd/Ctrl-F) from the menu bar. Your Reduce Noise settings will now apply to the entire image.

This next image shows the default settings. *Figure 7-17* These settings are a good place to start. (If you change these settings, the next time you open the filter the new settings will replace the default ones.) If the default settings aren't satisfactory, I suggest taking the following steps.

4. Start by setting the Strength value to 0. Slide the slider to the left, or enter the value in the box. This turns off luminance noise reduction, leaving you only with chromatic noise reduction. (Preserve Details, which is tied directly to the Strength value, will not be an option when Strength is set to 0.) Leave Sharpen Details set to 25% for now. *Figure 7-18*

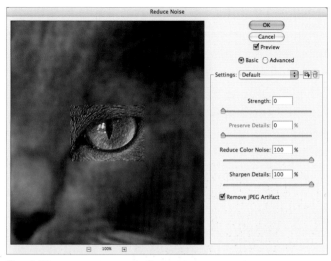

Figure 7-16

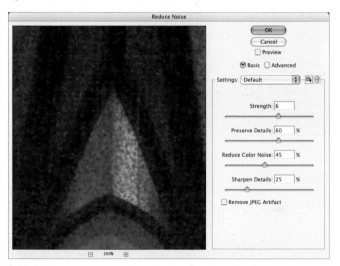

Figure 7-17

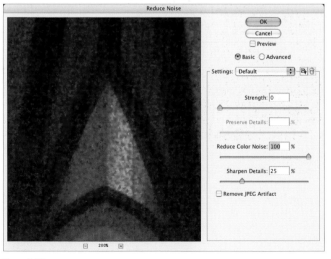

Figure 7-18

5. Experiment with different Reduce Color Noise values. Since this works only on the chromatic channels, this should not affect details of your image, only its colors. With the example shown here, nothing I did with Reduce Color Noise, even setting it to 100 percent, helped noticeably.

6. If Reduce Color Noise isn't enough, I suggest you set Strength, which works on the luminance (brightness) channel, to 10, its full value. Set Preserve Details to 0. The effect should be quite obvious, and image detail will surely suffer. (Mac users: withhold your judgment until the flashing bar below the percentage number stops signaling completion of processing. This can take some time depending on the size of your image or your settings. This won't be an issue for most Window users.) *Figure 7-19*

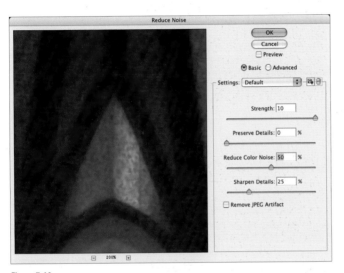

Figure 7-19

7. Now you have a choice: either dial the Strength value back, or increase Preserve Details. These two settings are related. Preserve Details simply provides parameters for Strength to work within, telling it to ignore (0) or preserve fine detail. After some experimentation, I came up with the proper combination of Strength and Preserve Detail to get what you see here. *Figure 7-20*

8. Try selecting Remove JPEG Artifact. Sometimes it helps, even when you are working with a RAW image that theoretically isn't compressed. (RAW data can be saved with compression, and sometimes you just don't know whether its has been saved this way.)

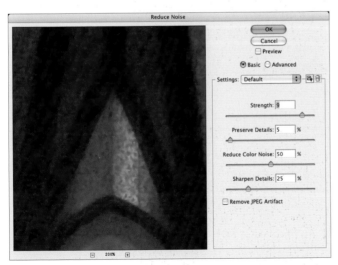

Figure 7-20

Advanced Settings for Reduce Noise

When you select Advanced, a Per Channel tab appears. *Figure 7-21*

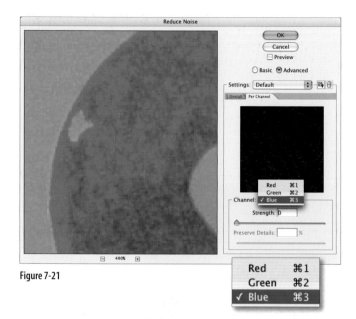

Figure 7-21

Using Advanced Settings Per Channel allows you to select individual channels based on the working color space and apply the Reduce Noise filter selectively. If you are working in RGB, for example, the red, green, and blue channels are available. If you are working in LAB, the Lightness and A B color channels are available. Since electronic noise often appears in one channel more than another, this can be quite useful. For example, typically in the RGB color space, it's the blue channel that displays more noise, but not always. *Figure 7-22*

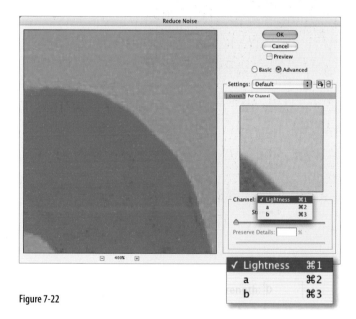

Figure 7-22

Using these settings, you can fine-tune your overall settings by boosting the noise reduction in a particular channel. You may find it useful to do all the adjusting in the individual channels. If you choose to do this, be sure to first adjust the Reduce Color Noise and Strength settings in the Overall menu to 0.

To use the Per Channel settings:

1. Select Advanced Settings.

2. Click on the Per Channel tab.

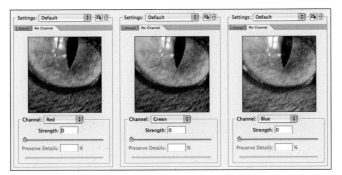

Figure 7-23

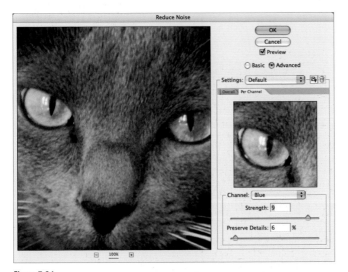

Figure 7-24

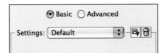

Figure 7-25

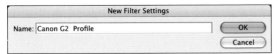

Figure 7-26

3. Cycle through the different Channels, observing the differences. *Figure 7-23* You can magnify/reduce the Color Channel grayscale display independently from the main color display window by holding your cursor over the grayscale display and Option/Alt-click to reduce and Cmd/Ctrl-click to magnify. To reduce the display in both windows simultaneously, place your cursor over either display window, and use Option/Alt+Shift-click; to magnify, use Cmd/Ctrl+Shift-click. Holding the Shift key while dragging will scroll both windows simultaneously.

4. Identify a channel that has noise. *Figure 7-24*

5. Adjust the Strength slider until the noise is reduced satisfactorily.

6. Adjust the Preserve Details slider accordingly.

7. To compare your changes with the original, place your cursor over either the color or the grayscale display, click, and hold. Both the color and grayscale displays will change. If this still doesn't remove all the noise, return to the Overall tab and make additional adjustments there.

Saving Advanced Noise Settings

When you find an optimal adjustment, you can save your settings and apply the setting later to another similar image. To save your settings:

1. Select the Save icon. *Figure 7-25*

2. When the New Filter Settings dialog box opens, type in a descriptive name. The next time you open the filter, your new setting will appear in the Settings pop-up menu. *Figure 7-26*

About Chromatic Aberrations

Chromatic aberrations show up as anomalous color shifts mostly on the outer perimeter of an image, in areas with distinct edge transitions. They are mostly evident when wide-angle lenses are used, but can appear with longer lenses as well. From a technical point of view, both Camera Raw and Photoshop provide nearly identical ways to fix Chromatic Aberrations

This image shows a shot taken by professional photographer Richard Morgenstein with a Canon 10D and a 14mm wide-angle lens. Although the chromatic aberrations are not visible at first glance, magnification will probably show some annoying anomalies in the edges of the chrome headlights. *Figure 7-27*

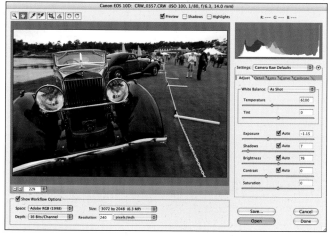

Figure 7-27

Reducing Chromatic Aberrations with Camera Raw

To use Camera Raw to reduce chromatic aberrations in images such as this:

1. Identify a likely area near the outer parameter of a likely candidate (for example, an image shot with a wide angle lens in bright lighting conditions with sharp edge detail).

2. Magnify the area using Camera Raw navigation tools. (Select the Magnify tool and hold your cursor over the area you wish to magnify. Click and drag a rectangle that contains the area you wish to magnify, then release the mouse. *Figure 7-28*

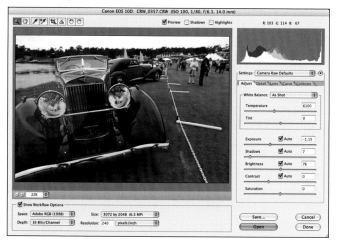

Figure 7-28

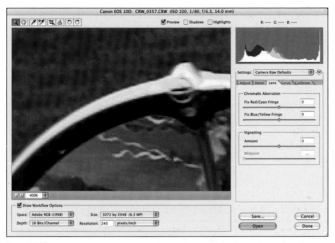

Figure 7-29

In the magnified image shown here, you can clearly see the color fringing so typical of this type of chromatic aberration. (When light passes through glass, different color wavelengths are sometimes separated and shifted in focus ever so slightly. To visualize this, think of a common prism and the rainbow it produces. This shift is recorded by the sensor and appears as a color fringe, such as shown here.) *Figure 7-29*

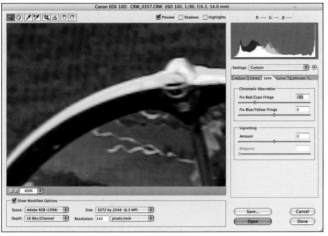

Figure 7-30

3. Select the Lens tab. Under Chromatic Aberration, select the appropriate slider. For this image, I chose Fix Red/Cyan Fringe and slid the slider to the left until I got what you see here. *Figure 7-30*

It's very useful to understand how these controls actually work. When I first started using the Chromatic Aberration controls, I assumed they worked by simply looking for edges and removing or desaturating colors. But this isn't at all how they work, and I should have figured that out by simply watching the effect of moving the control sliders radically one way or another. Try that yourself on an image and you'll see what I mean.

You should notice a subtle distortion of your image, growing in intensity from the center of the image out to the edges. In fact, the distortion is limited to select colors that are actually expanding or shrinking (i.e., distorting) based on your settings. For example, if you chose Fix

Red/Cyan Fringe, then either the red or cyan colors will be affected. If you chose Fix Blue/Yellow Fringe, only these colors will be affected. *Figure 7-31* In the next section, I'll use illustrations to show more clearly what I'm talking about.

The key point here is: there are important practical implications. First, don't crop your image, apply Chromatic Aberration controls, and then expect good results. The color distortions are based on a lens model, and the minute you crop you've changed that model. Second, don't expect this to work on other aberrations such as a dead pixel or a highlight blooming that appear in the dead center of an image. The effect is more powerful at the edges of your image, and diminishes as you move closer to the center. And finally, the results you get will vary depending on the lens you use.

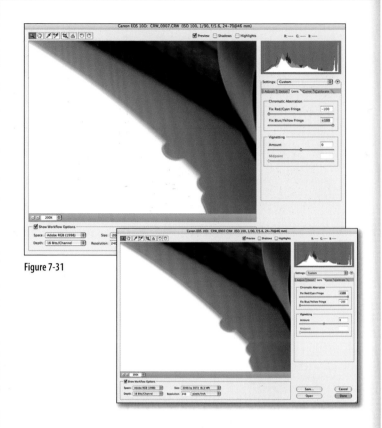

Figure 7-31

Reducing Chromatic Aberrations with Photoshop's Lens Correction Filter

Photoshop's new Lens Correction filter offers an alternative environment to fix chromatic aberrations. To access the filter, select Filter > Distort > Lens Correction from the menu bar. *Figure 7-32*

There is no difference between the Chromatic Aberration controls in Lens Correction filter and Camera Raw's controls. None at all. They use the same underlying code to do the job. They both work on 16-bit files. The Lens Correction filter, however, allows you to magnify your image to a larger percentage—1600 percent, compared to the 400 percent Camera Raw offers. It also does much more than just fix chromatic aberrations.

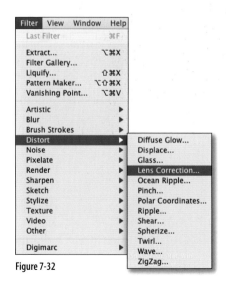

Figure 7-32

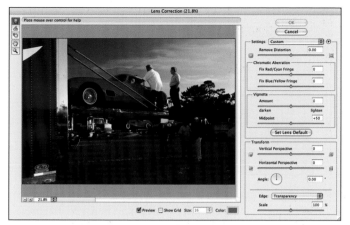

Figure 7-33

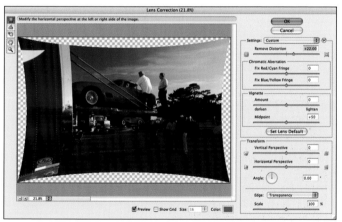

Figure 7-34

The Remove Distortion slider, for example, is a nifty way to correct barreling and pin-cushioning effects produced by some lenses. As you'll see later in the chapter, you can use the filter to remove (or add) vignetting—just as you can in Camera Raw. The Transform commands open a lot creative options—all beyond the scope of this book. I really love how you can use the Edge setting to add black (or transparent) borders. The Lens Correction filter is a really a nice addition to Photoshop's native filter set. *Figure 7-33*

To use the Chromatic Aberrations controls in the Lens Filter, simply refer to the previous section, "Reducing Chromatic Aberrations with Camera Raw". I suggest you deselect Show Grid, to get a clear view of your image. (The grid is handy when you use the Transform commands.)

I do, however, want to use the Lens Correction filter to illustrate better how the chromatic aberration controls work. I may be beating a dead horse, but sometimes it helps to understand how something works—and I've found so many people just don't get this one. Anyway, look at this image. *Figure 7-34*

I used the Distortion controls to "correct" for—in this case, non-existent—lens barreling. You can see how the image distorts inward. (Moving the Remove Distortion slider to the left corrects for pin-cushioning and distorts the image outward.) Well, imagine this same distortion specific to a select color instead of a global distortion. This is what happens when you use the chromatic aberration controls. The selected colors shrink or expand, incrementally, but enough to bring the colors back in line.

> By the way, just so you don't think you are going crazy. If you use the Edge: Background Color (found at the bottom of the Lens Correction filter), you'll always get a black border, regardless of which color you select in the Background swatch. I assume this will be fixed in subsequent versions of the filter. *Figure 7-35*

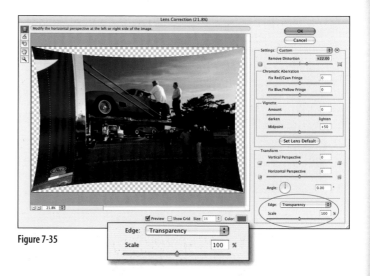

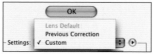

Figure 7-35

Saving Lens Correction Settings

To save custom Lens Correction settings specific to Chromatic Aberration:

1. Select Save Settings from the pop-up menu. *Figure 7-36*

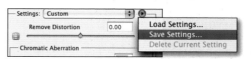

Figure 7-36

2. Type in a descriptive name for your setting. *Figure 7-37*

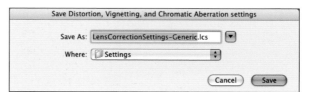

Figure 7-37

3. Load and apply your saved setting by selecting from the Settings pop-up menu. If it doesn't appear in the menu, select Load Settings from the pop-up menu next to the triangle and navigate to the appropriate location. *Figure 7-38*

Figure 7-38

Vignetting (darkening at the corners of the frame) can be caused by a mismatched filter/lens hood or a lens (e.g., using a filter on an ultra wide angle lens). It can also be caused by using wide angle lenses not optimized for digital capture (i.e., not optimized for even brightness across the frame). It's one of the easiest things you can fix in Camera Raw. Conversely, you can also add a vignette to your image, which will draw attention a specific part of an image.

Diminishing or Adding Vignetting

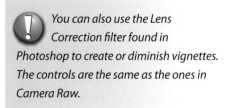

Figure 7-39

To add or diminish a vignette:

1. Select the Lens tab.

2. Adjust the Amount slider left or right. The edges will darken or lighten from a central radial point. *Figure 7-39* In this case, photographer Luis Delgado Qualtrough actually darkened the edges of his image to bring more attention to his subject. (The image, by the way, is part of quad-tych titled *Dream*, commissioned by a bookstore.)

3. Use the Midpoint slider to expand or decrease the range of the effect. You cannot, however, create multiple interest points. Adding a vignetting effect is therefore most effective when your image contains a single point of interest that you want to emphasize.

> *You can also use the Lens Correction filter found in Photoshop to create or diminish vignettes. The controls are the same as the ones in Camera Raw.*

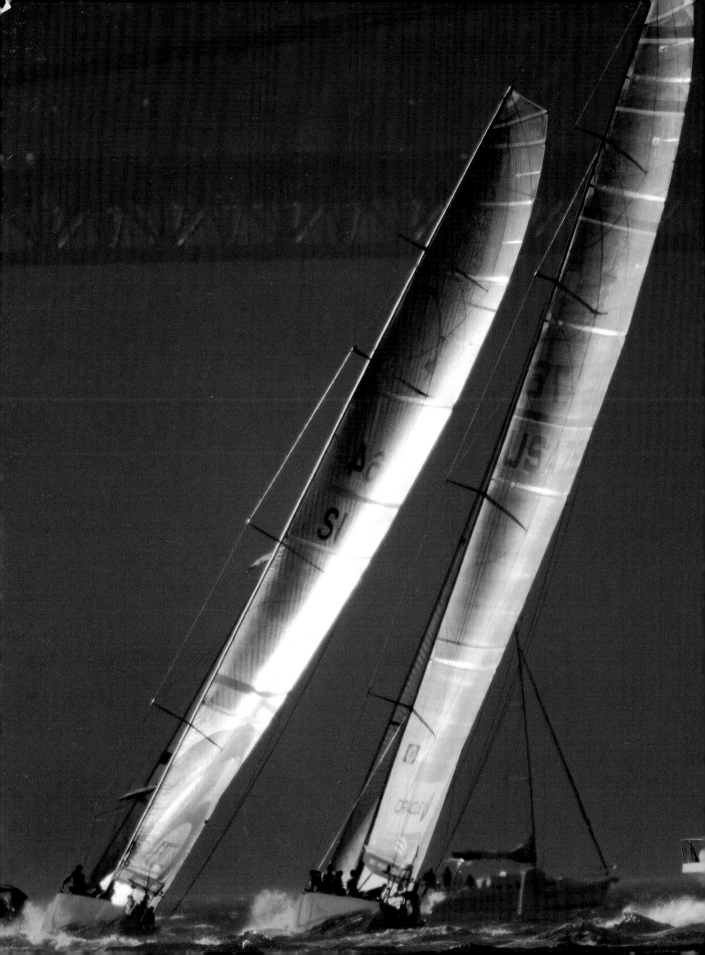

CHAPTER EIGHT

Better Black & White Images with RAW

Like most photographers, I hold a special place in my heart for black and white photography. If you take away the red, greens, and blues and replace them with subtle shifts of luminance, you'll find form and shape are emphasized. A beautiful black and white image is a welcome respite to the eyes and mind in a world full of oversaturated and gaudy color.

In this chapter, I'll show you a couple ways to use Camera Raw and Photoshop to generate a wide range of tones and tints from your RAW files and make black and white images that rival—and even surpass—traditional film shooting and processing techniques.

Chapter Contents

RAW Is Inherently Grayscale

Using Camera RAW to Generate Black & White Images

Shooting Considerations for Black & White Images

Using Calibration Controls to Fine Tune and Tint

Advanced Localized Black & White Control

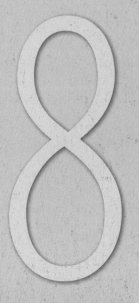

RAW Is Inherently Grayscale

A photographer I know questioned the validity of converting a color digital image to black and white, or technically, grayscale. His point of reference was the traditional film world where he'd never shoot color film when he wanted a black and white result. He was comforted when I explained that in reality all digital images are fundamentally grayscale and they aren't "converted" to grayscale. Sensors only record luminance values for color-filtered pixels. The characteristic color value of each pixel is recorded so Camera Raw knows what color values to assign to a particular pixel.

This first image, for example, is a RAW file "frozen" at a stage before color was interpreted, so the image displays only grayscale information. *Figure 8-1* (Photo courtesy of Jack Holm.)

Granted, this is a far cry the way Eastman Kodak's Tri-X or Ilford's FP4 capture light, but with a little careful post-processing of a RAW file, you can come pretty darn close to imitating the look and feel of those venerable black and white films.

I'll show you a couple of ways to do this: one way is very simple and quick, while the other is more complicated and requires advanced Photoshop techniques. However, this second technique delivers fabulous results with ultimate control.

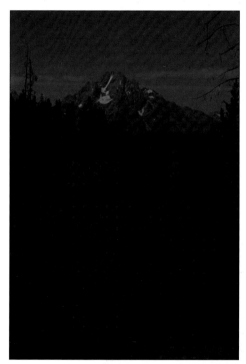

Figure 8-1

With Photoshop it has always been deceptively easy to turn a color image into black and white. Image > Mode > Grayscale and, viola, you are done. But with no user options, the results are totally unpredictable and often unsatisfactory. Many photographers prefer using Photoshop's Channel Mixer, which gives them more control over the way red, green, and blue values are mixed. Other photographers use third-party filters, which they claim gives them even better results with more controls. Some advanced Photoshop users work in the LAB color space and use a conversion method that requires multiple adjustment layers and masking techniques. Here, I'll show you ways that shooting RAW and using Camera Raw provide a great alternative method for creating black and white images.

Using Camera Raw to Generate Black & White Images

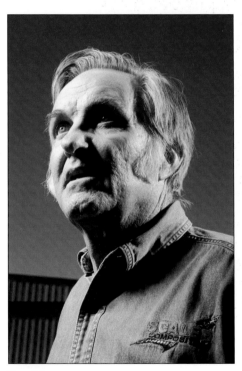

Figure 8-2

Using Camera Raw Saturate Controls

When it comes to working with RAW files, I've found Camera Raw's Saturate control, or a combination of the Saturate and Calibrate controls, produce results that actually rival or better other aforementioned methods. I'll show you what I mean now. And later in the chapter, I'll show you a really amazing way to use both Camera Raw and some classic Photoshop layer masking techniques to give you precise control over your black and white conversion.

Let's start by looking at an easy way to use Camera Raw to produce a grayscale image from a RAW file. I'll use a real-world example. The photo shown here was taken by John Carnett, staff photographer for *Popular Science* magazine. It's a portrait he took of Burt Rutan, the man behind StarShipOne. When John got the assignment, he immediately visualized the image in black and white. When he shot it using a Canon EOS 1DS, he used very hard side lighting to evoke a desert cowboy feel. *Figure 8-2*

The process John used to produce a black and white version for the magazine was simple. Let's walk through it:

1. From Bridge or Photoshop, open the RAW file in Camera Raw. John worked in the Adobe RGB (1998) 16 Bits/Channel to get the optimal color gamut.

2. In Camera Raw, adjust the Exposure, Shadows, Brightness, and Contrast controls to their optimum tonal settings. (In this example, John decreased his Exposure setting by .9 stop but left the other settings alone.) *Figure 8-3*

3. In Camera Raw, slide the Saturate slider as far left as you can, to a value of –100. *Figure 8-4*

4. Tweak the exposure controls to get the final look you want. Use the histogram for reference.

5. Select Open and do your final processing, if any, in Photoshop.

How does desaturate in Camera Raw compared with desaturate in Photoshop? The results shown here show desaturation done in Photoshop (Image > Adjustments > Desaturate). Note the obvious banding in the sky. *Figure 8-5*

Next you'll see the same image, but this time desaturation was done in Camera Raw. *Figure 8-6* The results are much better. I've seen similar qualitative differences when I applied this test to other images, but with some images the difference is not so obvious. I suspect one of the reasons you get better results in Camera Raw is the desaturation occurs in the LAB color space, which is always a better space for this kind of work. Camera Raw also has more data to work with, because of the nature of RAW.

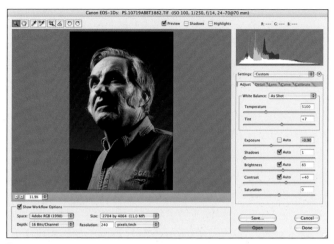

Figure 8-3

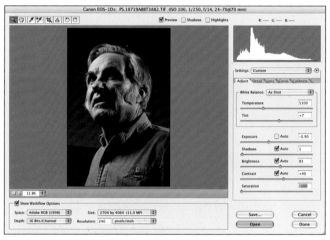

Figure 8-4

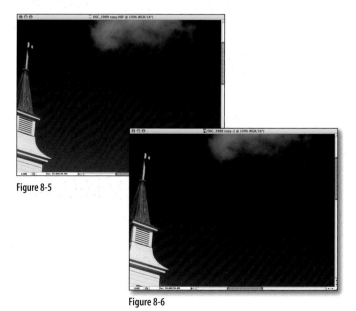

Figure 8-5

Figure 8-6

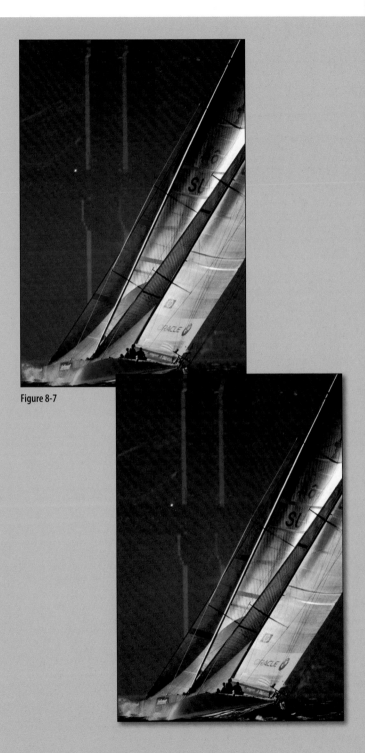

Figure 8-7

Shooting Considerations for Black & White Images

Some shots work better in black and white than others. There are no hard and fast rules. If you are trying to create a particular mood, or evoke a certain era in time, for example, rendering the final image in black and white is appropriate. However, a black and white image can be plain boring if there is neither good composition nor compelling content.

For example, John McDermott's vertical shot of two America's Cup yachts, shown here in both color and black and white, works very well either way because of the dramatic lighting and striking composition. Figure 8-7

Of course, content and composition aren't all that go into making a good black and white image. You need a range of tonal values, and that's where proper exposure comes in. Most digital cameras aren't capable of giving you a black and white preview. You can, if you want, tape a sheet of dark green acetate or cellophane over your LCD to get an approximate sense of grayscale. You can also employee the old fashioned method of "previsualizing" in black and white with your mind's eye. After all, most of the greatest black and white images of all time where taken using a "color" viewfinder and this method.

Imitating a Grainy Film Look

If you want to simulate the grainy look of say, Tri-X film, you can do so by increasing the noise of your digital image or using a Photoshop filter. Here are a few ways to go:

- *With your camera, increase the sensitivity of the sensor by boosting the ISO.*

- *In Camera Raw, increase the sharpening setting to its maximum. With your image open in Photoshop, take the effect further by using the Unsharp Mask filter (Filter > Sharpen > Unsharp Mask).*

- *In Photoshop, use the Add Noise filter (Filter > Noise > Add Noise).*

Any of these methods, or a combination of them, will produce an effect that approximates the "grainy" look associated with many black and white films. Figure 8-8

For the image shown here, I did the following:

1. *I desaturated the image using Camera Raw's Saturation control.*

2. *In Camera Raw, I increased Sharpness to its maximum.*

3. *In Camera Raw, I set Color Noise reduction to 0.*

4. *I opened the file in Photoshop.*

5. *I applied Photoshop's Add Noise filter with the settings shown here (Filter > Noise > Add Noise). Figure 8-9*

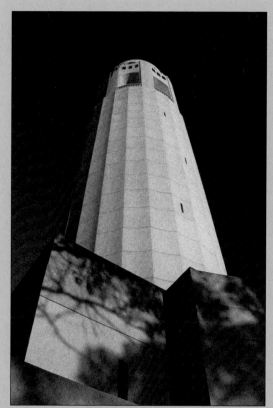

Figure 8-8

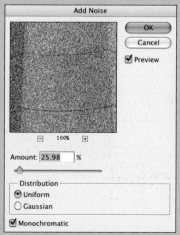

Figure 8-9

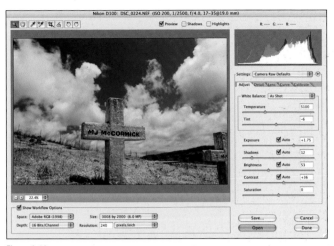

Figure 8-10

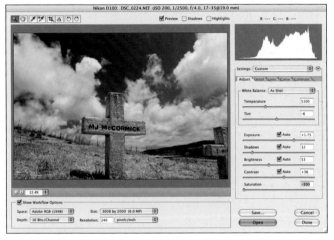

Figure 8-11

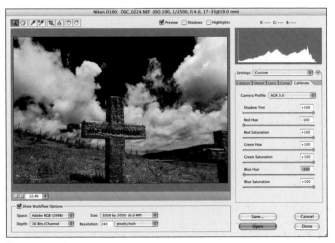

Figure 8-12

Using Calibrate Controls to Fine Tune and Tint

With Camera Raw's Calibrate controls, you can fine-tune your desaturated image to make it more dramatic or add subtle color tints. Yes, I know, the Calibrate controls weren't created specifically for this task. They are technically there to help you compensate for the difference between the actual behavior of your camera and Camera Raw's built-in profile for your camera. There's nothing intuitive about using these controls to fine-tune or tint your image, but if you have patience, you can come up with some effective results.

Let me show you what I did to fine-tune the image shown here. *Figure 8-10*

1. Open the RAW file in Camera Raw.

2. Set the Saturation control to –100. *Figure 8-11*

3. Select the Calibrate tab.

4. Adjust the Calibrate controls as shown here. Basically I set the sliders to +100, except for the red hue, which I set to –100. *Figure 8-12*

Now the image looks as if it were shot with either a polarizing or a dark red filter. I can also save these settings and apply them to other images. To do this, click the triangle next to the Settings menu and choose Save Settings from the pop-up menu.

Here's what I did using the Calibrate controls to slightly desaturate and subtlety color tint the image shown here. *Figure 8-13*

1. Open the RAW file in Camera Raw as shown. Note that I adjusted the Exposure setting slightly but left the Saturation control at 0.

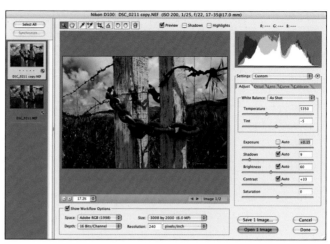

Figure 8-13

2. Select the Calibrate tab and adjust the Calibrate controls. *Figure 8-14*

There really wasn't any logic in my particular choices here. I just used trial and error until I got the results I liked.

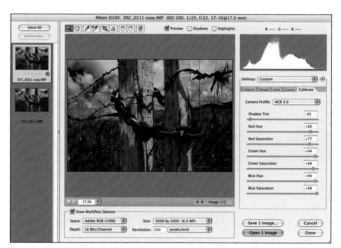

Figure 8-14

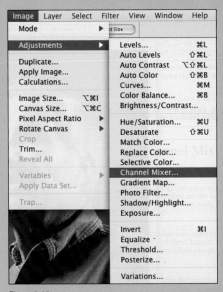

Figure 8-15

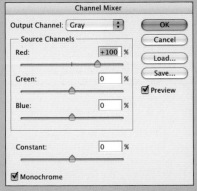

Figure 8-16

Using Photoshop's Channel Mixer to Convert to Grayscale

Here's a quick step-by-step plan for using Channel Mixer to convert your RGB image into grayscale. This method doesn't take full advantage of the potential of a RAW file. But for some images this method is quite adequate and it is relatively fast.

1. *Open your RAW file in Camera Raw.*

2. *In Camera Raw, set Exposure controls to optimize your color image. Don't desaturate. It's best to work in Adobe RGB, 16 Bits/Channel, which gives you a wide color gamut. The more colors you have, the more effective Channel Mixer will be later.*

3. *Open the RGB file in Photoshop.*

4. *Select Image > Adjustments > Channel Mixer from the main menu, or select Channel Mixer as an adjustment layer, in which case a layer mask can give near infinite local control.*
    Figure 8-15

5. *In Channel Mixer, check the Monochrome box. Figure 8-16*

6. *Adjust the Red, Green, and Blue sliders to obtain the desired effect.*

Advanced Localized Black & White Control

For the most part, the methods I've shown you so far apply a global effect over the entire image. For some images this is fine, but for others, it's helpful to paint the effects into specific areas. Granted, this takes time, and requires more advanced Photoshop skills. But the trade off in time is more than made up for in the control you gain.

Step One: Desaturate in Camera Raw

The method I use is a variation of a method shown to me by the photographer Bill Atkinson. Bill desaturates his images in Photoshop in the LAB color mode, while I prefer using Camera Raw. This is what I do as a preliminary step using Bridge and Camera Raw. Afterwards, I'll work entirely in Photoshop to get the exact look I want.

1. In Bridge, select the RAW file and make a duplicate (Edit > Duplicate). *Figure 8-17*

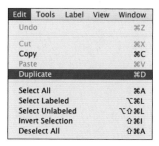

Figure 8-17

2. Then open both the original and the duplicate in Camera Raw. *Figure 8-18*

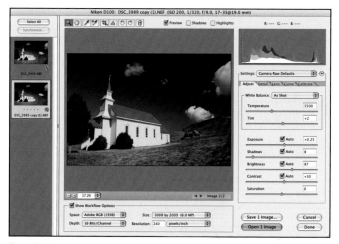

Figure 8-18

3. Select one of the copies and set the Saturation slider to –100 to desaturate it. *Figure 8-19*

4. Select the second image, optimize the Exposure, Shadows, and Brightness controls but leave the Saturation controls alone.

5. Select All and open both images—one in color, the other desaturated—in Photoshop.

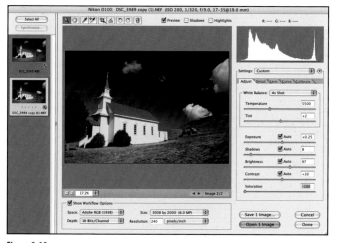

Figure 8-19

Concerned About Hard Drive Space?

Duplicating RAW files as I've done in this example can quickly fill your hard drive. You can delete the duplicate file when you are done. You can also do the following as an alternative method:

1. Open your original RAW file from Bridge in Camera Raw.

2. Perform tonal corrections but keep color saturated.

3. Open in Photoshop.

4. Go back to Bridge and open the same RAW file again in Camera Raw.

5. Set Camera Raw's Saturation slider to –100.

6. Open in Photoshop.

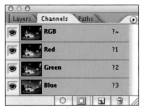

Figure 8-20

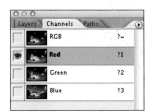

Figure 8-21

Now you have two versions of the RAW file, one saturated and the other not.

Up to this point, the process has been relatively straightforward. I created a color version which, as you'll soon see, I'll break into separate color channels. I created a desaturated version that will serve as an underlying base. I'll then combine luminance values from the appropriate RGB color channels with the base image to get exactly the effect I want.

In the first example, I'll show you how to create a dramatic sky. This closely imitates a look you might have gotten in the old days if you had shot the same scene with black and white film and a red filter over your lens. Then I'll show you how to use the same basic technique to differentiate between subtle shades of green, and how to improve a black and white portrait.

Imitating a Red Filter

First, let's start with a technique that emulates the classic red filter with black and white film. I begin with both the desaturated image and color RGB image open in Photoshop, then:

1. Select the colored image, and open the Channels palette. *Figure 8-20*

2. Examine the red, green, and blue channels separately. Do this by selecting the layer of the channel you wish to examine. *Figure 8-21* You should note how each color channel displays a grayscale version of the image, with slight variations depending on the channel.

As you can see in my example image, the Red channel contained a very dramatic sky. *Figure 8-22* Since this was the effect I was looking for, I selected it. (Click on the image window, then used the keyboard command Cmd/Ctrl-A)

3. Make a copy of the Red channel image. (Cmd/Ctrl-C).

4. Next, paste a copy of the Red channel image into the grayscale version. Select the grayscale image, make sure the Layers palette is showing, and then paste (Edit > Paste or Cmd/Ctrl-V). You should see the red channel appear on its own layer above the Background layer. *Figure 8-23*

5. After pasting, create a Layer mask. First, select the pasted Layer—in this case Layer 1. Click on the Layer mask icon found at the bottom of the layer palette.

6. Your layer palette should now look something like the one shown here. *Figure 8-24*

7. Now, select the mask by clicking on its icon in the Layer palette.

8. Fill the mask with black. Select Edit > Fill from the menu bar and use the settings shown here. This masks the entire contents of the top layer. Next you will paint and "reveal" only the parts you want to show through. *Figure 8-25*

9. Select the Brush tool from the tool bar. Choose an appropriate sized brush. (You can use the bracket keys to increase or decrease the size of the brush.) *Figure 8-26*

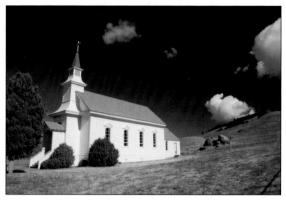

Figure 8-22

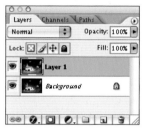

Figure 8-23

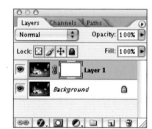

Figure 8-24

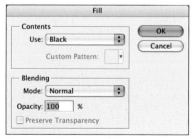

Figure 8-25

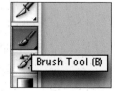

Figure 8-26

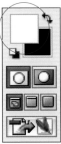

Figure 8-27

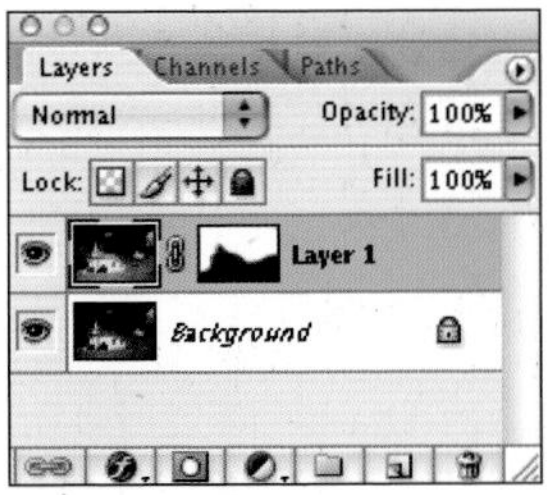

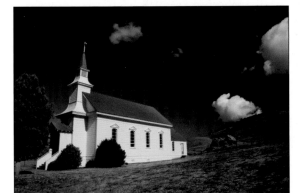

Figure 8-28

10. Make sure the foreground swatch at the bottom of the tool bar is set to white. (The keystroke X will switch the background and foreground colors alternatively.) *Figure 8-27*

11. Make sure the layer mask is selected by clicking on it in the Layer palette. Then paint the areas you wish to reveal. (Lighter colors reveal. Darker colors mask). For more on using layer masks refer to Adobe's excellent online help. *Figure 8-28* You can further control the effect by lowering the Opacity value either in the Brush tool options bar, or in the Layer palette.

When you are finished "painting" you can fine-tune the results by applying Levels or Curves to either or both layers, or simply call it a day. My final results are shown here. *Figure 8-29* Note that I also used the red channel image to bring out the contrast of the tree on the left.

![Church image]

Figure 8-29

Imitating a Blue Filter

In this next image, taken by photographer John McDermott, I followed the same procedure as outlined previously. However, instead of copying and pasting the Red channel from the colored image, I brought over the Blue channel instead. Here is the original color image. *Figure 8-30*

As I had done with the previous image, I desaturated one version of the RAW image in Camera Raw. The sky and rolling hills look fine, but the grape vines in the foreground lack contrast. *Figure 8-31*

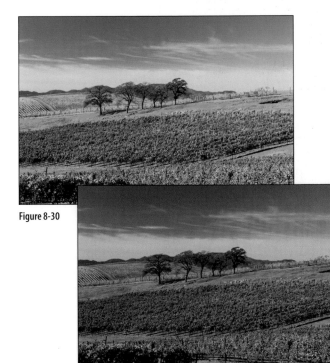

Figure 8-30

Figure 8-31

After I opened both the desaturated and the color versions in Photoshop, I examined the channels of the color version and saw the blue channel captured the grapevines nicely. I copied that channel and pasted it into the color version. *Figure 8-32*

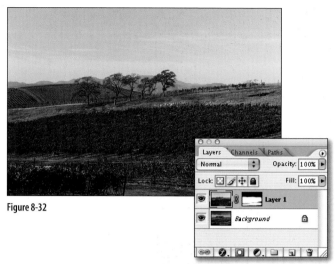

Figure 8-32

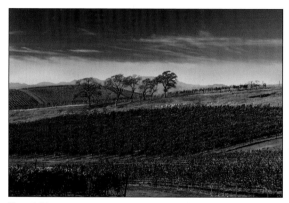

Figure 8-33

Here's the Layer palatte after I applied a Layer Mask and "painted" selectively to combine the best of both layers. *Figure 8-33*

In the final image, after I've tweaked the levels a bit, you can see a dramatic contrast that was lacking in the original desaturated image. *Figure 8-34*

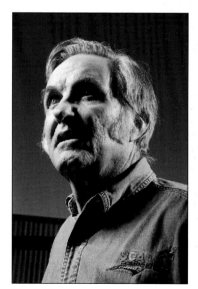

Figure 8-34

Improving a Portrait Shot

I couldn't resist trying this technique on John Carnett's portrait of Burt Rutan. I used the Red channel to bring out the logo on his shirt and darken the sky. Here, you can see the desaturated imaged from Camera Raw. *Figure 8-35*

Figure 8-35

In the Red channel, you can clearly see the logo and wording on the shirt. *Figure 8-36*

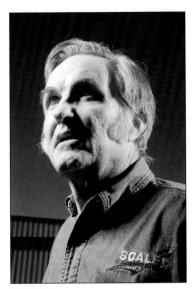

Figure 8-36

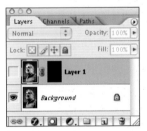

Figure 8-37

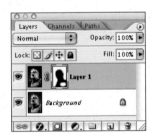

Figure 8-38

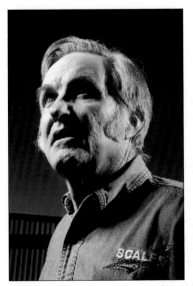

Figure 8-39

After copying and pasting the Red channel onto the base image, I applied a Layer Mask and filled the Layer Mask with black. *Figure 8-37*

Finally, I "painted" selectively to combine the best of both layers. You can see the altered Layer Mask here. *Figure 8-38*

Note the logo on Burt's shirt—originally in Red—is now readable. I also darkened the sky by revealing the Red channel information for that area. *Figure 8-39*

> In Chapter 5, Advanced Tonal Control, I told you how to create images with extended latitude using Photoshop's Merge to HDR command. Well, there is no reason you can't use this method to create dynamite grayscale images as well. After you create your HDR file, select Channel Mixer and its Monochrome mode. You'll be able to mix reds, greens, and blues, as described earlier.

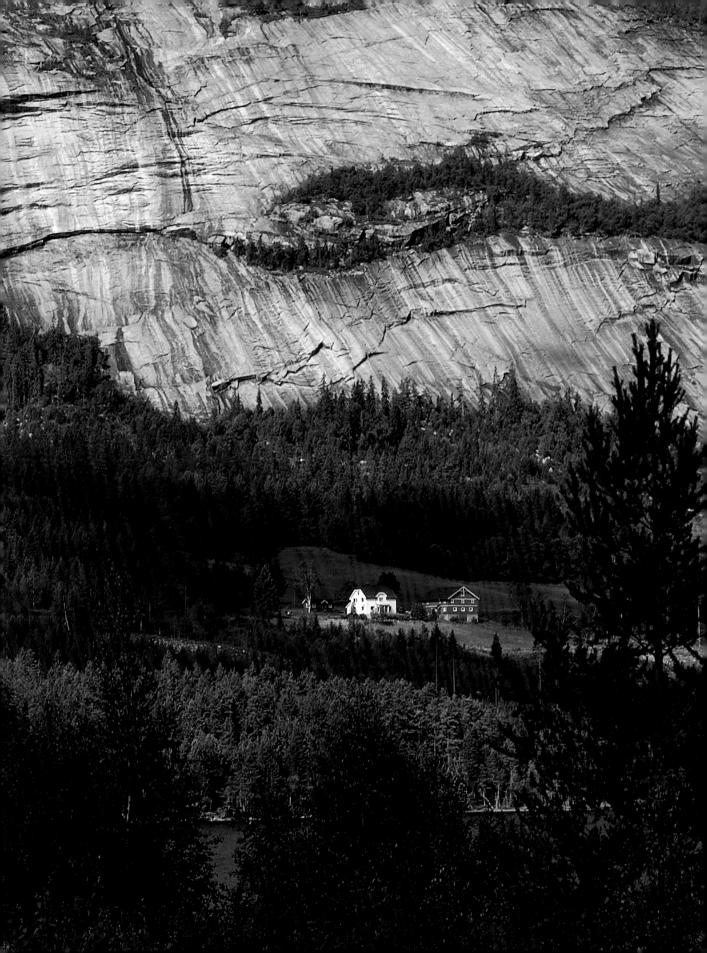

CHAPTER NINE

Archiving & Working with DNG

DNG stands for digital negative, and it is Adobe's answer to the confusing world of multiple RAW data file types. By converting and saving your proprietary RAW data file into the DNG format, you can archive your precious photographs and accompanying metadata in an open format that is more likely to be compatible with future software applications. You also have the option of packing your original RAW file into a DNG file, thereby increasing the odds that your image will be preserved intact for future viewing. This chapter will show you how to save and archive DNG files using either Camera Raw or the free, standalone, Adobe DNG Converter.

Chapter Contents

Archive Strategy: Hedging Your Bets

Saving DNG Files

Converting to DNG with Camera RAW

Using Adobe DNG Converter

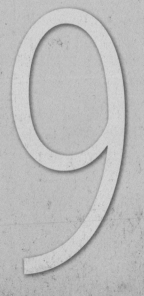

Archive Strategy: Hedging Your Bets

Will the RAW data files produced by your digital camera today be decipherable 5–10 years from now? No one knows for sure. Proprietary RAW files often contain encrypted data, potentially readable only by proprietary software. Camera companies argue they need encrypted and copyrighted data to maintain a competitive advantage, but what happens when no one dares (or bothers) to support these numerous formats? It's the photographer with thousands of unreadable files who potentially suffers.

What about the long-term reliability of Adobe's DNG format? Are you taking a chance converting and saving your proprietary RAW files in that format? Again, the honest answer is yes. There is no guarantee DNG will be supported in the future. *Figure 9-1*

There isn't anything particularly complicated or proprietary about the DNG format. Thomas Knoll, its creator, based DNG on the venerable and widely supported TIFF file format. Since it is an open format—publicly documented—anyone with coding skills can use or write to it with ease, without paying royalties.

When faced with an unknown future, I can see no reason why you shouldn't hedge your bet and save both the original RAW file and a DNG file separately. If you want to be more efficient, you can embed an exact copy of your original RAW file into the DNG file and trash the original, but then you are assuming there will always be software capable of extracting the original file from the DNG. Assuming that DNG is the best hope of ensuring future accessibility to our images, let's move on to creating and saving DNG files. *Figure 9-2*

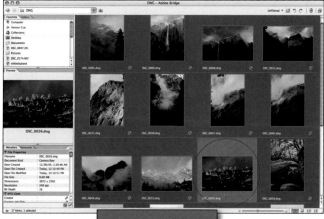

Figure 9-1

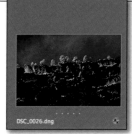

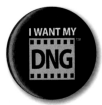

Figure 9-2

You can either use Camera Raw or the free, downloadable standalone Adobe DNG Converter application to convert and save your RAW files in the DNG format. Either approach allows you to convert single images one at a time or save multiple images in the DNG format. In this section, I'll discuss some of the variables you'll need to consider.

Saving DNG Files

From a time-saving standpoint, when converting entire folders full of RAW images, I've found the standalone Adobe DNG Converter more efficient than using Camera Raw. *Figure 9-3*

Regardless of which method you use— Camera Raw or the DNG Converter—you can choose whether to embed the original RAW file into the DNG file. This will more than double your file size, but it's a handy way of keeping all the original data and the DNG file in one place. (At this time, you'll need the Adobe DNG Converter to extract the original RAW files. More on that later.)

Figure 9-3

When you work on a DNG file in Camera Raw, process settings and other metadata is written directly to the DNG file, where it remains intact until updated. Here's a screen shot of a DNG file opened in a text editor. Figure 9-4 The Camera Raw settings are clearly part of the header information. No separate sidecar files are required, and this is a definite advantage—there is no chance of separating or losing the sidecar data, as is the case with using propriety RAW files.

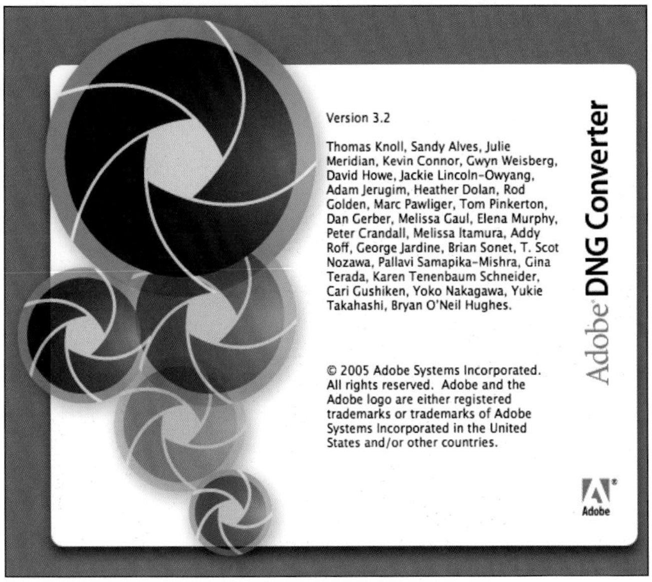

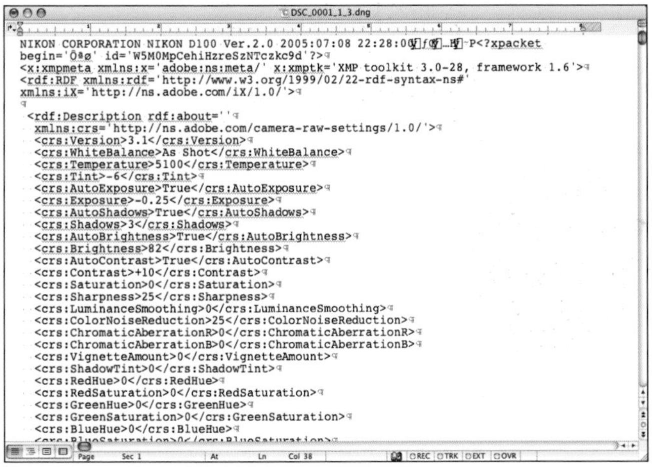

Figure 9-4

When to Convert to DNG?

At what point in the workflow should you convert your RAW files to DNG? Before you do anything to the original RAW file, or later, after you've used Camera Raw to tweak white balance, exposure, etc.? The answers to these questions depend on what you are doing. Let's look at some different approaches.

CONVERTING ONE FILE AT A TIME

If you are working with one portfolio quality image at a time, or just a few, it really doesn't matter when you convert. *Figure 9-5* It's a matter of personal preference. You can convert your original RAW file into a DNG without applying any Camera Raw settings, then work on the DNG file and apply custom Camera Raw settings later. You can also open the original RAW file in Camera Raw, apply custom settings, and then save the file as a DNG. Your Camera Raw settings will be written into the DNG file and—as long as you select Done in Camera Raw when you are finished—a sidecar file will be created for the original RAW file.

CONVERTING LARGE NUMBERS OF IMAGES AT ONCE

If you are working with an entire photo session of native RAW files, here are a couple of workflow scenarios. The good thing about Scenario 1 is much of the heavy lifting is done outside of the Photoshop/Bridge/Camera Raw environment, thereby freeing the applications for other purposes. The good thing about Scenario 2 is that you end up with a native RAW file whose Camera Raw settings match those of the converted DNG file. *Figure 9-6*

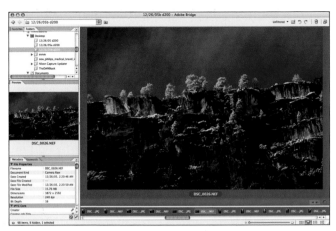

Figure 9-5

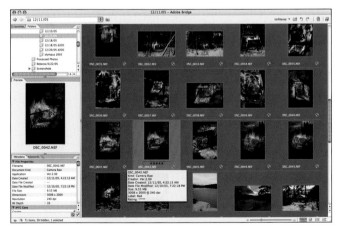

Figure 9-6

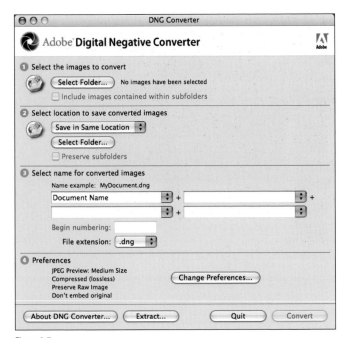

Figure 9-7

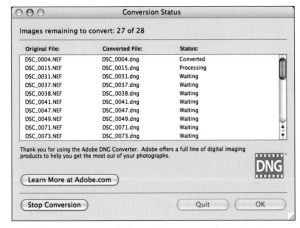

Figure 9-8

Scenario 1.

1. Download RAW files from your digital camera.

2. Open the Adobe DNG Converter and batch process all the images into DNG. *Figure 9-7* (I'll show you specifically how to use the DNG Converter later in the chapter.) The conversion process may take some time, depending on your DNG Converter settings. If you choose to embed the original RAW file or use full-sized previews, it can take longer. The good news is the processing is done outside the Bridge, Adobe Camera Raw, and Photoshop environments, thereby freeing up these applications/plug-ins. *Figure 9-8*

3. Open the DNG files in Camera Raw and apply the necessary settings (white balance, exposure, etc.).

4. Select Done. Photoshop will be inoperable until the updating process is complete, but you'll still be able to use Bridge.

Scenario 2

1. Download RAW files from your digital camera.

2. Apply custom Camera Raw settings to the native RAW files via Bridge, or open the images in Camera Raw and globally apply the settings. *Figure 9-9*

After you are finished applying custom settings to your native RAW file, you have two choices. In either case, you'll end up with custom settings attached to your native RAW file:

- In Camera Raw, select Save, and convert your files into DNG. (I'll show you shortly in detail how to do this.) Be sure to select Done when exiting Camera Raw. Otherwise, your custom settings won't be saved along with the native RAW file. *Figure 9-10*

- Or, select Done and exit Camera Raw. Use the Adobe DNG Converter to batch process the tweaked RAW files into the DNG format.

If you chose to have Camera Raw do the converting when Camera Raw is hosted by Photoshop, and you select done *Figure 9-11* while Camera Raw is converting the files, this dialog box appears in the Photoshop environment and remains until the conversions are done. Even though Photoshop is inoperable while the conversion is taking place, you'll still be able to work in Bridge.

The advantage of using Adobe DNG Converter, of course, is it is a standalone product and works independently outside the Photoshop/Bridge/Camera Raw environment. *Figure 9-12*

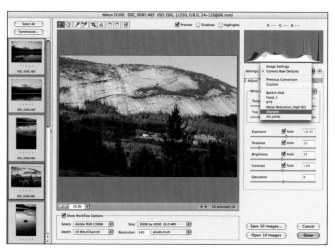

Figure 9-9

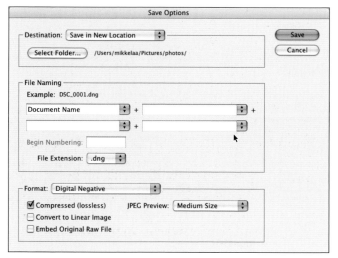

Figure 9-10

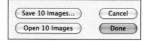

Figure 9-11

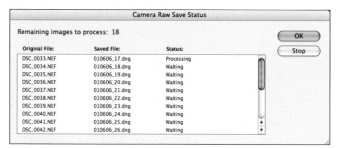

Figure 9-12

Regardless of whether you are working on one image or a series of several images, here is the basic step-by-step process for using Camera Raw to convert your RAW files into the DNG format. I'll get more specific about converting multiple files later in this section. If you use Camera Raw to convert you'll also be able to save your custom settings to the native RAW file.

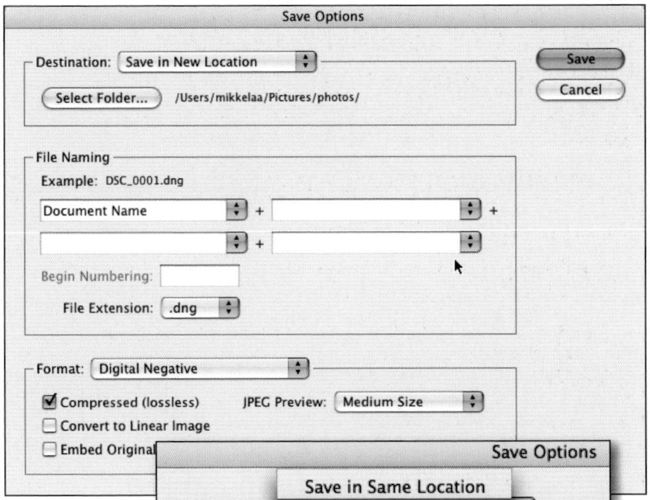

Converting to DNG with Camera Raw

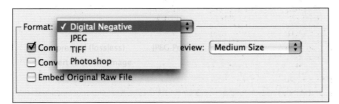

Figure 9-13

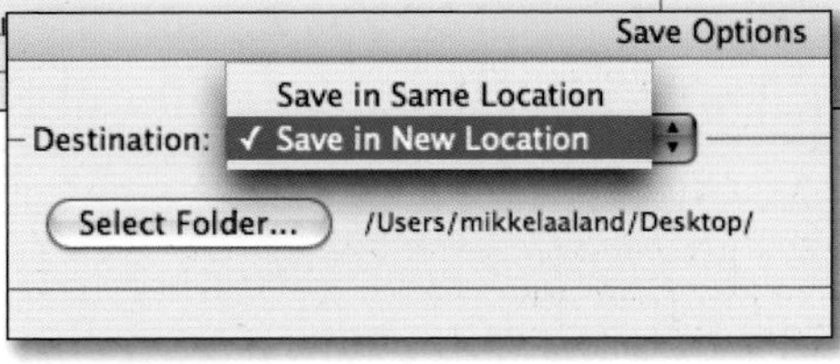

Figure 9-14

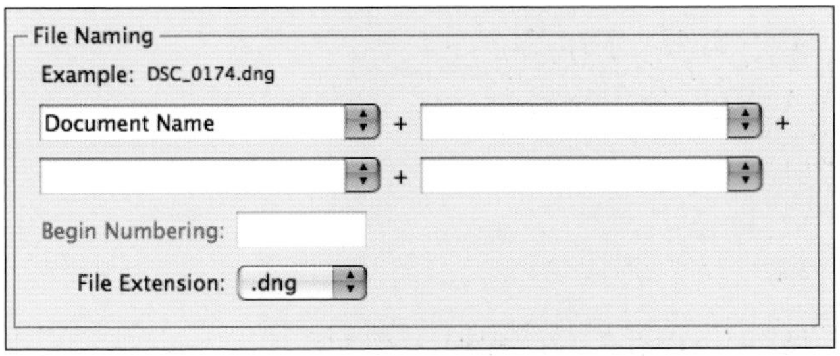

Figure 9-15

Figure 9-16

To convert:

1. Open your native RAW file(s) in Camera Raw. It doesn't matter if Camera Raw is hosted by Photoshop or Bridge.

2. Use Camera Raw to adjust or tweak your image(s). (If your images need no adjustment, you can obviously skip this step.)

3. Chose Save from the bottom of the Camera Raw dialog box. The Save Options dialog box appears. *Figure 9-13* (In the future, you can skip this dialog box by holding the Opt/Alt key when you select Save.)

Choose a Destination from the pop-up menu. You can select Save in New Location or Save in Same Location. If you choose Save in New Location you can select a separate destination for your converted images. *Figure 9-14*

Choose a File Naming protocol. The choices here are similar to those you get with the Batch Rename command. *Figure 9-15*

From the Save Options dialog box, you can also save your RAW file into other file formats such as JPEG, TIFF, or PSD, by selecting from the Format pop-up menu. (You can select and save only one file format at a time. If you want to save multiple file formats you'll need to refer to Chapter 10.) *Figure 9-16*

When you choose a Format, an appropriate extension is selected. The file extension for DNG is *.dng*, obviously. (Uppercase is also an option.) There are a few other options here. *Figure 9-17*

- Select Compressed (lossless) and your DNG file will be about a 1/3 smaller than the original RAW file with no trade off in quality or flexibility.

- Select Convert to Linear Image and your file will be more than 3 times the size of the original RAW file. Since it is separated into separate red, green, and blue channels, you've essentially lost all the advantages of saving RAW data. Adobe claims that in some instances, saving a demosaiced file can improve compatibility, particularly if the camera sensor contains an unusual mosaic pattern that all converters do not support.

- Select Embed Original Raw File if you want an exact copy of the original RAW file embedded within the DNG file. This will create a file about 2/3 larger than the original RAW file. At this time, you'll need the Adobe DNG converter to retrieve the embedded file from the DNG file.

When you select Save, you return to the Camera Raw workspace and you'll get this Save Status message at the bottom of the window: it may take some time, depending on the number of files you are converting and the options you choose. *Figure 9-18*

If you click on the Save Status link, you'll get a full dialog like the one shown earlier.

When Camera Raw is hosted by Photoshop, and you select Done or Cancel while the process is occurring and try and work in Photoshop, you'll get the dialog box again.

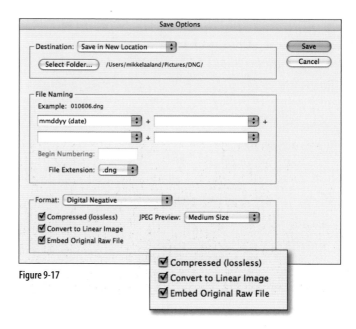

Figure 9-17

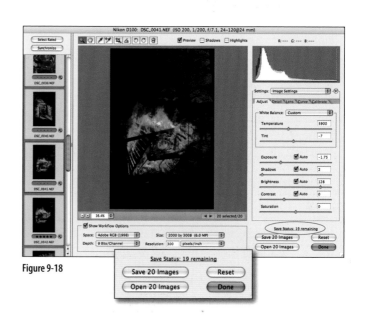

Figure 9-18

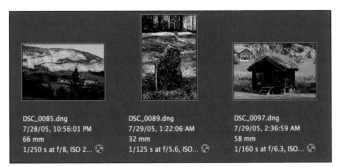

Figure 9-19

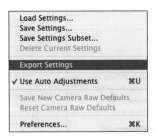

Figure 9-20

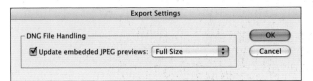

Figure 9-21

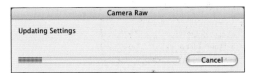

Figure 9-22

You won't be able to use any Photoshop controls while the dialog box is present, but Bridge will still be fully operable. You can cancel the process at any time.

Updating DNG Files

After you create a DNG file, you can work on the file in Camera Raw just as you would a native RAW file. When you are finished adjusting exposure, applying sharpening, etc., select Done in Camera Raw. If you haven't changed your Camera Raw preference to update previews, the update process should be very quick. Camera Raw simply changes the metadata to reflect your changes. If you change your preference to update the preview image, it'll take longer, because Camera Raw must rewrite the entire DNG file. *Figure 9-19*

You'll see a difference in the embedded preview only if you use other applications such as iView Media Pro or Photo Mechanic. Camera Raw creates its own previews on the fly. If you have multiple images open in Camera Raw, you can selectively apply the update preview image command to one or more images. To do this:

1. Select the image(s) you wish to update.

2. Select Export Settings from the drop-down menu. *Figure 9-20*

3. Select Update embedded JPEG previews. Choose a preview size. *Figure 9-21*

4. Wait as Camera Raw updates the settings. The time it takes to update will depend on how many images you selected and the size of the preview. *Figure 9-22*

DNG File Handling Preferences in Camera Raw

You can control how Camera Raw handles DNG files in the Preferences dialog box under DNG File Handling. *Figure 9-23*

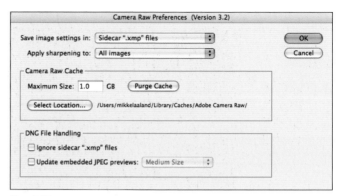

Figure 9-23

Select Ignore sidecar ".xmp" files if you are working with legacy DNG files created with older versions of Photoshop/Camera Raw. These earlier versions created DNG files with sidecar files. This can potentially cause problems if sidecars with the same file name are available for both the DNG and original RAW file. Selecting Ignore sidecar ".xmp" files is a good idea because it prevents Camera Raw from using the wrong sidecar.

If you choose to Update embedded JPEG previews, you are offered a choice of Medium Size (default) or Full Size. *Figure 9-24* These previews are not used when you open a DNG file in Camera Raw, but are used by cataloging programs such as iView Media Pro. *Figure 9-25*
Essentially, when you save a full resolution file, you create a very useful "soft proof" that reflects your Camera Raw adjustments. This proof is always part of the DNG file and can also be printed with very good results. (At this time, the full resolution preview isn't read by all third-party applications. This will change as DNG becomes more widely supported. Photoshop is not even capable of independently reading any of the DNG JPEG previews. You have to go through Camera Raw to view a DNG file.)

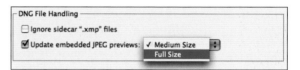

Figure 9-24

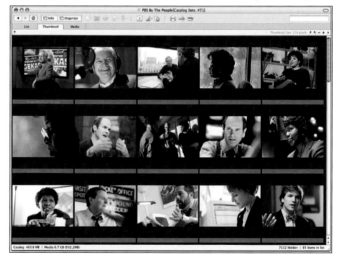

Figure 9-25

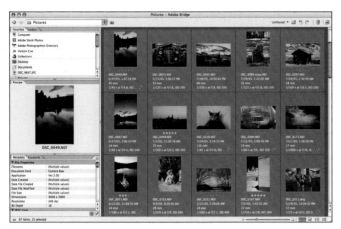

Figure 9-26

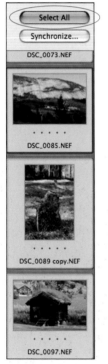

Figure 9-27

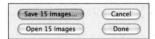

Figure 9-28

Converting Multiple Files with Camera Raw

If you want to convert a folder of images to the DNG format using Camera Raw, this what you should do:

1. Open Bridge.

2. Navigate to the folder containing the images you wish to convert to DNG. (You can also open files from within Photoshop, but it's so much easier to do it from within Bridge.) *Figure 9-26*

3. Select All the image files (Edit > Select All or Cmd/Ctrl-A).

4. Open the selection with Camera Raw (File > Open in Camera Raw).

5. In Camera Raw, click Select All from the top left of the work area. *Figure 9-27*

6. Apply any necessary Camera Raw settings that you wish to apply to all the RAW files. (White Balance, Exposure, Sharpening, etc.)

7. Select Save. (The number of images should be noted on the Tab.) *Figure 9-28*

8. Set the Save Options preferences as described in the earlier section. (In the future, you can bypass this dialog box by holding the Opt/Alt key when you select Save.)

9. Select Save from the Save Options dialog box.

10. A Save Status line appears at the bottom of the Camers Raw window. You can select Done at any time.

Using Adobe DNG Converter

You can use the Adobe DNG Converter to convert single RAW files or entire folders full of RAW files. I find it most efficient to use the DNG Converter when I want to convert an entire shoot worth of images. At this time, you will need the DNG Converter to extract original RAW files from a DNG, regardless of whether you used Camera Raw or the DNG Converter to embed them in the DNG file.

It's likely that you received a copy of the converter when you purchased the Photoshop CS2 update, or if you downloaded the latest version of Camera Raw. However, to insure you have the latest version, check *www.adobe.com*. The converter is free. *Figure 9-29*

Adobe DNG Converter

Figure 9-29

After you download the DNG Converter and open the standalone application, depending on the version you are using, you'll get a window that looks like this: *Figure 9-30*

At this point you should:

1. Select the images you want to convert. You can select a single RAW file, or an entire folder and subfolders.

2. Select a location for the converted images. If you are archiving your images, you may want to choose Save in New Folder or Select Folder and save the DNG files in an offsite location.

3. Select names for the converted images. You can leave the fields blank if you wish, and the original file names or numbers will be used and appended with the *.dng* extension.

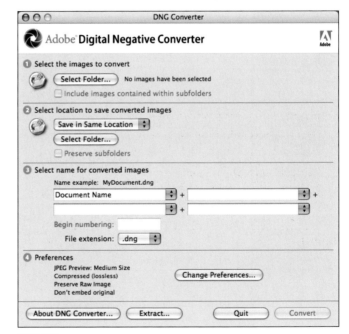

Figure 9-30

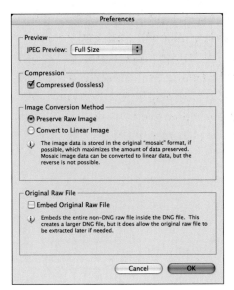

Figure 9-31

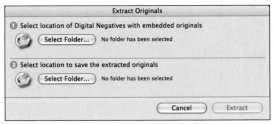

Figure 9-32

4. Select Change Preferences and this dialog box appears. *Figure 9-31* These are similar options to the ones in the Camera Raw Save Options dialog box I discussed earlier.

5. Select OK to take you back to the main window.

6. Select Convert to start the conversion process. The amount of time it will take depends on the number of images and the various Preferences you've selected. Processing is done independently of Photoshop, Bridge, or Camera Raw.

Using the DNG Converter to Extract Original RAW Data

If you have chosen to embed an original RAW file with your DNG file, your only option (at this time) for extracting the file is to use the Adobe DNG Converter.

To extract a RAW file from a DNG file:

1. Open the Adobe DNG Converter.

2. Select Extract from the bottom of the dialog box. This dialog box will appear. *Figure 9-32*

Select the location of the DNG file with the embedded original and select a location to save the extracted originals. The extraction is very quick. While the original RAW data is now available as a separate file, it is not accompanied by a sidecar containing any Camera Raw settings you may have applied to the DNG file. When you open the original RAW file in Camera Raw, it'll open with the default settings.

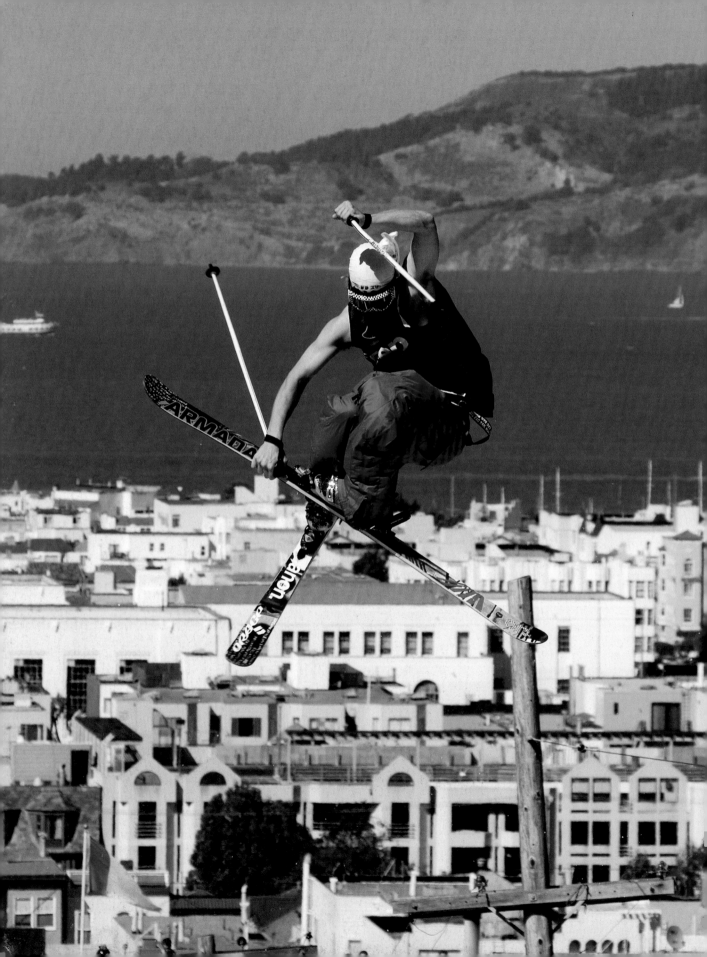

CHAPTER TEN

Converting & Delivering RAW

You'll rarely share your RAW files with friends or deliver them to clients, just as you rarely shared your negatives in traditional photography.

Up to now, for the most part, the discussion centered on getting a certain look or feel out of your RAW files. In this chapter, I'll show you how to use several of Photoshop CS2's automated tools and features to easily convert one—or several hundred—RAW file(s) into a form ready for delivery.

Not surprisingly, there are many ways to use Photoshop CS2 and its three distinct environments—Bridge, Camera Raw, and Photoshop—to help you convert and deliver your RAW images. While there is no single, one-click process that will take you everywhere you want to go, there are several automated commands, which when used on top of each other, should do the trick.

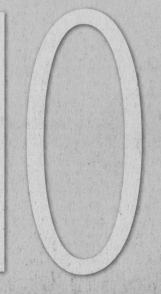

Chapter Contents

Using Bridge + Image Processor to Convert RAW Files

Applying Custom Camera Raw Settings to Multiple Images

Using Camera Raw's Save Command

Automating Contact Sheets, Picture Package & Web Photo Gallery

Using Batch & Actions

Writing Custom Scripts

Using Bridge +
Image Processor to
Convert RAW Files

Probably the easiest way to convert RAW files into a more readily shared file format is to use Bridge and the built-in Image Processor script. Image Processor can produce up to three versions of your RAW file: a JPEG, a TIFF, or a PSD file. Depending on your needs—any of these files produced by Image Processor can be thought of as a final deliverable—ready to be sent by email, posted on an FTP site, burned on to a CD, or incorporated into a printed or electronic contact sheet.

You can launch Image Processor from either Bridge or Photoshop. In Bridge, select Tools > Photoshop > Image Processor; in Photoshop, choose File > Scripts > Image Processor. Either method will bring up the screen you see here, albeit with slight variations in the user interface. *Figure 10-1*

> *You can also use one of the other Photoshop CS2 automated processes and quickly turn the TIFF or PSD files into a printable—or electronically delivered—contact sheet, picture package, or web photo gallery, ready for sharing. I'll get into this subject a bit later in the chapter—and also show you how to do this directly from a RAW file.*

To illustrate how Image Processor works, I'll turn to the work of photographer Maggie Hallahan, who uses Image Processor quite frequently. I'll demonstrate her process using a shoot she recently did for Corbis, her stock photo agency. The event she photographed was a mid-October ski jump in the middle of crowded San Francisco, featuring trucked-in snow and world-class ski jumpers.

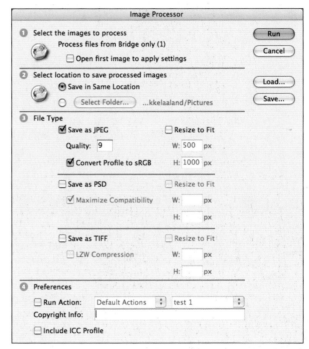

Figure 10-1

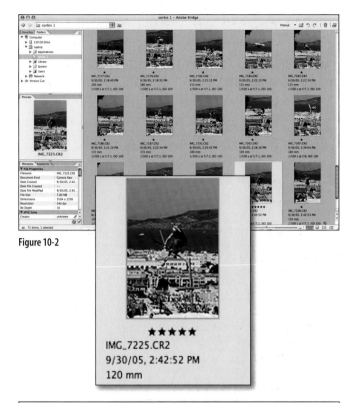

Figure 10-2

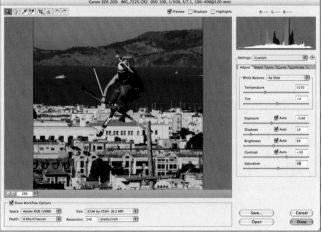

Figure 10-3

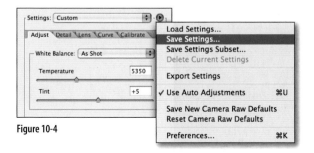

Figure 10-4

Maggie always begins her process by downloading camera files using a FireWire card reader onto to her portable's internal hard drive. Back in her studio, she puts all the images from a shoot into one folder and backs up the images on an external drive. She then uses Bridge to edit and sort the RAW files (See Chapter 2). She also adds copyright information and other metadata, such as a description of the contents of the shoot (using File Info), and a custom XMP metadata template. (Do this by choosing Edit > Select All. Then, choose File > File Info > and apply metadata template to all via pop-up menu. Again, for more on this, see Chapter 2.) Maggie ends up with a Bridge window that looks something like the one shown in here. *Figure 10-2*

Let's follow what Maggie does next step-by-step:

1. Open a representative image in Camera Raw and process it to get a look you like. In Maggie's case, for the ski jump images, there wasn't much to do. She increased saturation slightly, but left most everything else alone. She set the Space to Adobe RGB (1998) and Depth to 8 Bits/Channel, because that's what the client required. *Figure 10-3*

2. Create a custom setting with a specific name. Maggie named hers ski_jump. (From the arrow to the right of Settings, select Save Settings, then type in a descriptor.) *Figure 10-4*

3. Select Done.

4. Back in Bridge, select all the images you wish to deliver. (Edit > Select All, or use Cmd/Ctrl-A). Maggie then applies the custom Camera Raw setting to all the images. (Edit > Apply Camera Raw

Settings > *Setting of Choice.*) For more on this, and how to create a custom setting, see the next section. Once the processing is complete, Maggie is ready for the easy part, using Image Processor.

5. Open Image Processor (Tools > Photoshop > Image Processor).
Figure 10-5

6. Set the settings as shown here.
Figure 10-6

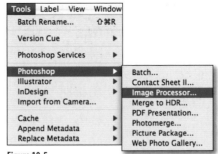

Figure 10-5

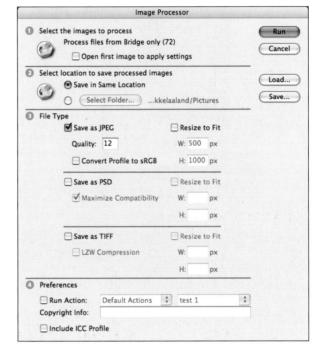

Figure 10-6

Here are more details on the various Image Processor options:

Select the Images to Process
If you are working from within Bridge, "Process files from Bridge only" is your only choice. (From Photoshop, you can navigate to a particular folder but, unfortunately, you can't use selected images from Bridge.) *Figure 10-7*

Open first image to apply settings
If you select this option, you can adjust the setting in the first image to your satisfaction and then apply the same settings to the remaining images. Maggie didn't do this because she had already applied a Camera Raw setting to all her RAW files before selecting Image Processor, which, in my opinion, is a better way to go. *Figure 10-8*

Select the Save Location for Processed images
You can process the same file multiple times to the same destination. Each file is saved with its own file name and— no fear—not overwritten. *Figure 10-9*

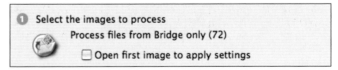

Figure 10-7

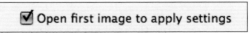

Figure 10-8

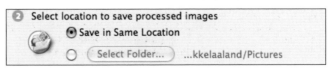

Figure 10-9

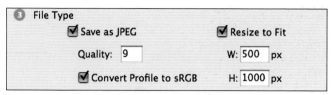

Figure 10-10

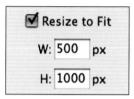

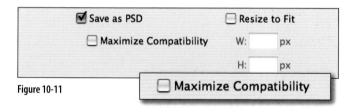

Figure 10-11

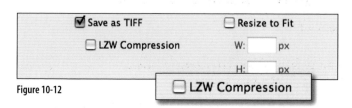

Figure 10-12

In the File Type area, you have the following choices.

Save As JPEG

Saves images in JPEG format within a folder called JPEG. *Figure 10-10*

Quality

Sets the JPEG image quality between 0 and 12. (Maggie always chooses 12 for maximum quality.)

Resize to Fit

Resizes the image to fit within the dimensions you enter in the Width and Height fields. The image retains its original proportions. (This is great if you want to quickly convert a series of images to a very specific size. You can also set your size in Camera Raw, which, in some cases, may produce better results.)

Convert Profile To sRGB

Converts the color profile to sRGB. (Again, you can choose a color space in Camera Raw.) Make sure that Include ICC Profile is selected if you want to save the profile with the image.

Save As PSD

Saves images in Photoshop format within a folder called PSD in the destination folder. *Figure 10-11*

Maximize Compatibility

Saves a composite version of a layered image within the target file for compatibility with applications that can't read layered images. It also increases file size significantly.

Save As TIFF

Saves images in TIFF format within a folder called TIFF in the destination folder. *Figure 10-12*

LZW Compression

Saves the TIFF file using the LZW compression scheme, which is lossless.

The Preferences section of the screen contains the following items: *Figure 10-13*

Run Action

Checking this box runs a Photoshop action loaded in the Actions palette. You can, for example, run an action that applies specific sharpening to an image based on output. However, keep in mind that the sharpening occurs before any resizing, making it useful only if you don't apply any resizing using Image Processor. (If you resize with Camera Raw, it won't matter.) I'll get more into creating and using actions later in the chapter.

Copyright Info

Includes any text you enter in the IPTC copyright metadata for the file. Remember, text you include here overwrites the copyright metadata in the original file, which is why Maggie left it blank.

Include ICC Profile

Checking this box embeds the color profile with the saved files.

7. When you've made all your selections, click Run. Image Processor converts and processes multiple files, using the original RAW data for each conversion. The amount of time it takes depends on several variables, including processor speed, number of files, and how many file formats are selected. The final images are neatly organized in appropriate folders. *Figure 10-14*

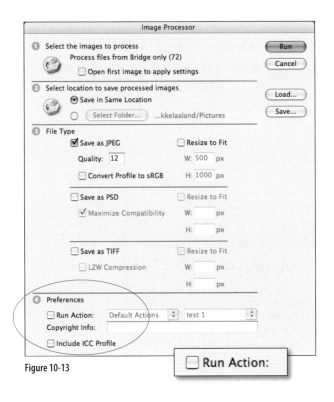

Figure 10-13

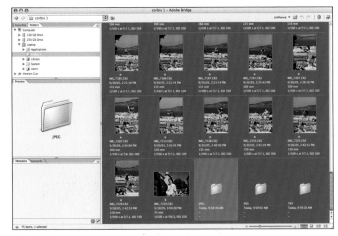

Figure 10-14

Applying Custom Camera Raw Settings to Multiple Images

If you have multiple RAW images that require similar adjustments, you can apply a custom setting to them all at once. Knowing how to do this quickly and efficiently is critical, especially if you don't want to spend your day in front of a computer screen. In this section, I'll go over using Camera Raw to accomplish this task.

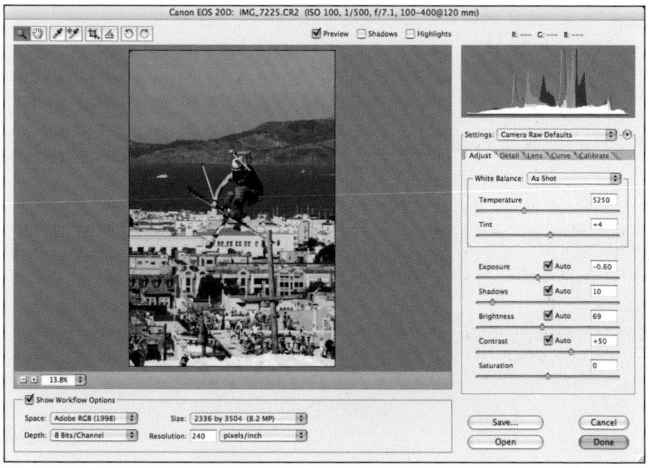

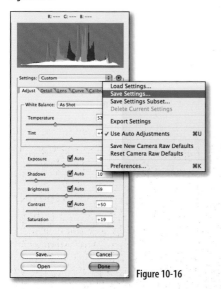

Figure 10-15

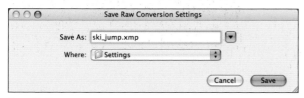

Figure 10-16

Figure 10-17

Here is a way to apply Camera Raw settings to multiple images in Bridge at once.

1. Select one key image that represents the majority of the images you are working with. In this example, Maggie Hallahan selected the shot of Olympic skier Jonny Moseley flying above San Francisco with crossed skis.)

2. Open the image in Camera Raw. *Figure 10-15*

3. Optimize the image using Camera Raw color and exposure and sharpening settings. (For more on this see Chapters 5, 6, 7, and 8.)

4. Select Save Savings from the Settings pop-up menu. *Figure 10-16*

5. Name your setting in the Save Raw Conversion Settings dialog and select a destination. Best to keep it in the default Settings folder—otherwise, the setting may not show up in Camera Raw's Settings pop-up menu, and then you'll have to manually navigate to it via the Camera Raw Load Settings option. (It might not show up as an option in Bridge either.) *Figure 10-17*

6. Select Done.

7. In Bridge, select the images to which you wish to apply the custom settings. Right-click (or Ctrl-click on a Mac) the selection. From the contextual menu, select your setting of choice. (In this

case, Maggie chooses ski_jump.) You can also select Previous Conversion, Camera Raw Defaults, or Clear Camera Raw Settings, if any of these are more appropriate. *Figure 10-18*. (You can also apply Camera Raw settings from the menu bar by choosing Edit > Apply Camera Raw Settings.)

8. You'll notice that the thumbs change, reflecting the new settings. A small icon with two triangles will appear at the bottom right of the thumb to indicate Camera Raw settings have been applied.

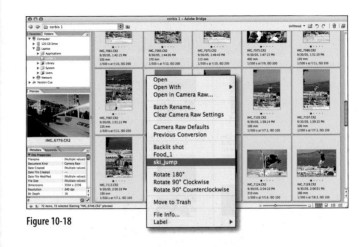

Figure 10-18

Save Settings Subset

You can create custom Camera Raw settings that contain specific Camera Raw adjustments, but not others. For example, you can selectively apply settings from Adjust tab controls, but not settings from the other tabs. To do this:

1. *Select Save Settings Subset... from the Settings pop-up menu. Figure 10-19*

2. *The following choices appear. You can deselect the ones you don't want applied. Figure 10-20*

3. *You can also choose from several pop-up presets. Figure 10-21*

When you select Save, you'll get the Save Raw Conversion Settings dialog box, where you can name the setting and select a destination. Again, it's best to keep settings in the default Settings folder. If you don't, the setting may not show up where you want them to.

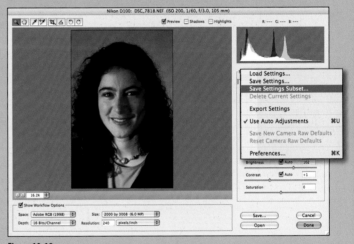

Figure 10-19

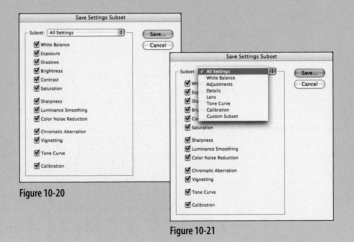

Figure 10-20

Figure 10-21

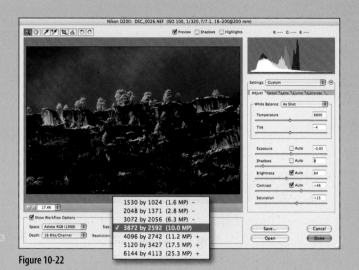

Figure 10-22

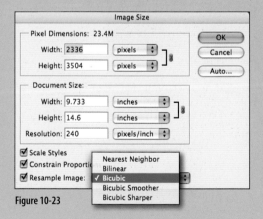

Figure 10-23

Where Should You Resize?

Many digital cameras produce images with pixels to spare, and there are many times when resizing down is necessary. On the other hand, there are times when you want more pixels and you want to sample up. Camera Raw offers preset Size options, both to sample up and to sample down. Then again, you can also resize in Photoshop via the Image Size dialog box. (Image > Image Size) Where is the best place to resize? This is what I suggest:

- *Resize in Camera Raw when speed and workflow are an issue. The quality is good, but you don't have as many size options as you would in Photoshop, and the options you have depend on the pixel dimensions of the original shot. Figure 10-22*

- *Resize in Photoshop when you need specific sizes not offered by Camera Raw, or if you want more control over the way resizing occurs. Figure 10-23 Not only does Photoshop provide a choice of interpolation methods (Bicubic, Bicubic Smoother, etc.) but also you can easily create an action or script to sample up or down in increments and add a slight sharpening at each step—the method acknowledged by many professionals as the best. (New Bicubic choices make incremental sharpening less desirable—Bicubic Sharper when sampling down, and Bicubic Smoother when sampling up—but I have no hard evidence to support this.) Third-party tools, like Genuine Fractals, are also available.*

Using Camera Raw's Save Command

You can convert multiple or single images to another file format directly from within Camera Raw. Using Camera Raw over Image Processor to convert is a matter of personal preference. In some cases you gain added control with Camera Raw—for example, renaming options—however, unlike Image Processor, Camera Raw only converts to one file format at a time.

Let's see how:

1. Open one or several images in Camera Raw. Using Cmd/Ctrl-R to open the files will insure Camera Raw is hosted by Bridge, which is what you want. That way, Camera Raw can run the conversion in the background while you maintain use of both Photoshop and Bridge. When you try to open ten or more images you get this polite reminder. Select OK. *Figure 10-24*

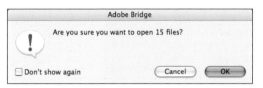

Figure 10-24

2. In Camera Raw, click on Select All at the top left. Now all the thumbnails on the left are selected and the Save button will reflect the total number of images. *Figure 10-25*

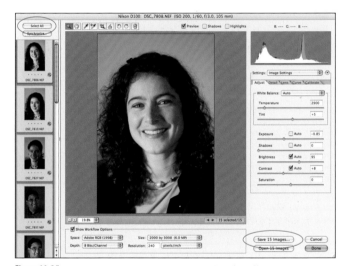

Figure 10-25

3. Select "Save *x* Images...". (In this example, it reads "Save 15 Images.") The Save File dialog box appears. *Figure 10-26* Here you can choose a destination for your converted images, custom file names, and format: TIFF, PSD, JPEG, or DNG. (I covered DNG in the previous chapter.) Each format offers different save options.

    a) JPEG, shown here, offers different quality settings.

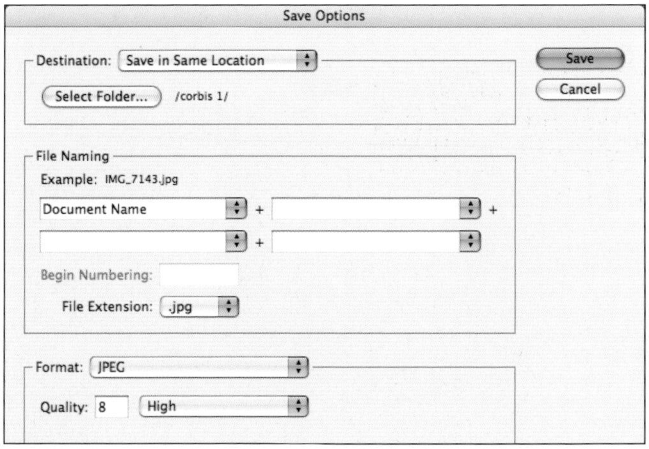

Figure 10-26

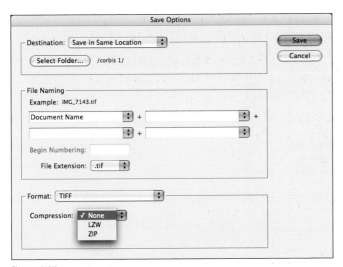

Figure 10-27

b) TIFF offers three types of Compression settings: None, LZW (which is lossless), and ZIP, which is also lossless. *Figure 10-27*

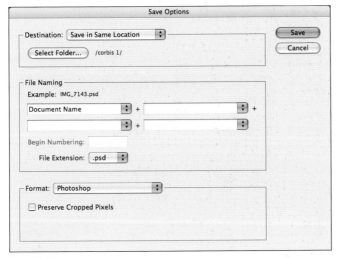

Figure 10-28

c) The Photoshop format is the only format that offers to "Preserve Cropped Pixels." If you don't select it, cropped pixels are discarded in the conversion. This is an option only if you have used Camera Raw's crop tool. *Figure 10-28*

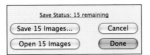

Figure 10-29

4. After selecting a file format (you can only select one at a time), select Save. You'll get a Save Status notice such as the one shown here. You are now free to select Done and return to Bridge, or you can select Open... and have your images opened in Photoshop. *Figure 10-29*

Archiving the Camera RAW Database

Camera Raw settings are saved as individual XMP sidecar files *Figure 10-30* or in a central Adobe Camera Raw Database. *Figure 10-31*

You choose which location by setting Camera Raw Preferences, accessed either through Bridge or in Camera Raw. *Figure 10-32*

Knowing where this data is saved is especially important when you go to archive your RAW files on an external hard drive or removable media. If your settings are saved as XMP sidecar files, it's very straightforward: simply transfer and backup the XMP files along with the original RAW files. They'll share the same file name, albeit with a different extension. If the settings are saved in a Camera Raw database, it's more problematic. For single or multiple images that are open in Camera Raw, selecting Export Settings from the Settings pop-up menu will generate XMP sidecar files if there aren't any. Short of that, you'll need to locate the Camera Raw database on your hard drive and archive it as well. Of course, all this is an argument for using the DNG file format, which saves the Camera Raw settings together with the image data in one file. (I covered DNG in Chapter 9.) *Figure 10-33*

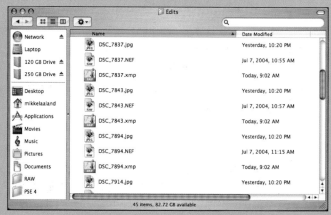

Figure 10-30

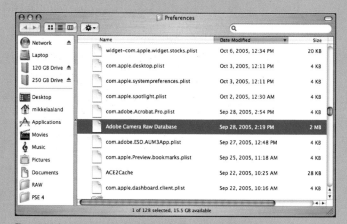

Figure 10-31

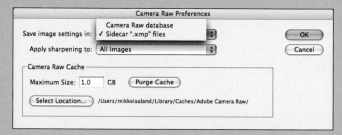

Figure 10-32

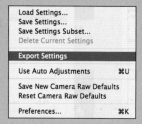

Figure 10-33

One of the most convenient ways to share files is via a printed or emailed contact sheet. In this section, I'll show you how to use automated techniques to make a printable contact sheet, a PDF file containing a emailable version of your contact sheet(s), and a Picture Package. I'll end this section by showing you how to create a Web Photo Gallery that's ready for posting on the Web.

Automating Contact Sheets, Picture Package & Web Photo Gallery

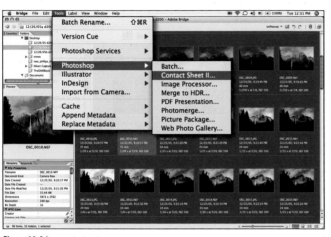

Figure 10-34

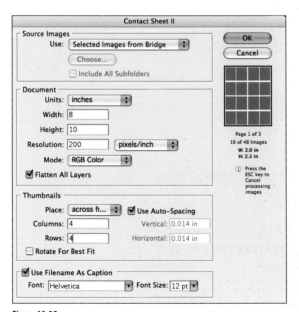

Figure 10-35

You can use these automation commands directly on a RAW file, or, if you've converted your RAW files into TIFFs or PSDs, you can apply them directly to these files. (If you apply the automation commands to JPEG conversions quality will suffer.) All the automation commands are available via Photoshop, but I suggest using them directly from Bridge, because you'll have direct access to images displayed in Bridge. (Using Bridge as a source is not possible when you start from Photoshop.) *Figure 10-34*

Here's what to do:

Creating a Printable Contact Sheet

We'll start by creating a simple printable contact sheet:

1. Select your RAW, PSD, or TIFF files in Bridge.

2. Select Tools > Photoshop > Contact Sheet II from the Bridge menu bar.

3. Select your Source Images (Selected Images from Bridge) from the Contact Sheet II dialog box. *Figure 10-35* Determine the size of your document and the resolution. If you want, select Use Filename as Caption, so the person viewing your work can reference their image choices. Click OK.

Converting the Contact Sheet to PDF

Once you've created it, you can print your contact sheet. But if you want to share your contact sheet(s) electronically via email, I suggest converting the sheet(s) into a PDF file. A PDF file can contain multiple sheets at a reasonable file size. It's best to do this from within Photoshop, after you have created your contact sheet.

To convert:

1. From within Photoshop, after Contact Sheet II has finished creating the contact sheets, select File > Automate > PDF Presentation. *Figure 10-36*

2. Select Add Open Files, Multi-Page Document, and then Save.

3. When the Save Adobe PDF dialog box appears, make the appropriate selections. *Figure 10-37* For example, if you want the optimal email size, select Smallest File Size from the Adobe PDF Preset pop-up menu.

4. You can also restrict viewing and printing by selecting the Security tab and selecting the appropriate boxes. *Figure 10-38*

Creating a Picture Package

Photoshop's Picture Package is a tool for automatically creating a variety of layouts with your images that otherwise would be very time-consuming.

To create packages:

1. Select your RAW, PSD, or TIFF files in Bridge.

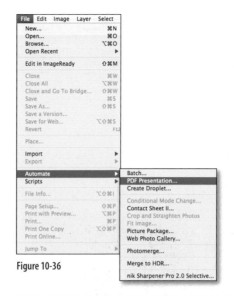

Figure 10-36

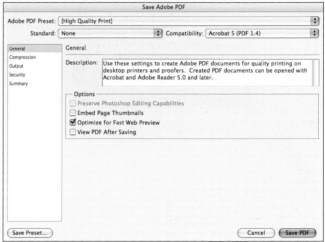

Figure 10-37

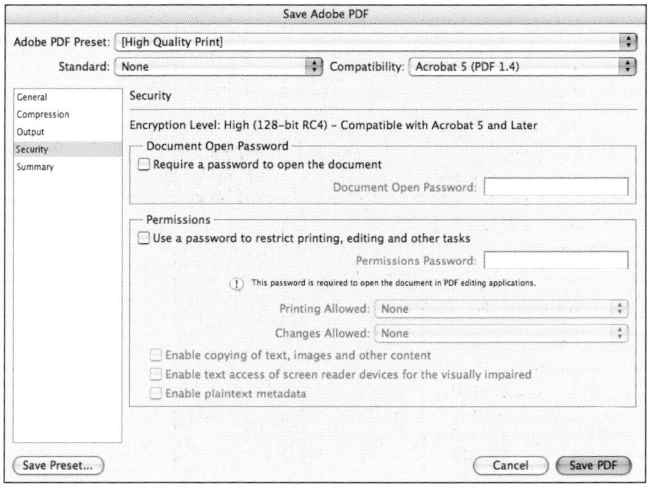

Figure 10-38

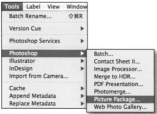

Figure 10-39

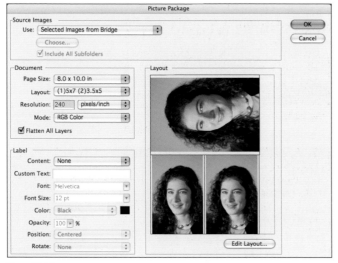

Figure 10-40

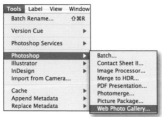

Figure 10-41

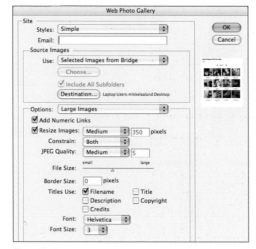

Figure 10-42

2. Select Tools > Photoshop > Picture Package from the Bridge menu bar. *Figure 10-39*

3. Select your Source Images (Selected Images from Bridge) from the Picture Package dialog box. *Figure 10-40* Determine page size, layout, resolution, and mode. You can add labels and custom text. Picture Package offers many options, including the ability to include a variety of different images on the same page. (For more on this, refer to Adobe's online help.) Click OK.

Creating a Web Photo Gallery

With the Web Photo Gallery command, it's easy to convert a folder or selection of RAW images into an interactive online gallery. Photoshop creates both thumbnail and full-size images, as well as the HTML pages and navigable links.

To use the Web Photo Gallery command:

1. From within Bridge, select the images you wish to share.

2. Select Tools > Photoshop > Web Photo Gallery from the Bridge menu bar. This will launch Photoshop if it isn't already open. *Figure 10-41*

3. Select your Source Images (Selected Images from Bridge) and a destination from the Web Photo Gallery dialog box. *Figure 10-42* Choose an appropriate style and enter descriptive text. Be sure Web Photo Gallery is set to include a filename under each image, so the person viewing your work can reference their image choices. Click OK. (For more on creating a Web Photo Gallery and posting your content on the web, I suggest you refer to Adobe's online help.)

Using Batch & Actions

Image Processor is great for its ease of use, and it does offer a modicum of control. But for another notch up, there is the Batch command combined with actions. Actions, of course, are a playable recordings of a series of commands and tasks, and they certainly are not new to Photoshop users. Photoshop power users have long used actions to automate even the simplest task—such as opening and closing files. The Batch Command is used to apply the action to an entire folder or selection of images.

If you want to apply an existing action to a batch, start by evoking the Batch tool from Bridge. Select Tools > Photoshop > Batch from the Bridge menu bar. *Figure 10-43*

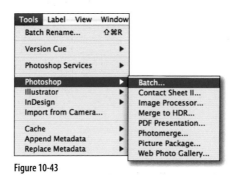

Figure 10-43

This opens the Batch dialog box in Photoshop. *Figure 10-44* Here you can select any preexisting action you have loaded.

Most of the time, you'll want to create a specific action for a specific batch of images. For example, I'm going to resample up a group of portraits to a specific size not available in Camera Raw. Since the final destination is a high quality printer, I'm going to resample up in increments and add a sharpening step after each resize. (Image Processor adds a sharpen Action before resizing, which isn't very useful.)

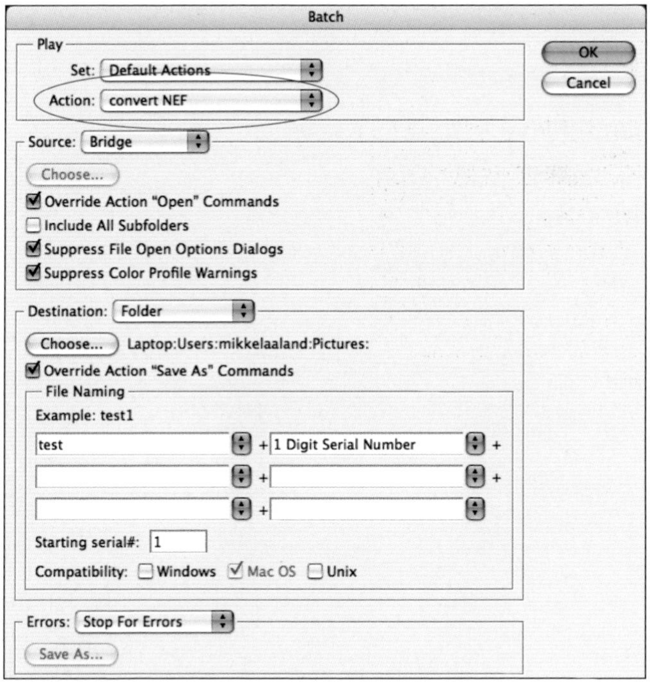

Figure 10-44

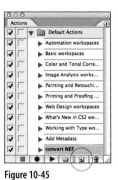

Figure 10-45   **Figure 10-46**

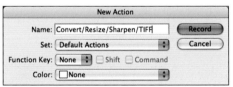

Figure 10-47

File	Edit	Image	Layer	Select
New...				⌘ N
Open...				⌘ O
Browse...				⌥⌘ O
Open Recent				▶
Edit in ImageReady				⇧⌘ M
Close				⌘ W
Close All				⌥⌘ W
Close and Go To Bridge...				⇧⌘ W
Save				⌘ S

Figure 10-48

Let's start by creating the action in Photoshop, and use Bridge to apply a Batch/Action to a group of selected RAW files. From Photoshop:

1. Open the Actions palette (Window > Action). *Figure 10-45*

2. In the Actions palette, either click the New Action button, or choose New Action from the Actions palette flyout menu. *Figure 10-46*

3. Name your Action. (I've named mine Convert/Resize/Sharpen/TIFF.) *Figure 10-47*

4. Click Record.

5. Open a RAW file using the Photoshop File > Open menu. It'll open in Camera Raw. (It doesn't matter which image you use. It's only the Camera Raw settings we are interested in capturing.) *Figure 10-48*

6. In Camera Raw, select the appropriate workflow settings. (I've selected Adobe RGB and 8 Bits/Channel. I kept the size at its original camera setting.)

7. In the Settings pop-up menu, select either Camera Settings or Camera Raw Default. Be sure to make the right choice. If you know Camera Raw Default is the way you want to go, fine. However, if you are working with RAW files that have been previously edited in Camera Raw with custom settings, you'll want to select Image Settings. This way, the settings particular to each image (from the Camera Raw database or sidecar XMP files) are applied when you batch process. *Figure 10-49*

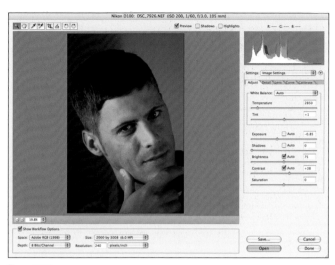

Figure 10-49

8. Select Open and wait until the RAW file is open in Photoshop.

9. Select File > Image Size from Photoshop's main menu. *Figure 10-50*

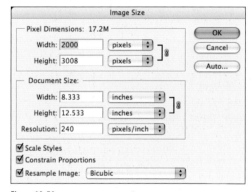

Figure 10-50

10. My final size is 20 inches by 30 inches, but I'm going to resample up in approximately 50% increments. First, I'll enter 12 inches in the Width box. As long as Constrain Proportions is selected, the Height is automatically set to 18.048. I'll also change my resample method from Bicubic to Bicubic Smoother. (If you resample down, I recommend using Bicubic Sharper.) *Figure 10-51*

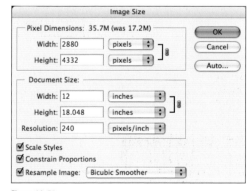

Figure 10-51

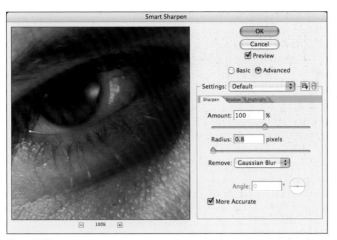

Figure 10-52

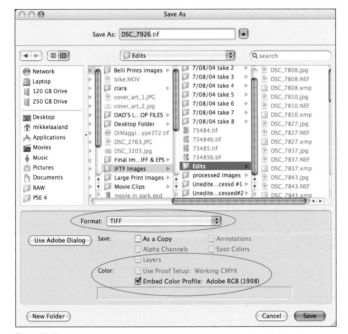

Figure 10-53

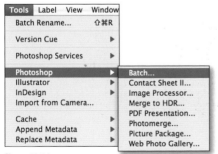

Figure 10-54

11. Select OK. Next, in Photoshop, I'll use the new Smart Sharpen filter to apply a slight sharpening, as shown here. Then I'll open Resize again and resample up to 20 inches x 30.083 inches. Again, in Photoshop, I'll apply a slightly higher Smart Sharpen Radius setting, because my file is now slighter larger. I know this is sounding slow and tedious, but because I'm recording all my steps, I'll have to do it only once. *Figure 10-52*

12. When you're done resizing (or whatever your action is), select Save As from Photoshop's main menu. It's not critical to change either the destination or file name. As you'll see later, when we get to the part about using Batch, you'll override this step anyway and keep the original file names intact. You'll choose a destination in the Batch options. The important thing here is to select the file format of choice and whether or not to embed a color profile. Select Save. *Figure 10-53*

13. In Photoshop, close your image and stop recording. To stop recording, either click the Stop button, choose Stop Recording from the Actions palette menu, or press the Esc key.

Now, let's go to Bridge and apply this Action to a batch of images, using the Batch command.

1. Select the RAW files you wish to process.

2. Select Tools > Photoshop > Batch. *Figure 10-54*

3. The Batch window opens. *Figure 10-55*

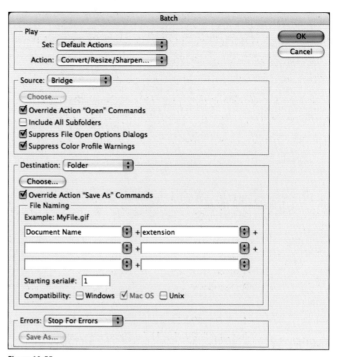

Figure 10-55

I've listed the settings that are critical for this work.

Critical Batch Settings

- *Play: Select correct Set and Action.*

- *Source: Bridge*

  Override Action "Open" Commands. **This ensures your Bridge files open, not the file named in the action.**

  Suppress File Open Options Dialogs. **This prevents the Camera Raw dialog box from opening for each RAW file being processed.**

  Suppress Color Profile Warnings. **If you don't select this option, you'll have to manually close the color profile warning for every image.**

- *Destination. Choose a Destination for the final images. Then select "Override Action 'Save As' Commands" This will apply the Save As file format choice, but keep the original file names or names chosen with File Naming options.*

- *File Naming. Change your document name and add sequencing information here, if wanted.*

- *Errors. Stopping for errors is generally recommended. However, if you are confident the process works, and want to avoid a possible delay, select Log Errors to File. The process will continue, even if a minor glitch occurs.*

4. Select OK. Depending on the complexity of the Action, the number of RAW files, and the speed of your computer, you may very well take the opportunity to go out and have lunch.

Scripts are much like Actions—they allow you to automate common tasks. However, they are much more powerful, because instead of recording and playing back a linear sequence of events, you can build in "if this > then that" logic. Scripts can be written in JavaScript (which plays on both the Mac and Windows platforms), Visual Basic (which is Windows-only), or AppleScript (which is Mac-only).

Writing Custom Scripts

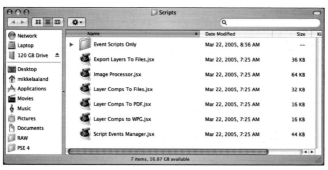

Figure 10-56

Image Processor, which I discussed earlier in this chapter, is a JavaScript. So is Import from Camera, which I discussed in Chapter 1. Scripts are good, and many people enjoy writing their own and sharing them via the web for free—or for a nominal charge. I have friends who do that—but I don't. *Figure 10-56*

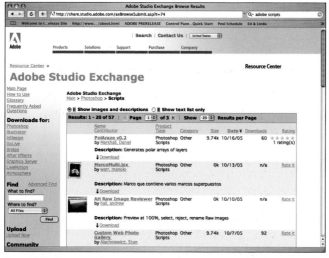

Figure 10-57

This is what I suggest. If you are like me, periodically check the Adobe web site for scripts that sound interesting (*http://share.studio.adobe.com*). *Figure 10-57* Follow the instructions for loading them. Try them out. See if they work. (I've downloaded a few dogs.) If you want to write your own, refer to the Adobe online help. Me, I'm tired of spending so much time in front of a computer. I'm done. I'm going out and shooting some photos!

Index

Numbers & Symbols

.exr files, 107
.xmp files (see sidecars)
16 Bits/Channel or 8 Bits/Channel command, 108
32-bit Preview Options, 107

A

ACDSee, 32
actions, 184
  applying to group of RAW files, 195
Actions palette, 184, 195
Add Noise filter, 154
adjustments, finishing in Photoshop, 89
AdobeLibrary*.jsx files, 11
AdobeScriptManager file, 11
Adobe Bridge (see Bridge)
Adobe Camera Raw Database, 190
Adobe web site, 199
AppleScript, 199
Apply Camera Raw Settings command, 41
Apply Metadata on Import, 12
Atkinson, Bill, 158
automation commands, Bridge, 191
Auto Adjustments, 58
Auto settings, 80
Auto White Balance setting, 7

B

batch, applying to group of RAW files, 195
Batch Rename command, 40, 171
Batch tool, 194–199
  critical settings, 198
Batch window, 198
Bicubic Sharper, 187
Bicubic Smoother, 187

black and white photography, 150–163
  advanced localized control, 158–163
  improving portrait shot, 162
  Layer Mask, 163
  red filter, 159
  shooting considerations, 153
  using Camera Raw to generate, 151–157
blending multiple images in Photoshop, 99–101
Blending Options (Photoshop), 101
Blue channel, 161
blur filters, 124
Bridge
  Additional Lines of Thumbnail Metadata (General
      Preferences), 27
  automation commands, 191
  Auto Adjustments, 26
  background color, 19
  Batch tool, 194–199
  cache, 21
  converting RAW files, 180–184
  creating duplicate RAW files, 95–97
  deleting images, 23
  display performance, 20
  exposure checking, 25
  files, renaming, 32
  Filmstrip view, 24
  host, 22
  image sharpness, 24
  importing images, 11
  Import Camera script, 11
  keywords, labeling, rating, and adding, 29
  Keywords tab, 30
  launching, 16
  Merge to HDR command, 105
  metadata, editing based upon, 27
  Metadata tab, 27
  setting to launch automatically, 16
  slide shows, 19
  viewing images as a slide show, 18
  viewing options, 17
Brightness tonal control slider, 76
Brush tool, 160

C

Calibrate controls, 86, 151, 156
Calibrate tab, 86
camera models
　Canon 1D Mark II, 40
　Canon EOS 1DS, 94
　Canon EOS 1Ds, 132
　Fuji FinePix S3 Pro SLR, 115
　Nikon D100 6MP, 111
Camera Raw, xvi
　Adjust tab, 53
　assign ratings with, 42
　Calibrate tab, 54
　color histogram, 52
　Color Sampler tool, 46
　Crop tool, 47
　Curve tab, 54, 82
　Defaults, 25
　　changing, 26
　deleting images with, 42
　depth, 38
　Detail tab, 53
　determining version, 36
　dialog box, 171
　editing photo shoots with, 40
　exposure, 25
　Exposure and Shadows clipping display, 63
　Exposure settings, 79
　for converting images, 188
　histogram, 68
　image orientation, 50
　Lens tab, 54
　maximum image size, setting, 39
　panorama, creating, 48
　previews, 173
　Preview option, 51
　ratings, 42–43
　resolution, 39
　resolution, setting, 39
　Save command, 188
　　file formats, 188

　　Photoshop format, 189
　　TIFF compression, 189
　Shadow and Highlight clipping warnings, 51
　size, 39
　Straighten tool, 49
　Use Auto Adjustments, 58
　using to generate black and white images, 151–157
　White Balance tool, 45
　Workflow Options, 38
　Zoom and Hand tools, 44
Camera Raw plug-in
　downloading, 37
Camera Raw settings
　Adobe Camera Raw Database, 190
　applying to multiple images, 185–186
　Camera Raw Defaults, 186, 196
　Camera Settings, 196
　Clear Camera Raw Settings, 186
　Previous Conversion, 186
　saving, 186, 190
　XMP sidecar files, 190
Canon 1D Mark II, 40
Canon EOS 1DS, 94
Canon EOS 1Ds, 132
Canto Cumulus, 32
Carnett, John, 151, 162
Centralized Cache File, 21
Channel Mixer, 107, 151
　converting RGB to grayscale, 157
chromatic aberrations, 142–146
　Photoshop Lens Correction filter, 144–146
　　saving settings, 146
　reducing with Camera Raw, 142–144
Cloudy (White Balance preset), 73
color bias compensation, 10
Color Noise Reduction, 133, 137
Color Range selection tool, 99
Color Reduction control, 133, 135
Color Sampler tool, 46, 66
color space, 7, 65
color space, choosing, 65
color targets, 9

Compressed (lossless), 172
Contact Sheets, 31
  converting to PDF, 192
Contact Sheet II dialog box, 191
Contrast tonal control slider, 76
converting RAW files
  Bridge, 180
  Camera Raw, 188
  DNG format, 167, 168
    folder of images, 175
    when Camera Raw hosted by Photoshop, 170
    with Camera Raw, 171–175
  Image Processor, 180
Convert to Linear Image, 172
Copyright Info, 184
Crop Custom settings, 48
Crop tool, 46, 47
Curve tab, 54, 82
custom-named settings, 62
custom camera profiles, creating, 86

D

darkening at the corners of the frame, 147
Daylight (White Balance preset), 73
default settings, 59
  reverting, 88
Desaturate command, 152
desaturate in Camera Raw, 158
digital negative (see DNG files)
Distributed Cache Files, 21
DNG Converter, 167, 169
  batch processing files, 170
  extracting original RAW data, 177
  using, 176–177
DNG files, 166–177
  converting, 168
    multiple using Camera Raw, 175
  handling in Camera Raw preferences, 174
  legacy, 174
  long-term reliability, 166
  opened in text editor, 167
  saving, 167
  updating, 173

down sampling, 187
Dr. Brown's Place-A-Matic script, 98
Duplicate command, 95
duplicating RAW files, 159
dynamic range
  extending, 102–111
  (see also HDR Files; Merge to HDR filter)

E

Embed Original Raw File, 172
Equalize Histogram (Photoshop), 108
evaluating images, 63–71
EXIF data, 27, 28, 33
ExpoDisc Digital White Balance filter, 7
exposure, 5, 25
  correct, 8
Exposure and Gamma (Photoshop), 108
Exposure and Shadows clipping display, 63
Exposure option, 107
Exposure settings, 79
Exposure slider, 70
Exposure tonal control slider, 76
Extensis Portfolio, 32

F

file formats, 5
  changing, 3
File Naming protocol, 171
Fill command, 160
Filmstrip view (Bridge), 17
Flash (White Balance preset), 73
Flourescent (White Balance preset), 73
FocalBlade, 116
Fors, Thomas, 86
frame, darkening at the corners of, 147
Fuji FinePix S3, 102
Fuji FinePix S3 Pro SLR, 115

G

Gaussian blur, 124
Genuine Fractals, 187
grainy look, imitating, 154

grayscale, 150
   converting RGB to grayscale, 157
   (see also black and white photography)
Grayscale command, 151
gray cards, 9
GretagMacbeth color test chart, 9

H

Hallahan, Maggie, 185
Hand tool, 44, 46, 117
hard drive space, 159
HDR files
   converting to usable form, 108–111
   saving, 107
   working with in Photoshop, 107
Highlight Compression (Photoshop), 108
high ISO, images shot at, 129
histograms, 8
   interpreting, 68
Histogram palette, 107
Holm, Jack, 150

I

images
   applying custom Camera Raw settings to multiple,
       185–186
   deleting, 23
   keywords, 29
   labeling, 29
   rating, 29
   resizing, 187
   saving as JPEG, 183
   saving as PSD, 183
   saving as TIFF, 183
   saving to set location, 182
   selecting to process, 182
Image Processor
   converting RAW files, 180–184
   Copyright Info, 184
   how it works, 180
   Include ICC Profile, 184
   launching, 180

   options, 182
   Run Action, 184
   versus Camera Raw for converting images, 188
Import Camera script, 11
Import from Camera command, 12
Include ICC Profile, 184
Info palette, 107
Inverse command (Photoshop), 100
IPTC data, 28
ISO, 6
   images shot at high ISO, 129
iView, 32
iView Media Pro, 173

J

JavaScript, 199
JPEG
   Image Processor, 180
   saving, 183
   when to shoot, 4
.jsx files, 11

K

keyboard shortcuts for Adjust and Curve tabs, 85
keywords, 29
Keywords tab, 30
Knoll, Thomas, 166
Krogh, Peter, 87

L

labels, 29
LAB color mode, 151, 152, 158
Layer Blending Options, 99
Layer Mask, 163
Layer palette, 160, 161
Layer Style dialog box, 101
LCD preview, 8
legacy DNG files, 174
Lens blur, 124
Lens Correction filter (Photoshop), 144–146
   saving settings, 146
Levels and Curves, 107

Linear Tone Curve setting, 83
Local Adaptation (Photoshop), 108
Luminance Smoothing, 121, 133, 135, 137
LZW compression, 183

M

Magnify tools, 117
masks
  creating, 99
McDermott, John, 153, 161
Merge to HDR filter (Photoshop), 102
  shooting for, 104–105
  using, 103
More Accurate mode (Smart Sharpen), 123
Moseley, Jonny, 185

N

NEF RAW file, 122
New Bicubic, 187
New Filter Settings dialog box, 141
Nikon Capture Editor, 122
Nikon D100 6MP, 111
Nik Sharpener Pro, 116
noise
  overview, 132
  Photoshop Reduce Noise filter, 137–141
    Advanced settings, 140
  using Camera Raw to reduce, 133–136
    saving noise reduction settings, 135

O

OpenEXR files, 107
Over/Under exposure, 8

P

PDF, converting from contact sheets, 192
PDF Presentation command, 192
Petersen, John, 103
.pfm files, 107
PhotoKit Sharpener, 116

Photoshop
  action, 184
  blending multiple images, 99–101
  Blending Options, 101
  Channel Mixer (see Channel Mixer)
  Equalize Histogram, 108
  Exposure and Gamma, 108
  finishing adjustments in, 89
  Highlight Compression, 108
  Inverse command, 100
  Lens Correction filter, 144–146
    saving settings, 146–147
  Local Adaptation, 108
  Merge to HDR command, 163
  Merge to HDR filter (see Merge to HDR filter)
  Place command, 97
  Preferences, 16
  Reduce Noise filter, 137–141
    Advanced settings, 140
  Smart Sharpen (see Smart Sharpen)
  Smart Sharpen filter, 137
  Unsharp Mask filter, 116
  working with HDR files, 107
Photoshop CS2, xvi
Photo Filter, 107
Photo Mechanic, 173
Picture Package, 192
  dialog box, 193
Place-A-Matic script, 98
Place command (Photoshop), 97
Portable Bitmap files, 107
portrait shot
  black and white photography, 162
Preserve Details, 139
preview, 67
  applying sharpening to preview images only, 119
  changing for HDR files, 107
  deselected, 118
previews, Camera Raw, 173
printable contact sheet, 191
ProPhoto RGB, 65

PSD
    Image Processor, 180
    saving, 183
.psd files, 107
Purge Cache for This Folder..., 26

Q

Qualtrough, Luis Delgado, 132, 147

R

rating images, 29, 42–43
RAW
    exposure, 5
    file format, 5
    loading time, 20
    overview, xv
    versus JPEG, 2, 4
    when to shoot, 4
Reduce Noise filter (Photoshop), 137–141
    Advanced settings, 140
    sharpening images shot at high ISO, 129
Red channel, 160–162
red filter, 159
Reichmann, Michael, 94
Remove JPEG Artifact, 139
Rename command, 32
Rename on Import, 12
resizing images, 187
RGB
    converting RGB to grayscale, 157
    values, 46
Richards, Mark, 132
Run Action, 184
Rutan, Burt, 151, 162

S

sampling, 187
Saturate control, 151
Saturation tonal control slider, 76
Save File dialog box, 188
Save Options dialog box, 171, 175, 177

Save Raw Conversion Settings dialog box, 186
Save Settings Subset dialog window, 122, 135
scripts, 199
Shade (White Balance preset), 73
Shadows slider, 70
Shadows tonal control slider, 76
sharpening, 6, 114–129
    applying to preview images only, 119
    fixing over sharpening, 121
    goal of, 114
    images shot at high ISO, 129
    No Sharpen, 122
    Photoshop Smart Sharpen (see Smart Sharpen)
    Photoshop Unsharp Mask filter, 116
    saving Detail Tab settings, 121
    third-party software, 116
    using Camera Raw feature, 116–122
    value set to 25, 120
    when to apply, 115–117
side-by-side image comparisons, 71
sidecars, with same file name for DNG and RAW files, 174
Smart Objects, 95, 97, 98
Smart Sharpen (Photoshop), 116, 123–128
    Advanced settings, 127–128
    blur filters, 124
    More Accurate mode, 123
    saving settings, 128
    selecting proper settings, 125–126
Smart Sharpen filter (Photoshop), 137
StarShipOne, 151
Story, Derrick, 77
Straighten tool, 46
Sundberg, Martin, 40

T

Temperature and Tint controls, 74
Thumbnails command, 17
TIFF
    compression settings, 189
    Image Processor, 180
    LZW compression, 183
    saving, 183

TIFF file format, 166

.tif files, 107

tonal control

advanced techniques, 94–111

simplifying, 77

sliders, 76

tonal distribution, 84

Tone Curve presets, 82

Tungsten (White Balance preset), 73

U

Undo command, 50

Unsharp Mask filter, 154

Unsharp Mask filter (Photoshop), 116

up sampling, 187

Use Auto Adjustments, 58

V

vignetting, 147

Visual Basic, 199

W

Web Photo Gallery, 31, 193

White Balance, 6

adjusting manually, 72

determining from a target, 75

filter, 7

presets, 73

tool, 74

White Balance tool, 46

Work Flow settings, 64

X

XMP data, 28

XMP sidecar files, 190

Z

Zoom level controls, 117

Zoom tool, 44, 46, 117

Better than e-books

Try it Free! Sign up today
and get your first 14 days free.
Go to *safari.oreilly.com*

Search
thousands of
top tech books

Download
whole chapters

Cut and Paste
code examples

Find
answers fast

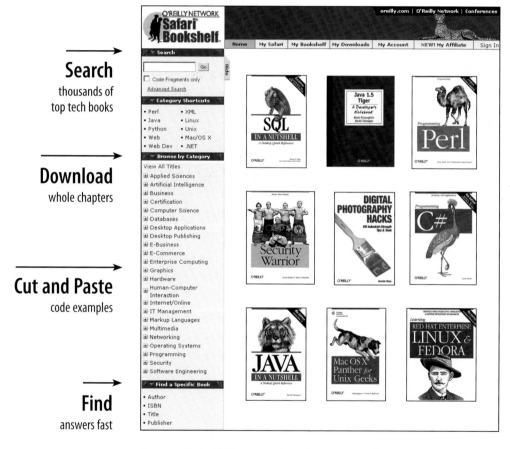

Search Safari! The premier electronic reference
library for programmers and IT professionals.

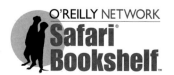

Related Titles from O'Reilly

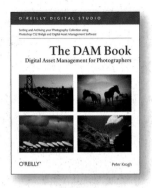

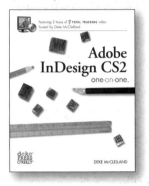

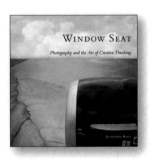

Digital Media

Adobe InDesign CS2
One-on-One

Adobe Encore DVD: In the Studio

The DAM Book: Digital
Asset Management for
Photographers

Digital Audio Essentials

Digital Photography: Expert
Techniques

Digital Photography Hacks

Digital Photography Pocket
Guide, *3rd Edition*

Digital Video Hacks

Digital Video Pocket Guide

Digital Video Production
Cookbook

DV Filmmaking: From Start
to Finish

DVD Studio Pro 3: In the Studio

GarageBand 2: The Missing
Manual, *2nd Edition*

Home Theater Hacks

iLife '05: The Missing Manual

iMovie HD & iDVD 6:
The Missing Manual

InDesign Production
Cookbook

iPhoto 6: The
Missing Manual

iPod & iTunes Hacks

iPod & iTunes: The Missing
Manual, *3rd Edition*

iPod Fan Book

iPod Playlists

iPod Shuffle Fan Book

PDF Hacks

Stephen Johnson on Digital
Photography

Window Seat: Photography and
the Art of Creative Thinking

O'REILLY®

Our books are available at most retail and online bookstores.

To order direct: 1-800-998-9938 • *order@oreilly.com* • *www.oreilly.com*

Online editions of most O'Reilly titles are available by subscription at *safari.oreilly.com*